'HOME AND AWAY': SPORT AND SOUTH ASIAN MALE YOUTH

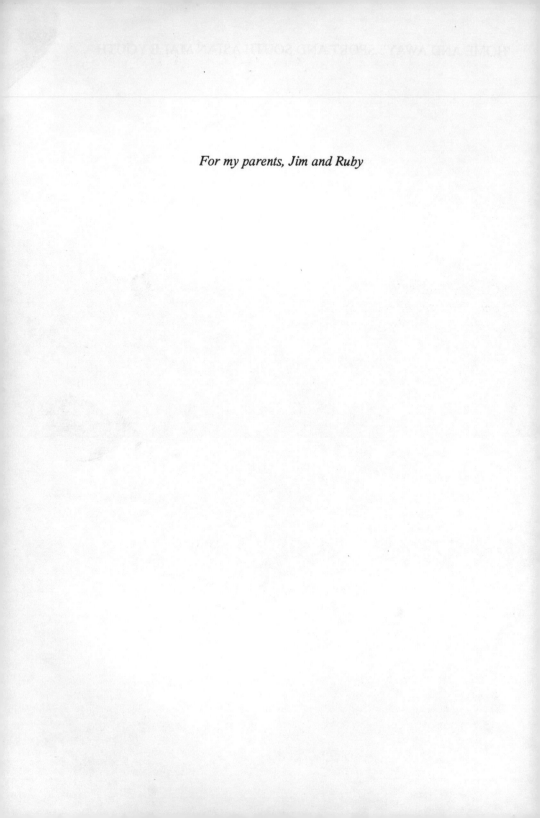

For my parents, Jim and Ruby

'Home and Away': Sport and South Asian Male Youth

SCOTT FLEMING
Faculty of Education and Sport
Cardiff Institute of Higher Education

Avebury

Aldershot • Brookfield USA • Hong Kong • Singapore • Sydney

Published by
Avebury
Ashgate Publishing Limited
Gower House
Croft Road
Aldershot
Hants GU11 3HR
England

Ashgate Publishing Company
Old Post Road
Brookfield
Vermont 05036
USA

British Library Cataloguing in Publication Data
Fleming, Scott
     Home and Away: Sport and South Asian Male
     Youth
     I. Title
     796.08995
ISBN 1 85972 017 X

Library of Congress Catalog Card Number: 95-79157

Printed and bound by Athenæum Press Ltd.,
Gateshead, Tyne & Wear.

Contents

Figures and tables		vi
Acknowledgements		vii
Abbreviations		viii
Preface		ix
1	'What it's all about': an introduction	1
2	'At home': a traditional cultural context	6
3	'Home from home': sport and cultural continuity	20
4	'Away from home': sport and cultural change	29
5	'Sorting it out': the research strategy	51
6	'In the field': life at Parkview School	68
7	'Taking each game as it comes': patterns of participation	96
8	'At the end of the day ... ': some concluding comments	122
Bibliography		132
Author index		151
Subject index		153

Figures and tables

3.1   Population of Britain by South Asian groups and country
        of birth, 1984-86   21

4.1   Socio-economic status of South Asians and 'whites' in
        Britain aged 16 and over in employment, 1981   33

6.1   Typology of South Asian males at Parkview School   69

Acknowledgements

This book is principally about the students of 'Parkview School', and I am very grateful to them. But it is also about the staff of the school, the members of local sports clubs, and the young people and fellow employees of 'Northbridge's' Playscheme Service. They provided me with much more than mere research data, and I am grateful to them too.

There are many other people to whom I am indebted. I would particularly like to thank Alan Tomlinson for his help, guidance, support and attention to detail, and Teddy Brett for his invaluable suggestions on an earlier incarnation of this book. Also Jim Atkinson and the Greater London and South East Regional Sports Council, for their help and collaboration in the project; and Ken Roberts and Sally Tomlinson for their encouragement. I am appreciative of the support and interest shown by my former colleagues at the University of Brighton, Lesley Lawrence and Graham McFee; the cooperation of my new colleagues, Steve Cooper and Huw Wiltshire; and the understanding and patience of Jo Gooderham and Pat Marks at Avebury.

Most of all, I would like to thank Beverley and Jordan, who have lived with this book for far too long, and have shown super-human tolerance of my moody obsessive behaviour and anti-social working habits; and more recently, Stewart and Matthew, who have been a reminder of what is really important.

Abbreviations

BAALPE	British Association of Advisers and Lecturers in Physical Education
BASS	British Association of Sports Sciences
BBC TV	British Broadcasting Corporation Television
BYRT	Bradford Youth Research Team
CRC	Community Relations Council
C4 TV	Channel 4 Television
CRE	Commission for Racial Equality
DES	Department of Education and Science
DoE	Department of the Environment
E2L	English as a Second Language
GCSE	General Certificate of Secondary Education
HMSO	Her Majesty's Stationery Office
ILEA	Inner London Education Authority
ITV	Independent Television
LEA	Local Education Authority
LCSR	London Council for Sport and Recreation
MBC	Metropolitan Borough Council
NATFHE	National Association of Teachers in Further and Higher Education
NFER	National Foundation for Educational Research
PE	Physical Education
PhD	Doctor of Philosophy
PSE	Personal and Social Education

Also, classes at Parkview School were referred to by the initials of the form tutor. Hence, 1MP.

Preface

During the late 1970s I used to travel to the Hawthorns on a 'football special' coach to watch West Bromwich Albion. It was at a time when black footballers had begun to make a real impact in what was then the first division, and the late Laurie Cunningham was being touted as the first black England international at senior level. In the West Brom team with him at that time were Cyrille Regis and Brendon Batson, and they formed a triumvirate that manager Ron Atkinson affectionately referred to as his "three degrees".

Travelling to the ground, in order to avoid the heavy traffic leaving the motorway, the coach took a route through the inner-city back streets of Sandwell. On nearing the drop-off point there was one particular road that the passengers on the coach would use to predict the result of the game. Down this road, when the coach passed a white person, a cheer would go up - a goal 'for'; when the coach passed a South Asian, there was a loud "boo" - a goal 'against'. Why?

1 'What's it all about': an introduction

Sport and ethnicity in Britain - some opening remarks

Throughout the history of organised sport there have been numerous examples of the way that it has acted as a powerful vehicle for the development of ethnic identity and the expression of ethnic pride. Minority ethnic groups are using sport as an increasingly important means of establishing cultural identity and asserting independence, and as Ken Roberts (1983, p.154) has observed: "some blacks see sport as an area for ethnic achievement where they can outplay whites at the latter's games, rules and grounds". There is now a clear recognition that cultural background impacts upon participation in leisure activities, and in recent years ethnicity has become a focal point for a great deal of attention amongst sports providers, academics, journalists, and broadcasters. In the main, though, the interest has focused primarily in African-Caribbean sportsmen, and to a lesser extent Afro-Caribbean sportswomen.

There are now over 1,323,000 people of South Asian origin living in Britain (Pumfrey, 1993); but, somewhat surprisingly, their sporting and leisure participation patterns have, until recently, been largely neglected, and therefore often misunderstood. That is not to say that South Asians have been completely ignored, and since the mid 1980s the apparently 'exceptional' sporting exploits of some young South Asians have been reported by the national media. Some relatively localised empirical studies have also considered sport and leisure related topics, and in conjunction with larger-scale survey investigations, these have made important contributions to increasing the overall level of understanding of South Asians, sport and leisure. Yet, importantly, some of these works have not always been greeted with unanimous approval; and it will become clear from later chapters that some work in this area is seriously flawed .

The sports participation of South Asian people in Britain has also been addressed by the physical education (PE) profession through the guidelines for what, at the time of their publication, was considered good practice; and in other analyses of the unique challenges faced by PE in culturally diverse schools. In general, though, the quality of these is very variable, and they have tended to adopt what Tony Bayliss

1

(1983; 1989) has termed the 'problems approach' to PE, placing so-called 'cultural restrictions' at the heart of the discourse.

A 'gap in the market'

Set against this backdrop of inadequate information and misunderstanding it has generally assumed that South Asians have been disproportionately under-represented in sports participation. There is evidence to tentatively support this proposition, but it has been based on research that was often speculative and typically characterised by being small-scale, anecdotal and lacking in rigour. In the major policy document 'Sport in the Community ... The Next Ten Years', the Sports Council (1982) firstly identified 'ethnic minorities' collectively as a "target group" for increased participation; and secondly offered suggestions about the sorts of schemes that would help to achieve the objectives of the 'Sport for All' campaign.

It had therefore been assumed that even though there was no substantive and specifically focused evidence to corroborate the notion of South Asian non-involvement in sport, action was nevertheless required. There were, of course, some important questions that needed to be addressed: What were the actual patterns of sports participation? Were the formal indicators for sports participation applicable to South Asians? What other sorts of sports participation might South Asians have been engaged in? What was the wider picture of South Asian leisure lifestyles? Did South Asians want to be involved in more sport? If so, what was required in terms of provision? And what, if any, were the barriers to them? The implication was clear - South Asians' involvement in sport did not seem to replicate the participation patterns of white middle-class British males, and was therefore identified as something of a problem. Perhaps most strikingly of all, the patterns of sports participation adopted by South Asians did not even seem to be remotely similar to those of the African-Caribbean communities, yet both were large and easily identifiable minority ethnic groups in Britain.

By the time that the Sports Council (1988) published its policy update document 'Sport in the Community - Into the 90's', other evidence indicated that South Asians were indeed under-represented in sports participation; but by this time it had become very evident that: "a lack of understanding [remained] about the needs of different ethnic minority groups, and in many areas service delivery is inadequate" (p.30). One such area of 'service delivery' concerned with complex sport-ethnicity relations was school-based sporting activity, and this should not be under-estimated. For it is through frequent and regular exposure to formalised PE lessons, organised extra-curricular clubs and teams, and informal 'play' that young people have the opportunity to formulate their own realities of sport and physical activity. Moreover, it is through these sources of social interaction, as John Hargreaves (1986) has observed, that ethnic tension and racial conflict enter school sport.

It would also be true to say that physical educators have been slow to respond to the needs of a multi-cultural society, and that the needs of minority ethnic groups have not been adequately catered for. For instance, there has been an apparent reluctance or inability to confront the important issues that face PE in a culturally pluralist society in some texts on the curriculum, and although Muriel Robinson (1989) does deal with a multi-cultural approach to primary school PE, she prefaces her discussion with the revealing comment that: "[PE and games] might not seem to be a relevant area" (p.135).

South Asians, in particular, have not featured prominently in the discourse about PE. For a considerable time after it was published, Field and Haikin's (1971) comments were indicative of the broad level of understanding about young South Asians and PE:

> The Asian child must feel himself [sic] to be an island, surrounded by a raging torrent of a sea, formed by new and frightening sounds - of children chattering in an unknown tongue, of the weird music of voice and piano, and the boisterous bouncing on wooden floors in physical education lessons. (p.57)

The research upon which this book is based was a real attempt to address the general lack of understanding, and therefore to plug a 'gap in the market'.

Sport, leisure and the 'sociological imagination'

The 'sociological imagination' provides an analytical framework for the study of sport and South Asian youth, and it does so in (at least) two ways. First, as C Wright Mills (1959, p.12) puts it, the sociological imagination: "enables us to grasp history and biography, and the relations between the two within society". That is to say, in order for individuals to fully comprehend their own inner lives, they must have an understanding of the wider historical context, and of the forces that construct and define the social world around them. These are the broad issues that are addressed in the early part of this book (i.e., chapters two, three and four). It is clear, however, that the historical development of sport and leisure is not a simple yet inevitable uninterrupted evolution from one generation to the next; and what follows is not an example of what Tomlinson (1982, p.50) has critically described as the: "'Book of Genesis' version of the social development in which sport x begat sport y, begat sport z and so on - until, in the end, all things are attributable to what came first". The absurdity of such an approach is well illustrated by Stuart Hall (1986, p.23):

> The study of popular culture has been somewhat bedevilled by this descriptive approach, tracing the internal evolution of popular pastimes, from hunting wild boar to collecting garden gnomes, strung together by an evolutionary chain of 'things' slowly becoming 'other things'.

Rather, as Hall and Tomlinson both go on to argue, it is the key social relations and cultural conflicts, as well as the moments of transition, that are significant. Hence the two broad themes of cultural change and cultural continuity are central to developing a fully contextualised understanding of the sporting involvement of South Asian youth in Britain; and these permit the shift from one perspective to another: from macro to micro, from the remote and impersonal to the most intimate (Mills, 1959; A. Tomlinson, 1984).

The second contribution that the sociological imagination makes to the understanding of the sporting and leisure pursuits of young South Asians is in the distinction it makes between "personal troubles" and "public issues" (Mills, 1959, p.14). As Tomlinson (1984, p.21) elaborates: "Sociological insight is particularly focused upon cases where personal troubles outgrow particular individual settings and become public issues of social structure". The point, in relation to South Asians especially, is well made by Jarvie (1991a). He argues that if one South Asian individual is denied equal access to opportunity and quality of experience, the cause might be a personal trouble; but if South Asians collectively are denied that access, the personal trouble transcends the individual level, and enters the public domain. Thus, by adopting an approach to research that emphasises the priorities of the sociological imagination, the needs of all parties associated with this set of research questions can be served effectively.

"The omission of the experience of women"

From the outset, it is important to emphasise that the focus in this book is almost exclusively concerned with South Asian <u>male</u> youth. This was for done for a great many reasons, some epistemological, some theoretical, and some practical. But in delimiting the work in this way, and in borrowing the sub-title (above) from Stanley and Wise (1983, p.17), the significance of gender as a central factor in the analysis of the sport-ethnicity relations as experienced by South Asians has not been overlooked. Rather, the emphasis is placed upon the youthful masculinity of young South Asian males; and this, in itself, is largely under-researched and often misunderstood.

The associations of sport, and especially PE, with masculinity are well established. Sport has been seen as having a masculine image, and the media represent sport as a quintessentially masculine domain (Carrington et al., 1987). Sport can therefore play an important part in the assertion and affirmation of masculinity. But as Sheila Scraton (1987) suggests, masculinity is not a static universal concept, and sub-cultural analyses of male subject groups are also explorations in masculinity. Hence, through an analysis of the social meanings and interactions of young South Asian males in sporting situations and environments, it is possible to develop a greater understanding of the construction of their masculinity. This is not an explicit issue that is addressed, but it is nevertheless a recurrent theme throughout the chapters that follow.

A note on terminology

The discourse of 'race relations' and studies of ethnicity has seldom adopted universality in the language used (Cole, 1993). On one level many of the subtleties are semantic and can be a distraction from the substantive arguments. For clarity, however, some of the working definitions of those terms that are widely and diversely interpreted are outlined here.

Ethnicity

Anthony Giddens (1989, p.726) suggests that ethnicity may be defined very simply as the "cultural values and norms which distinguish the members of a given group from others". This is, of course, somewhat over-simplified; but a valid point of departure for discussion nonetheless. Importantly, as David Gillborn (1990, p.7) points out, "[it] concerns the sense and expression of ethnic difference". That is to say, the self-realisation of the cultural difference and separateness between ethnic groups:

> ... with people of one culture realising its distinctiveness and utilising its distinctive resources (be they emotional, symbolic, cultural, political economic etc.) in interactions with outsiders. Both presuppose an awareness of difference and a degree of contact and interaction with non-ethnic outsiders. (Khan, 1976, p.223)

Ethnic group

Definitions of any ethnic group have tended to emphasise three main features of belonging to that group, where people:

(1) possess a distinctive culture;
(2) interact in such a way to be socially distinct; and
(3) identify themselves with a common set of beliefs and values which constrain and direct their goals. (Lyon 1973, p.2)

Thus, an ethnic group is one whose members share a distinct awareness of a common cultural identity - for example, a long shared history and cultural tradition, a common geographic origin, language, literature and religion (MacDonald et al., 1989); and this cultural identity separates them from other groups around them (Giddens, 1989).

South Asian

A definition of South Asian is directly related to a traditional cultural origin, and refers to those people who: "share in the heritage of the civilizations of old Hindustan prior to British conquest. Roughly, it is those people who believe that the Taj Mahal is an object of their history" (Modood, 1988, p.397). In this context, it is not restricted to individuals who have migrated to Britain from India, Pakistan, Bangladesh or East Africa, but rather includes those migrants from the Indian sub-continent and their progeny.

2 'At home': a traditional cultural context

The role that sport plays in the lifestyles of young South Asians in Britain is influenced by the wider cultural influences that South Asian youth cultures are exposed to. A full socio-cultural context must therefore include those elements of the traditional culture of the Indian sub-continent that continue to define and shape the experiences of young South Asians, as well as other influences from contemporary popular culture in Britain itself. These are the themes that are examined in the three chapters that follow. In this, the first of them, the development of sport in the Indian sub-continent is briefly contextualised for its socio-cultural and historical significance.

India is the home of one of the world's oldest and most influential civilisations (Benn, 1991a). Other ancient civilisations - in Greece, China, Babylonia - can be traced back as far as the ancient Indian civilisation, but none has retained its culture to quite the same extent. The history of sport in India is perhaps over five millennia old (Haynes, 1985), and dance, physical activity and exercise therapy have been an established part of Indian culture ever since (Deshpande, 1970; Vatsyayan, 1976). The great variety of traditional forms of sporting and leisure activity have their roots in indigenous folk culture (Bose, 1970), and these reflect the heterogeneity of the sub-continent with its staggering multiplicity of social, linguistic and ethnic groups.

Yet in spite of this rich history popular pastimes - especially in rural areas throughout the region - it was the imperialist games of the Raj that became the central sporting activities of the Indian sub-continent (Cashman, 1979; Bose, 1990).

Sport and the Raj

Once trading links had been established with India in 1591, the British seized political power, and used a major military force to maintain it (Vadgama, 1984; Stoddart, 1982). By the early nineteenth century, the British dominated the region, and given the delicate internal political climate and the potentially volatile diplomatic situation that existed with neighbouring Russia, it was important for the British Army to remain in a state of physical preparedness. Moreover, in a country rife with 'exotic' diseases, fitness was seen as all-important, and sporting activities

6

became an obsession (Miles and Khan, 1988). Equestrian pursuits that emphasised the skills of warfare were widely practised by cavalry officers, with horse-racing, polo and various forms of hunting particularly popular.

But more than merely acting as preparation for military conflict, sport was considered to engender the sort of 'moral fibre' and *esprit de corps* which were highly valued commodities in times of war (Mangan, 1985). The significance of sport was not only concerned with physical fitness and being competitive, but also in the traditional values of fairness, honesty, straightforwardness and a respect for authority that developed alongside a sense of solidarity, duty, and service through team games (Mason, 1990; Holt, 1989). As a result, cricket in particular, became an important feature of Imperial sport, and so too, to a lesser extent, did hockey.

Sport and leisure were complementary to the world of the British military in India; but in the absence of other forms of entertainment, sport also became a compensation for the military lifestyle and a source of diversion. Importantly too, sport and leisure activities became a source of cultural expression in an unfamiliar society - a reminder of home in a strange environment (Holt, 1989). From the outset, sport served both to establish and maintain a separate social status from the indigenous population (Ford, 1977), and to assert ethnic identity and 'superiority'.

Later, however, the desire to assert social status was replaced by a more pressing need to build cultural bridges with the indigenous population. At a time when there were fears of internal insurrection, good relations with the local aristocracy were clearly advantageous in order that routine governmental and administrative tasks could be undertaken with comparative ease (Holt, 1989). As a significant, and even integral part of British imperial lifestyle in India, sport was a crucial element in the process of the assimilation of the indigenous rulers into the culture of the Raj. The implications for the development of sport in the sub-continent were profound; for not only were the Indian rulers exposed to unfamiliar forms of sporting activity imported from Britain, but also to a British value system. Sport was then propagated amongst the elite families of India through the schools patronised by the nobility, which were modelled on the English public school system of the mid-Victorian era. The 'cult of athleticism' was pervasive, and at a time when many Maharajahs were, as Ross (1983, p.29) puts it "exceedingly plump and unhealthy", and there were concerns that their children would emulate them. Physical activity became a central part of the process of schooling the aristocracy in India, with athletics, gymnastics, cricket, football, tennis and rackets all popular. Of these, it was cricket that captured the imagination of the Indian nobility most of all. It was a fashionable, high-status sport played in the commercial cities of Bombay, Calcutta and Madras, and helped to uphold the hierarchical social order. It also helped to further the process of Anglicisation, and inculcated the personal attributes associated with the English public schools - 'manliness' and teamwork - which were deemed to be character-building (Cashman, 1979).

Other sports imported by the British did not receive the same aristocratic patronage, and their subsequent development reflects this. Hockey, for example, was less fashionable than cricket amongst the Indian nobility and was less glamorous. Yet in spite of this, Holt (1989) argues that it was hockey rather than cricket that became India's national sport, and on the evidence of international success it would be difficult to argue with his assessment: India won the Olympic hockey tournament in 1928 (the first year that India competed), 1932 and 1936; after

Partition, Pakistan won in 1960 and 1968, were silver medalists in 1956 and 1976, and were bronze medalists in 1972.

Like hockey football has always had a broader appeal than cricket in India (Bose, 1990); but it was regionally based, and did not gain acceptance in certain areas of India. It did, however, develop in the industrial centres where Muslim populations were concentrated (c.f., Mason, 1990). Racket sports also flourished, and the international success enjoyed by post-partition Pakistan in squash is remarkable, especially given the absence of adequate facilities that characterised its place in the sporting life of the sub-continent. Squash was never a mass participation sport, but in the distinctive Anglo-Indian institution of the 'club', which provided an ideal meeting place for both civilians and the military, one of the principal attractions was the sporting facilities, including squash courts (Miles and Khan, 1988). As the local indigenous population became involved in the organisation and administration of the club, the influence of squash spread and before long many clubs employed their own Indian professional players (Khan and Randall, 1982).

The development of polo followed a different pattern, a consequence of a pre-imperial history of thousands of years in Asia (Stoddart, 1982). The nature of the game played by the Indian indigenous population in Northeast India was very different in character from that which the British adopted. The traditional game of south and central Asia was skill-oriented rather than result-oriented, and had no goals. Participants played as individuals displaying their skills of ball-control on horseback for as long as possible. Yet in order to fulfil the military purpose the British required a variation of the game emphasised teamwork, strategy, and leadership; and the game was therefore changed to suit their needs. Not surprisingly, there was substantial resistance to the British form of polo amongst the indigenous 'tribesmen', but the Indian Maharajas embraced it unreservedly, as they had most other elements of British culture. As a result, even among the indigenous population, two forms of the game developed, with the Indian nobility adopting the British result-oriented version. In so-doing, the Maharajas became central to the subsequent development of polo, and this form of the game became predominant. A 'polo cult' developed, and through their patronage of polo, the Maharajas were able to demonstrate their importance to the Raj (Holt, 1989).

Sport, national identity and ethnic pride

Sport in India became significant in its symbolism for the assertion of ethnic identity and national pride. In view of the centrality of the Raj in the history of the Indian sub-continent over the last two centuries, and the emphasis placed on sport under that regime, it is not surprising that Vadgama (1984, p.125) remarks that: "Nothing could better illustrate the relationship between India and Britain than the history of sporting contact between the two nations". More than this though, in a geographical region characterised by intense conflict, sport acted as a metaphor for political, religious, ethnic and national rivalries; and judging by the accounts of contemporary sports stars from the sub-continent, it continues to do so.

In a new or different political, economic or social system, sport has often acted as an indicator of international worth; and the drive for sporting success has been used as a measure of national insecurity (Caldwell, 1982). It is no coincidence therefore, that politicians from India and Pakistan have not been slow to court the popularity of successful sports stars, and bask in the reflected glory. For a nation dominated by Imperialist rule, sport provided a means by which the indigenous population of India could symbolically confront the dominant minority group, and challenge the prevalent notion of white superiority. Through sport, it was possible to express national and ethnic identity. When Indian-born Ranjitsinhji played cricket for England, he was able to demonstrate to the Indian people that he was able to succeed in competition with and against the British, and it was at 'their own game':

> It was the idea of Ranji, the awareness that it was an Indian who had become the greatest batsman in the world, that contributed more than anything else to the Indian cricketer's realisation of his own possibilities. (Ross, 1983, p. 243)

Cricket therefore became a source of great pride to the people of the Indian sub-continent who were familiar with Ranjitsinhji and his successes.
Football also took on the role of asserting ethnic pride and became a metaphor for the India v. England contestation. In the Football Association Shield Final in 1911, a team of barefoot Indians - Mohun Bagan - defeated the East Yorkshire regiment. The game became legendary in nationalist history:

> The club's historian would later describe the match as "a red-letter day in the history of Indian football - a day that has gone down in the history of the nation's struggle for freedom and independence... It gave hope and pride to all Indians and sustained and strengthened the peoples' feelings of patriotism and helped to rouse national consciousness". (Bose, 1990, pp.17-18)

There were also political implications in the outcome, for it indicated to the Indians that their relationship with the British was changing "from one of patron-client to equal partners" (Stoddart, 1982, p.83).
After Independence and the departure of the British, increasing urbanisation during the 1950s and 1960s caused cricket to grow in popularity throughout India and Pakistan. Nationalism was to the fore, as the international aspect of Test cricket elevated a mere game to a patriotic cause to be argued over five days at a time (S. Mukherjee, 1988). Success on the cricket field would boost the national psyche immeasurably, and players were awarded superstar status. For relatively poor and developing countries, sporting heroes took on a special significance, and become emblematic of national aspiration. When Abid Ali struck the boundary that gave India victory in the Oval Test match of 1971, over 4000 miles away in Bombay, crowds poured onto the streets, shouting, gesticulating and blowing horns (Bose, 1990). Buses were stopped and commandeered, and the traffic came to a standstill as a delirious Indian public celebrated the triumph (Ray, 1987). This elation was not restricted to success at cricket. The hockey-playing exploits of Dyan Chand (scorer of six goals in the 1936 Olympic hockey final) propelled him to the level of national sporting hero (Holt, 1989), and squash world champion Hashim Khan reflects on the overwhelming reception that he received on his return from victory in England in 1950:

Governor General and his officials come close to greet me. They give me a party and make speeches and I receive an excellent watch with engraving... There is a reception at airport with five hundred guests and then I am in an open car riding slow through city and every sidewalk is full of people waving, and there are many children because Chief Minister closes all schools this day I come home. Never I think a squash player can have so much honor [sic]. (Khan and Randall, 1982, pp.32-33)

More important, as Miles and Khan (1988, p.47) observe, Pakistan, a country that was less than five years old, had a world champion. The boost to national pride and morale was immense.

An even clearer indication of the importance of sporting success is apparent from the reaction to success in India versus Pakistan sporting encounters. For these have not only articulated ethnic hostility and religious conflict, and have put a severe strain on already fragile Muslim-Hindu relations; but have also been a clear manifestation of national rivalry and political differences (Kureishi, 1989a; 1989b). In this regard they have come to represent a continuation of the Indo-Pakistan 'cold war' (Ahsan, 1989). Indeed, such are the high passions that have been generated through sporting encounters between India and Pakistan that the game of cricket *per se* takes on secondary importance. When former Pakistan cricket captain Imran Khan comments that "One's country's hopes and one's self-respect are riding on the result of a [Test match] series" (1988, p.44), it is hard to argue that nationalism has not been a strong motivating force behind success on the field of play - or perhaps more appropriately, the field of combat.

Sport on the Indian sub-continent has therefore been a source of national, regional and ethnic pride; and a battleground for political, religious, cultural and class rivalries. Yet these issues are not just concerned with sport. They are manifestations of the whole social order - of which sport is only a part.

Religion, culture and social division

The Indian sub-continent is a heterogeneous mix of a number of religions: Hindus, Muslims, Sikhs, Christians, Jains, Buddhists, Parsis and some Jews (Weightman, 1985). Of these, the three religious groups that wield the greatest influence - both numerically and in terms of power - are Hindus, Muslims and Sikhs. Islam and Hinduism, however, are much more than merely the sources of spiritual guidance and social affiliation, they are "cores of elaborate cultural systems that have dominated world societies for centuries" (Eitzen and Sage, 1983, p.269). Religion is both a cohesive and a divisive force (Taylor and Hegarty, 1985), and as a pervasive feature of culture it has helped to define and re-define the social customs and lifestyles of the inhabitants of the sub-continent. As the single most important bond in the affirmation of community social solidarity, the contribution of religion to sport and leisure is profound. As Wissmann (1972, p.100) contends: "An adequate view of sport phenomena must be orientated towards historical observations in which a conditional connection between sport and religion can be seen more clearly".

Hinduism refers to a complex religious and cultural tradition which has evolved organically in India since protohistoric Hinduism over a period of about 4,000 years (Cole 1991). It has always been concerned more with the practical realisation of religious values at every level, than with the performance of rites and rituals (Weightman, 1985); yet a lot of time is devoted to ritual behaviours and the annual cycle of festivals. Many of these are concerned with the seasons, and the festivals have provided the origins for many of the leisure activities of the Indian sub-continent.

In addition, Wissmann (1972) has also identified in Hinduism the links that exist between physical exercise and religious purpose, especially in relation to dance and yoga exercises. These, he suggests,

> Do not only serve the purpose of religious cognition but also, through the gestures accompanying their execution, make the performer and viewer conscious of religiously motivated Indian theories of the nature of the human body. (Wissman, 1972, pp.102-103)

The notion of *Ahimsa*, which has its roots in Jainism and is concerned with 'non-injury of life', is also considered to have had an effect on the development of sport in India. As Folkert (1985) puts it:

> Ahimsa has come to embody one's willingness to separate oneself not merely from acts of injury and killing, but also from the entire mechanism of aggression, possession and consumption that characterises life in this world. (p.24)

Hence cricket, an activity that was relatively non-violent, and a non-contact game, gained widespread acceptance in India. Towards the end of the nineteenth century Indian society was governed by codes of behaviour that even regulated human contact, and cricket did not violate any such taboos. By the same token, neither did hockey or racket sports.

In contrast, a commitment to *Ahimsa* was clearly incompatible with football - a semi-contact game that became, and still remains, a lower class game (Cashman, 1979). Part of the explanation for the failure of Hindus to adopt football as unreservedly as their Muslim counterparts was undoubtedly concerned with *Ahimsa*; but also, Stoddart (1982, p.80) suggests, in part because "Hindus, with their reverence for cows, could not embrace a game which involved kicking a leather ball".

Clearly there are some glaring inconsistencies in this analysis of the influence of *Ahimsa*. The big game hunting that was popularised by Hindu princes and the 'leisured class' (Ibrahim, 1991) was an example of violence and blood-letting that does not adhere to the main tenet of *Ahimsa*. The nobility apart, however, hunting was not practised by Hindus; and blood sports only received any real support in those regions heavily influenced by Islamic culture (Cashman, 1979), where there was no such concern with 'non-injury'. Wrestling and *kabaddi* are also anomalous with the notion of *Ahimsa*, for both were very clearly full contact sports with a explaining that while wrestling enjoys considerable popularity, "as a body contact sport it has less status than cricket". That is to say, wrestling and football became identified as low status sports, and this was indicative of the hierarchical ranking of sporting activities according to social acceptability; non-contact elitist activities imported by the British and popularised by the Indian nobility were at the top of the scale, and violent non-exclusive sports were at the bottom.

Islam, sport and leisure

Islam is a strong and simple, non-sacerdotal, monotheistic religion based on egalitarian principles, and is, quite simply, "a guidance and a way of life for the totality of human experience" (McDermott and Ahsan, 1980, p.5). It is the view of Muslims that "there are few if any aspects of individual and social life that are not considered to be expressions of Islam" (Welch, 1985, p.123).

Yet, as Ibrahim (1982; 1991) observes, there is no comparable term in Arabic for 'leisure'. This, he argues, is more than a mere peculiarity of translation, and is, in fact, illustrative of the Muslim attitude to sport and recreation. Unlike Christianity and Judaism, he contends that "Islam never sanctified time or frowned on leisure activities" (Ibrahim, 1982, p.208); and consequently there is an emphasis in Islam on 'recreational' activities. He cites two of the *hadith* - the sayings and deeds of the Prophet Muhammad: "Recreate your hearts hour after hour for the tired hearts go blind. Teach your children swimming, shooting, and horse-back riding" (Ibrahim, 1982, p.200). Islam therefore encourages participation in sport and physical activity, but such participation must be in accordance with the *Shari'a* (the Islamic principles): that all sports that do not provide spiritual, physical, mental and economic benefits to Muslims are prohibited (Yusuf Ali, 1946).

Islam and sport clearly have a close relationship, and as current international Muslim sports-stars have discovered, Islam helps to provide many of the personal qualities necessary for success at the very highest level (C4 TV, 1986). Jahangir Khan, for example, displays a real conviction in the power of Islam to affect his sporting performances: "I learn a lot of discipline from my religion. Not to drink alcohol, not to do many other things. In our religion there are so many things which help sportsmen" (Miles and Khan, 1988, p.148). More importantly the spiritual dimension of Jahangir's success on the squash court was never neglected: "The word most frequently used was *Inshallah* - God willing. All the training in the world would not help them [Jahangir and his coach Rahmat Khan] unless they had the blessing of *Allah*" (Miles and Khan, 1988, p.137). English-born Featherstone Rovers player Ikram Butt is the first (and as yet only) South Asian to be playing professional rugby league in England; and he makes the further observation that his commitment to Islam, and the sense of fate and destiny that is a part of the Muslim way of life, help him to cope with defeat and failure on the field of play (Hadfield, 1995; ITV, 1995).

The one element of physical activity that has been restricted by Islam is in relation to dance, though there is a problem of definition of what is actually meant by 'dance'. Celebratory and ritualistic folk dances generally do not seem to contravene Islamic social mores. There are, for example 'dervish dances' that are still very much a part of Pakistani culture (I. Khan, 1990), and also mass devotional dances that accompany some festivals in Pakistan. In contrast to these expressions

12

of cultural dance, it is 'display' forms of dance that are problematic for some Muslims. These are the dance forms that violate social taboos concerning modesty and *izzat*, which is concerned with male family pride. The *Qur'an* does not forbid dance, and it would be inappropriate to refer to it for specific guidance, but as Hedayatullah (1977, p.395) explains:

> The later Muslims who formulated the *Shari'a* and became its guardians, in the course of time built up a huge super-structure of social morality... The medieval Muslims had forbidden these pastimes [dancing, singing, etc.] for the ordinary Muslim although they were part of life in Muslim royal circles and in the religious exercise of the Sufis.

The situation is elaborated upon further still by a Muslim woman who was the organiser of some fund-raising activities in Britain - of which dance, music and performance were central elements:

> I believe that music is not religiously acceptable in front of men, but it is fine when only women are present. It is for happiness, and our religion does not prohibit you from being happy. Otherwise the events would be far too boring. Some [religious] people are too extreme. (Cited in Werbner, 1992, pp.5-6)

In this case, popular cultural forms might, on the face of it, appear to be at odds with perceptions of the established socio-cultural mores of strict adherence to Islam. An important point to note, however, is the variable approach to being a Muslim evidenced in this woman's remarks, and also the heterogeneity that this demonstrates. Clearly not all Muslims adhere to Islam in exactly the same way, and through expressions of popular culture, there is a sense in which more strictly committed modes of behaviour (or 'high culture') are mediated, whilst still retaining the central tenets of Islamic teaching and lifestyle.

Sikhism and Sport

Sikhism is a relatively modern religion being founded in 1469 (Cole, 1991), and was a reaction to the traditional standards and practices of Hindu and Muslim piety of which Guru Nanak - the founder of Sikhism - was severely critical (Cole, 1985). It emphasises tolerance, co-existence and equity - especially between men and women; but as Cole (1985, p.253) indicates:

> Sikhism has never succeeded in separating itself completely from its Hindu parent. In fact Hindus would regard Sikhs as heterodox Hindus. As a minority tradition existing in the midst of such a Great Tradition, not to mention the strong presence of Islam, it may seem remarkable that Sikhism has survived at all.

Its continued survival owes much to two distinct factors which have implications for the development of sport in the Indian sub-continent. First, the concentration of

Sikhs, particularly in the Punjab; and second, the willingness of Sikhs to confront hostility and to wage war effectively.

An important role for sport was to ensure preparedness for war, and many different kinds of sporting activity have obvious military utility. Indeed, some sporting activities may even have a religious association with the object of waging the 'Holy War' (Wissmann, 1972). In terms of regionalism, however, the influence of Sikhism may be more profound. Although it is not a function of Sikhism as such, the distribution of centres of particular sporting excellence indicates a propensity for hockey, and hence hockey has become popular in those areas where Sikhs are concentrated - the Punjab and northern India (Cashman, 1979).

At the same time though, there are other sports for which Sikhs have not generated the same enthusiasm. Cricket is one such example. Cashman (1979) cites the evidence of the under-representation of Sikhs in the Indian national cricket team. Sixteen years on, the number of Sikhs who have played international cricket has increased, but they still remain a disproportionate minority.

Sport and contemporary social division

Sport in India and Pakistan is characterised by the sort of social inequality that is representative of the lifestyles of the people of those countries, particularly in the forms of: elitism, caste, nepotism and regionalism. In addition, sport is affected by corporate and commercial institutional interest, and the unequal treatment of women.

Social Elitism

The history of sport in India is very largely the history of aristocratic involvement and princely patronage of exclusive sporting activities. In recent years some sports have undergone changes, and there has been a broadening of the social base of the participants in certain sports. Yet, participation is clearly structured around class divisions (Khan and Murphy, 1983). There are some sports that remain solely the preserve of the privileged few, and there are others that are predominantly for foreign visitors - "horse-riding, trekking, big game fishing, fly fishing, scuba diving and mountain climbing" (Camerapix, 1989, p.292). For the populace of the sub-continent, post-Imperial sport has generally become more accessible, but even in sports where there is widespread appeal, participation is restricted. Cricketers have tended to come from the social elites (J. Williams, 1989), and despite Cashman's claims about an expanding social base, they still do.

A cursory glance at the life-history of some of the international sports stars who have been accorded 'super-hero' status in the sub-continent indicates a background characterised by elitism. Imran Khan enjoyed a very fortunate and privileged start in life (Khan, 1988); and Sunil Gavaskar also experienced the sort of comfortable and supportive home-life that enabled him to develop into the most prolific accumulator of runs in the history of Test cricket (Bose, 1990). There were others too who were not from such affluent backgrounds as these, but who had the benefits of a university education or middle-class wealth (Crace, 1992). The class-bound nature of much post-Imperial sport in the Indian sub-continent is shown even more clearly by the absence of international cricketers of working-class backgrounds. With a handful of notable recent exceptions from Pakistan - Abdul Qadir (Berry, 1987), Tauseef Ahmed (Khan, 1988) and Javed Miandad (Gati, 1988) - sport in general, and cricket in particular, has not provided young working-class men from the Indian sub-continent with a ladder for upward social mobility. But even these who are from less privileged backgrounds than most cricketers, are not amongst the truly impoverished or the 'absolutely poor'.

Social elitism also applies to other sports. The Amritraj family of Indian tennis players enjoyed a very comfortable middle-class upbringing in the entrepot city of Madras (Amritraj and Evans, 1990); and even the working-class squash-playing Khan family was atypical in the sense that Hashim Khan's father was the Chief Steward of the Officer's Club near Nawakille - "an excellent position" (Khan and Randall 1982, p.16). For both of these families, who have become central in the history of their respective sports in the sub-continent, there was real and unusual privilege in terms of access to facilities and resources.

Although participation in these sports is still the domain of the middle and upper classes, it has been suggested that the spectator appeal of the sports spectacle transcends class barriers. Yet the cost of attending a Test match in one of the Indian cities is clearly prohibitive for many working class Indians, and would be beyond the scope of India's 70% of the population "earning less than the average income per head of the population" (Kerawalla, 1980, p.217). Thus, in addition to being stratified in terms of participation, it would also seem that cricket is not a sport that is easily accessible to all as a spectator activity. Bose (1990, p.251) claims that, "Indians, at least urban Indians, love cricket to distraction", yet the reality is that although large sections of the urban Indian population are deeply interested in the game, they are prevented from actually attending important international cricket matches.

Caste

The other sort of social stratification that influences sporting involvement, and is unique to South Asian religious and cultural groups, is discrimination based on the Hindu caste system. There are three main characteristics which van den Berghe (1988) considers to be the minimal definition of caste:

(1) endogamy, i.e. compulsory marriage within the groups.
(2) ascriptive membership by birth and for life, and hence, hereditary status;
(3) ranking in a hierarchy in relation to other such groups.
(van den Berghe, 1988, p.45)

In India, until the twentieth century, an individual's place in the social order was ascribed rather than achieved, and was determined by 'an accident of birth'. Throughout the twentieth century, however, the influence of caste has declined and been replaced by differential access to opportunities based on class. That is not to say that it no longer exists, but it remains more as a "social and ritual framework" than a "source of authority and regulator of action" (Brown, 1985, p.252).

Indian society may be characterised by class struggle, but the influence of caste is still an important factor in the social order. There are both single-caste and multi-caste villages, as well as towns and cities differentiated by caste; and these all have different religious beliefs and practices which are manifested in the social structure (Weightman, 1985). Interaction between castes is affected by this; and the underlying principle of social hierarchy persists and denies equal access to opportunities for low-caste Hindus in a number of areas of the day-to-day life, including sport and leisure. The implications are potentially very serious:

> The [caste] system results in the most minute discriminations being made in the sphere of interpersonal relations... If a member breaks his [sic] caste's purity rules, the pollution he [sic] incurs can affect the whole caste group, so the social sanctions against the offender can be severe. (Weightman, 1985, p. 210)

There is a conscious drive to minimise, and ultimately eradicate caste consciousness, but deep-rooted caste prejudices continue to create inequality in all walks of life (Kerawalla, 1980). Thus, caste adds another dimension to social stratification amongst Hindus, and reinforces the unequal distribution of facilities and resources for leisure activities and pursuits.

Nepotism

Cricket in Pakistan is riddled with nepotism, inefficiency, corruption and constant bickering (I. Khan, 1988; Crace, 1992). Imran Khan himself was fortunate in the favouritism shown to him by family members at the start of his career, and he acknowledges it, particularly with regard to selection (Khan and Murphy, 1983). With eight of Imran's cousins having played first class cricket in Pakistan - two of them captaining the national side, and an uncle who chaired the group of the regional selectors, the familial connections with the cricket establishment were strong.

Nepotism is also a feature of cricket selection in India. Sunil Gavaskar's uncle, Madhav Mantri, made four Test appearances for India in the early 1950s, and by the time Gavaskar was making his first class debut, Mantri was a member of the selection committee. For Imran Khan and Gavaskar, accusations of favouritism may have lacked validity as they were both destined for cricketing greatness; but they were both perceived to be benefiting from corruption and nepotism. The explanation is simple:

> With the commercial organisations in charge, nepotism and favouritism are rampant since they are not under any pressure from their supporters or members... Corruption and nepotism are common in team selection. (Khan and Murphy, 1983, p.129)

Indeed familial connections are evidently very important in the development of contemporary sport in the sub-continent, and the list of influential families is lengthy. In addition to those already referred to, it includes amongst others: the Amarnaths and the Nazars (Sharma, 1983), the Manjrekars (Bose, 1990), and the Krishnans (Amritraj and Evans, 1990).

Regionalism and Urbanism

In spite of recent claims about declining regionalism (Berry, 1992), cricket in India is concentrated in the two main centres of Bombay and Delhi, while the two main power bases in Pakistan are in Lahore and Karachi. In each country there is a great divide, factions are polarised, and there is even feuding amongst the players from the major cities. The reasons why cricket especially became centralised in the large conurbations are concerned with more than just the effects of urbanisation. Cricket has always been a 'princely enclave', and it largely remains so (Holt, 1989). But the explanation for this revolves around the aristocratic pursuit of glamour. Cashman (1979, p.185) elaborates:

> Cricket has retained its aristocratic image. It is regarded as socially prestigious to attend a test match... It is a frequent complaint of cricket-lovers that many of the socially privileged present have no real interest in the game and exclude the more serious students of cricket.

As a result cricketers rank as highly as film stars, with the trappings of fame and material wealth to match (Cashman, 1979).

The second source of patronage cited by Cashman, that of corporate business interest, has been central in the recent development of sport in the sub-continent. In conjunction with some of the public utilities and the armed forces, these large institutions provide much of the support necessary for the continued success of elite sport. Cricket, football and hockey have all benefited from this institutional patronage, and so too has *kabaddi* at the highest levels of national competition (Walia, 1991). Underpinning the projection of high institutional profile is the influence of the media, but the media are very largely preoccupied with cricket and all sports are not all promoted equally. This serves to further consolidate the position of cricket as a glamorous, high-profile, urban sport.

Different sporting activities have developed more fully in different parts of the sub-continent, and some of the reasons for this have already been addressed. The outcome has been, for example, that football has developed in West Bengal and Kerala (Stoddart, 1982), cricket in the states of southern and western India, and hockey in the Punjab (Cashman, 1979). In addition, there is a good deal of regional rivalry; not just in these sports, but in the more traditionally South Asian activities like *kabaddi*. The 1991 national competition was blighted by accusations of bias by officials, with Tamil Nadu suffering in both the men's and women's finals. The accuracy of the claims is, in one sense, immaterial; for what is more important is that the players concerned believed that they had been cheated, and that the reason, they thought, was because they came from a southern state (C4 TV, 1991a).

Sport and Gender

The role of women and sport in the sub-continent is an extremely complex issue, and in general terms women are not granted equal access to sporting opportunities. There is a popular perception that Muslim women are restricted most of all. In the Islamic state of Pakistan there is an on-going debate on women and sport, and it has been suggested by Lyons (1991a) that the main difficulty facing women is the lack of facilities. While it is certainly true that women require the use of separate facilities that are seldom available, and schools for girls are not as well equipped as schools for boys (Hardman and Khan, 1989), the suggestion that this is the contributory cause of female under-representation in sport fails to acknowledge Muslim modes of behaviour in relation to women and the full nature of the gender dynamic in Muslim cultures. It is equally misleading to attribute the restrictions placed on females in sport to 'Islamic fundamentalism', for this implies that sport is not restricted for all non-fundamentalists, and to attribute women's under-representation in sport to 'fundamentalism' is to over-simplify to the point of misrepresenting the complex and multi-faceted cultural situation facing Muslim women in Pakistan.

Hindu women, like their Muslim peers, are religiously the equal of men (Weightman, 1985; Welch, 1985), yet for many Muslims and Hindus the domestic roles of men and women are very different. With primary responsibility for household management and child rearing, many Hindu women are severely restricted by the amount and quality of their leisure time. For Sikh women too, theoretical equality is not manifested in lifestyle experiences that are 'identical' to those of men; and in that sense, is no different in principle from the experiences of many women from other cultures from other parts of the world, as Weightman (1985, p.222) remarks:

> There is little reason to think that the Hindu woman is at any greater disadvantage than women elsewhere in the world, as the presence of women in many leading positions in India conclusively demonstrates.

In other words, women occupy a disadvantaged position in terms of access to power in many walks of life and in many different cultures; and to assume that the position of Hindu women is any 'worse' or 'more severe' than the position of women in other cultural groups is a manifestation of a Eurocentric approach to the understanding of other cultures that associates cultural difference with value-laden negative characteristics.

Sport, however, would seem to be one area of public life in India that provides an exception to this generalisation, for, as Callaghan (1991) observes, sport in India is, at best, only "almost becoming emancipated". There are very few Indian women sports stars; though Sonita Godara Anand - the 'marathon tigress' - is an obvious exception. The other activity in which women have made some headway, at least in terms of parity of access and opportunity with the men, is in *kabaddi*. The national women's competition attracted similar levels of interest to the men's competition (C4 TV, 1991a); and some of the players, for example, Susheela Sundaram and Suvra Bannerjee are superstars of their sport.

But even these women, who have forged a successful sporting career for themselves, have experienced cultural difficulties; some of a very subtle kind. Suvra Bannerjee explains her parents' reaction to her participation in kabaddi:

> At first my parents did not like me playing kabaddi. Girls are not encouraged to take part in sport. They were worried about what other people would say. But gradually my father accepted the idea, and he

18

convinced my mother. Now my parents agree that women should take part in sport. (C4 TV, 1991a)

In those few sentences she makes a very important point about the participation in sport by women.   There are clearly defined cultural expectations about gender specific behaviour, of which female participation in sport does not feature as an accepted norm; indeed participation by women is even seen to be almost unacceptable behaviour that requires legitimisation by men in order to receive widespread approval.

The traditional cultural context for South Asians in Britain

What is clear therefore, is that sport in the Indian sub-continent is an elitist, male-dominated, urban, institutionalised phenomenon that has been significantly influenced by the legacy of the Raj; and it is characterised by class, caste, ethnic, and gender inequality. There is a strong political will to effect real change (Callaghan, 1991), but the influences of traditional culture will take considerable time to erode. It is these influences that impact on the lives of South Asians living in Britain. Their attitudes and perceptions are fundamentally shaped by their experiences of sport in the traditional culture of their ethnic origin, and by those of their parents and grandparents

3 'Home from home': sport and cultural continuity

The lifestyles of young South Asians in Britain are characterised by some elements of cultural continuity, and other elements of cultural change. In this chapter, the traditional elements from the culture of origin that impact on contemporary South Asian cultures in Britain are examined. This represents an analysis of the factors from a socio-historical and cultural contextualisation of the traditional 'home' culture, and the ways in which they continue to affect the experiences of young South Asians in a different cultural situation, the new 'home'. Hence, as the proportion of British-born South Asian continues to rise, there may be many who have never experienced the traditional culture of origin at 'first hand'. Yet there are features of traditional South Asian cultures that continue to profoundly shape the daily lived experiences of young South Asians in Britain; and in a very real sense then, this is a discussion of factors that are 'home from home'.

The heterogeneity of South Asian youth

The demographic profile of Britain's minority groups has been steadily increasing in both absolute and relative terms during the last forty years (Todd, 1991). Recent estimates indicate that minority groups now account for 2,577,000 (4.8%) of the population (Pumfrey, 1993). South Asian groups constitute over half of Britain's minority population, and of these over a third were actually born in Britain (see table 3.1).

The South Asian communities in Britain are also characterised by heterogeneity, and are, as Tessa Lovell (1991) acknowledges, not a lumpen mass of people who all share the same lifestyle patterns and uniform culture. Researchers in the areas of leisure studies and the sociology of education have, for the most part, acknowledged some degree of differentiation amongst South Asians. When they have not, it has usually been in an attempt to generalise about South Asians collectively and contrast them with other broadly defined ethno-cultural groups; or to comment on the shared experience of racism.

Table 3.1 Population of Britain by South Asian Ethnic Group and Country of Birth, 1986-88.

Ethnic Group	Total (thousands)	(% of all minorities)	% born in UK
White	51,470	(-)	96
All minorities	2,577	(100)	45
Indian	787	(31)	37
Pakistani	428	(17)	46
Bangladeshi	108	(4)	32

(Source: adapted from tables 3.1 & 3.3 in Pumfrey, 1993, pp.32-34)

With regard to physical education, however, there has been a lack of awareness and sensitivity to cultural diversity; and recommendations for the PE profession, whilst valuable in highlighting important issues, were often based on stereotypes and 'false universalism' (see Raval, 1989; Fleming, 1994). Research that has acknowledged South Asian heterogeneity, has typically sought to isolate one or two individual lifestyle characteristics and has attempted to document the way in which they impact on sport and leisure. Analyses have inevitably been guilty of over-simplification, for these lifestyle choices are influenced by more than a single variable. Blanket generalisations about South Asians are misleading, and must, as Sally Tomlinson (1983; 1986a) points out, be rejected in favour of a more sophisticated exposition. Yet consideration of the principal influences does enable the construction of a framework for multi-variable analysis, and also helps to contextualise the simplistic understanding of South Asians in sport that prevailed until the mid-1980s.

Place of family origin

In spite of the shared national origins from the sub-continent that pre-date Partition in 1947, and Bangladeshi Independence in 1971, the country of family origin has often been identified as a key factor that influences the leisure pursuits of South Asians in Britain. This, in itself, seems unremarkable since definitions of ethnicity typically include country of origin as a fundamental premise; but it is a distinctly questionable practice to generalise about all South Asian youth on this basis. Nationality of origin is a very crude variable when applied to the Indian subcontinent, which is, after all, about half the area of the USA with major regional areas with their own geography, climate, language, customs, and even food (Brown, 1985). Furthermore, as Gajendra Verma and his colleagues (1991) observe, "Before

Independence, India consisted of about 600 semi-independent kingdoms... there were fifteen major languages and over 1,600 minor languages and dialects" (p.3).

The one aspect of sport and leisure that has received attention in academic and professional discourse, and about which certain national characteristics do apply, is concerned with South Asian dance forms. Lashley (1980b, pp.71-72) elaborates:

> The children of Asian background can be ... divided into four groups:
> (1) those from India whose religions are mainly Hindu based. Dance and music are an important part of their religion and culture;
> (2) those from Pakistan where dance is not an important part of their culture and girls in particular do not normally participate in dance;
> (3) those from Bangladesh to whom music is an essential part of their culture and much more widely practised than dance;
> (4) those from East Africa who will have a combination of the above but whose movement and music sense will have been heightened by their African experience.

Lashley's description employs 'country of origin' as the organising theme, but he also indicates the importance of religion, gender and culture; and in that sense his comments are based on a multi-variable appreciation of South Asian cultures.

As an alternative to national boundaries, regional variables offer a more appropriate geographical analysis of sporting and leisure pursuits and patterns. Coventry LEA (1980) considered these and outlined the location of the areas of origin of "the majority of immigrants [sic]" (p.9), but these descriptive data provide no more than background material that form no part of the subsequent guidelines for good practice; and the implications for PE and sport of an individual's ancestry being the Mirpur border, the Punjab, or the Gujerat are neither examined, nor made explicit. The experiences that some young urban South Asians from the sub-continent had of the education system in that particular country, and of PE in particular, are, of course, of direct relevance. Cherrington's (1975) survey of first-generation Indians indicated that in India:

> Physical education is significantly restricted in scope... When we questioned subjects about PE they talked about games (e.g.,. hockey, cricket), but perhaps more significantly about drill, exercises, marching and arm swinging. (p.36)

And rather than differences, there were certain similarities reported by the first-generation Pakistanis:

> The personal experiences of our Pakistani subjects suggested that PE is a low priority subject in their country. It mainly takes the form of games such as hockey and football for boys and netball and badminton for girls. Subjects did no gymnastics as we know them but did do 'exercises'. (p.36)

Evidently nationality, or even geographical region of family origin, is of less importance in defining ethnicity and ethnic identity than religion. Livingstone (1977, p.9) makes the point with regard to Pakistanis: "In most Pakistani families the emphasis is on religion, i.e. the Moslem religion"; though the same would apply about Hindus and Sikhs in other areas of the Indian sub-continent.

Religion

There has been a tendency in the British tradition of ethnic studies to treat religion as a factor of only peripheral significance (Beckerlegge, 1991). Yet cultural diversity among the South Asian communities in Britain has frequently been seen as a direct consequence of religious differentiation; and when a single factor affecting ethno-cultural heterogeneity has been isolated, it has often been religion that has been identified as the most important.

The South Asian cultural groups in Britain are a rich mixture of at least three broadly distinctive denominational religions (Verma and Mallick, 1981) and each has its own unique characteristics: the caste and polytheistic tendencies of Hinduism; the egalitarian reformational nature of Sikhism; and the uncompromising non-sacerdotal orthodoxy of Islam with its rejection of British pluralism. Each has its own festivals, for example, Hindus celebrate *Navaratra, Diwali*, and *Kali Puja*; Sikhs celebrate *Diwali* and *Gurpurb*; and Muslims celebrate *Eid-ul-Fitr* and *Eid-ul-Adha* (Duncan, 1985). These are sacred traditional religious festivals, and central aspects of South Asians' lifestyles in Britain.

In the acknowledgement of the cultural diversity amongst South Asians, and the leisure choices that are made, consideration has occasionally been given to the socio-religious context of different groups. This has often taken the form of brief and necessarily superficial descriptive accounts of what are considered to be the principal features of the religion, and the preoccupation with the 'problems approach' has created a focus on the perceived 'religious/cultural constraints' that are thought to restrict active participation in sport and leisure - and importantly, also on the coping strategies that have been sought for the 'problems' and 'difficulties' that are encountered by young South Asians.

Muslims and Islam Muslims in Britain are fragmented into different sects and factions, and are themselves a heterogeneous collection of people (Nielsen, 1987; Ruthven, 1991); but there has been some degree of consensus amongst Muslim groups in the demands that they have made in response to what they see to be the inadequacies and short-comings of mainstream education. One of the prominent issues facing educational policy makers has been the role of single-sex schools for Muslims, and as Khan (1985, p.33) has observed, "the debate has been marked by anger and misunderstanding and has produced a good deal of confusion on all sides". The reaction to Muslims becoming collectively more assertive has typically taken the form of a minor moral panic, as Islam is often seen as presenting the greatest set of practical issues and concerns for educationalists in general, and physical educators in particular (Semple, 1992).

The teachings of Islam place a high priority on egalitarianism between the sexes, but this manifests itself in different roles for men and women. For those who have a Eurocentric perspective on Islam, the place of women in Muslim communities often seems to be unemancipated and far from equal to the position of men. It has also been claimed that Muslims consider western culture to lack a fixed sense of moral values, to present a spectacle of moral anarchy and degeneracy (Hurst, 1985), and that this significantly affects the way in which sport, PE and leisure are perceived. The different roles of men and women are at the heart of the cultural concerns about sport and PE, for Islam is often seen to be incompatible with some of the established practices in PE. The lifestyles of many different groups of Muslims in Britain are based, in varying degrees, on a traditional view of the value of upholding family status and honour. Great importance is placed upon *izzat* - male family pride, and this is often expressed through the concept of female family modesty (Pettigrew, 1981). Many Muslim men are concerned that participation in sport is culturally unacceptable since it offends traditional customs of modesty, and will therefore result in family disgrace (Wolverhampton BC, 1985). The mixing of the sexes during adolescence is contrary to Islamic teaching, and while the wishes of some Muslim parents to have their children educated in single-sex schools has caused considerable controversy (Khan, 1985), it is in PE lessons where the situation for many young Muslims and their parents is most acute (Semple, 1992). In many primary schools, as Williams (1989b) observes, mixed PE classes have been the norm for some time, but there have been vociferous demands from some Muslim community leaders for separate PE classes for males and females (Griffiths, 1982).

One of the main areas of concern for many young Muslims and their parents is in relation to the clothing worn for PE and sport, yet it was not until the mid-1980s that there was any concerted policy to address the issue. The precise nature of the concern is that PE kit is seen as revealing and 'shameless'. There is some anxiety that men will see Muslim girls and young women in this state (Leaman, 1984); the possible consequences of which are potentially very serious - even to the point, as Taylor and Hegarty (1985) note, of ruining the marriage prospects for that young woman and her siblings.

The attitude of physical educators in general, is outlined by Williams (1989b, p.164):

> Restrictions are more marked for older [secondary school aged] girls, however levels of modesty expected in mixed company are such that some adaptation may be necessary in for example changing arrangements and dress... Muslim culture demand[s] that women should cover their legs. This requires no more than minor adaptations in schools where it is not common practice to allow the wearing of tracksuits.

There are also some specific guidelines for what should be acceptable to young Muslims and their parents (Duncan, 1985). Occasionally though, the compromise measures described above by Williams may be unacceptable; and in spite of the absence of the statutory right of parents to remove their children from the secular school curriculum (Semple, 1992), many Muslim parents wish to retain the right of withdrawal on these religious/cultural grounds (Sarwar, 1983).

The concept of modesty has also been the focus of some considerable attention in relation to changing facilities and after-sport showering. On one level the issue is merely one of respecting an individual's right to privacy whilst acknowledging the importance of personal hygiene; and the response that has been recommended by Rotherham MBC (1988) implies the adoption of a 'colour-blind' approach. Other guidelines of good practice, however, indicate a greater sensitivity to the needs of Muslims:

> Girls, particularly Muslims, may be reluctant to shower especially within a communal context and allowances should be made for this, possibly by allowing them to shower earlier than the rest of the class or to use private showers if available. (Coventry LEA 1980, p.35)

The focus here, and in this sense it is the norm rather than the exception, is on Muslim girls and women; but as Parker-Jenkins (1991) has noted, standards of modesty apply to both males and females. Seldom have Muslim males featured in any of the recommendations pertaining to appropriate dress, but the Leicestershire Education Authority Working Party on Multi-Cultural Education (1983, p.40) did suggest that for Muslim males, "The minimum part of the body which must be covered is from the waist to the knees". This principle is advanced for the modesty incumbent on Muslim males whilst showering too: "Boys and Girls must be allowed to cover themselves during showering... They should be allowed to shower with their swimming costumes on" (Sarwar, 1983, pp.22 &14).

Given this concern associated with traditional Muslim view of modesty, it is not surprising that swimming is one particular element of the PE curriculum that is seen as fraught with difficulties. The typical reaction has been to suggest single-sex swimming lessons, with same-sex teachers; though Williams (1989b, pp.164-165) suggests that establishing community links is also essential:

> ... in this situation the school has first to persuade the community that swimming is an important life skill and then look for ways of enabling children to learn to swim. If community leaders can be convinced that swimming is important and can influence parents then a compromise may be reached whereby girls arc allowed to join in mixed swimming classes.

Importantly, though, as with other areas of potential conflict for Muslims, guidelines still advocate the ultimate right of Muslim parents to withdraw their children from lessons on these religious grounds (Sarwar, 1983).

Swimming as a leisure activity for Muslim women has also received some attention from facilitators, enablers and policy-makers. Dixey (1982) reported a scheme in which swimming was introduced to a group of women of Pakistani origin at the Fairfax Community School in Bradford, and suggested that it might have provided a 'useful model' for other schemes. In it, community education provision expanded from a basis of English language classes to include health, fitness and swimming; the women were taken to and from the swimming pool in a mini-bus and privacy was ensured by excluding men from the pool area. Although the Fairfax scheme was considered a success, there were some important issues generated by it. First, there was a real sense that something culturally taboo was smuggled in under the guise of something more acceptable: "Emerging from under the umbrella of language lessons, the project gained legitimacy in the eyes of the community" (Dixey, 1982, p.108). Indeed it may have been that male sections of the community were actually misled or even deceived. For example: "In order not to alarm the male section of the community, it was necessary that the publicity for the project was 'low key' and not overly visible" (Dixey, 1982, p.108). Second, the concept of 'unequal effort for equal opportunities' has important implications, especially in this instance where free transport was provided, there was no charge for admission, and the pool was made inaccessible to other members of the community. Third, the scheme was a short-term project and at the time there was no guarantee that participation in swimming by this section of society would continue after the scheme had finished. In spite of these reservations, however, some of the key principles of the Fairfax project have been adopted with success elsewhere (David, 1991), and the sort of attention to detail demonstrated in it, has become a blueprint for increased sports participation amongst Muslim women's groups (Lyons, 1989).

A final religious consideration of particular relevance to PE teachers, that applies uniquely to Muslims, is that of the daily fast during the Islamic holy month of *Ramazan*. This matter, like other elements of Muslim culture has been surrounded by a lack of clear understanding. But as levels of awareness have increased, the implications for PE and sport have been made explicit:

> Children who are fasting may feel weak and tired during the day. Strenuous physical exercise may make them feel worse... Those children who go swimming may be concerned about swallowing water - strictly speaking this would be breaking the fast - so they will spit it out. (McDermott and Ahsan 1980, p.47)

As the physical education profession demonstrates an enhanced understanding of the importance of nutrition for physical activity, there is some evidence of increasing tolerance in response to observance of *Ramazan*. But behind the apparent tolerance, lies an inherent reluctance to compromise. As Yates (1986, p.71) explains:

> School can also be seen as jealous of its own cultural territory. The incursion of non-indigenous cultural behaviour is not automatically welcomed. Allowing Muslim girls to wear trousers or opt out of games is sometimes seen as a concession rather than a right.

The appropriateness of clothing for PE and sport is one of the issues that has not been questioned from within the PE profession as effectively as it might have been. The knee-jerk reaction to relieve a perceived problem has dealt primarily with the symptoms. But Robinson (1989, p.135) has suggested a different approach that tackles the cause rather than the effect:

> Sometimes a compromise over required clothing can be reached, and schools need to be ready to ask themselves **why they are asking for certain forms of dress** and whether there are alternatives. [Emphasis added]

The 'problems' approach to Physical Education for a culturally pluralist society offers a series of remedies to the problems and difficulties that different cultural groups encounter in PE and sports participation; the aim, as Bayliss (1989, p.19) remarks, "is to ensure participation with minimum disruption to the programme". Cultural differentness is often treated with suspicion, and Muslims are affected by this perhaps more than any other sizeable minority ethnic group. For example, Cherrington (1975, p.34) reveals the level of intolerance that surrounded Muslims observing of *Ramazan* were subjected to: "[Teachers] suspected that some non-practising Muslim children used fasting as an excuse to avoid PE". For some, that may, of course, have been true; but to have addressed the matter in this way, as Bayliss (1989) argues, made the assumption that the 'problem' lay with the young Muslims, and not with related issues of racism and inappropriate curricula.

Sikhs and Sikhism The religious and cultural position of Sikhs in relation to PE and sport has focused primarily on the religious behaviour and adornments that characterise Sikhism. The 'Five Ks' are described simply by Bayliss (1983, p.3) as:

No shaving or cutting of hair (*Kesh*)
The wearing of a steel bangle on the right wrist (*Kara*)
The wearing of a special comb (*Kangha*), and a turban to cover the hair
The wearing of a long white undergarment, shorts (*Kaccha*)
The wearing of a small ceremonial dagger (*Kirpan*).

Like other groups defined by religious criteria, Sikhs are not an homogeneous group, and observance of the 'Five Ks' will vary. Some will be relatively lax in their observance, others will adopt some of the five, and others still will be very devout in their strictness. The religious and cultural symbolism of the 'Five Ks' is significant for each of the five makes a statement about Sikhism. The *Kesh* is symbolic of complete devotion to God, and the *Kangha* of self-discipline. The *Kirpan* acts as a symbol of self-reliance and as a reminder of the Sikh's duty to defend their faith. The *Kara* indicates solidarity in the unbroken circle of Sikh brotherhood, and the *Kachh* symbolises purity and spiritual freedom (Rotherham MBC, 1988). Therefore, to treat the *Kara* as 'jewellery', in the way that has sometimes occurred, minimises its cultural symbolism, and implies that it is merely a decorative item. Anne Williams (1989b) has remarked, some Sikhs may object to the removal of the *Kara*; and the response from PE teachers has often been to seek another 'remedy': "If there is a problem then the *Kara* can be taped over for physical education so that it does not constitute a danger to others or to its wearer" (p.165).

The notion of female modesty is not restricted to Muslims. Traditional Sikh culture also demands that women should cover their legs (Coventry LEA, 1980). The suggestions from the PE profession (and others) for Muslims apply to Sikhs too, and require no more than 'minor modifications'. Interestingly too, Eleanor Nesbitt (1991) has remarked that many Sikhs enjoy dance, and especially *bhangra*, but she also comments on the objections raised by devout Sikhs, that dance is a distraction for young people from the Guru's teaching.

Hindus and Hinduism It should already be evident that generalising about one of the religious groups originating from the Indian sub-continent is fraught with difficulties, and may ultimately lead to very damaging 'false universalism'. In view of the caste system which creates social differentiation in India, and the polytheism of Hinduism, there would seem to be more differences between groups of Hindus than there are similarities. It has been suggested that caste distinctions persist and

27

play a major role amongst Hindus in Britain (Michaelson, 1979b), but the more general view seems to indicate that caste is largely irrelevant (e.g., Jackson, 1981), or relevant mainly to the Brahmins - the hereditary priestly caste, ritually the most pure - and the lower castes (Jackson and Nesbitt, 1993). Significantly, it seems that although caste consciousness may exist, there is little evidence of caste discrimination (Kanitkar, 1981), and that there is no operational caste structure in place in Britain (Tambs-Lyche, 1975). Lyon (1973) goes further and contends that social stratification based on caste has been replaced by class relations. Whilst caste therefore has an important, and even central role in maintaining the social order amongst Hindus in India, its relevance in Britain is, at most, only peripheral to the wider issues affecting Hindus in particular, and South Asians more generally.

Hinduism is perhaps the religion about which there is greatest difficulty in making any sort of general comment in relation to PE, sport and leisure. There are no obvious religious taboos that are violated by participation, though there are certain superstitions associated with women washing their hair on certain days of the week. The influence of Jainism and *Ahimsa* should not be ignored (as already discussed in chapter two), but Hindu socio-cultural mores would seem to be more compatible with active involvement in sport. Consequently Hinduism receives the least attention from the physical education literature; it is presumably seen as posing fewest 'problems'. In the apparent absence of religious factors that might directly restrict participation in PE lessons, the influences that do impact on Hindus' involvement are socio-cultural. These are, of course, shaped by the Hindu faith, but the mechanisms through which they operate are more indirect.

4 'Away from home': sport and cultural change

In this chapter some of the broad spheres of influence that reflect cultural discontinuity and change are considered in relation to the leisure lifestyles of South Asian youth in Britain. First, the cultural diversity of South Asian youth is highlighted emphasising two key elements of South Asian lifestyles in Britain: generation and class. Though, like the other factors already considered, these do not work in isolation, but produce a complex framework of inter-related variables. Second, the work-leisure relation is addressed in the context of the socio-economic position in which many South Asians are situated. Third, the flawed concept of 'race' is considered because of its profound implications for the ways that young South Asians are stereotyped. Such stereotypes directly reflect an under-lying logic of racism, and though in educational discourse this is often unintended, in other contexts manifestations are considerably more malevolent. This is the focus for the fourth part of the chapter. Finally, some of the documented participation patterns of the sporting and leisure involvement of South Asian communities are addressed. Together, these five sections in conjunction with the themes and issues raised in previous chapters, provide an important backdrop for a contextualised understanding of the sporting and leisure lifestyles of one particular community of South Asian males - Parkview School - which is examined in detail in chapters six and seven.

Generation

It has often been said that South Asian youth in particular is "caught between two cultures", and as such faces a set of unique and distinctive problems. Pilkington (1986, p.148) quotes an unnamed writer who observed that: "Asian youth suffer very distinctly from inhabiting a different world at home from that at school"; or as the CRC (1976, p.7) observe: "Their world is neither the 'old' nor the 'new' but both". This is, of course, somewhat misleading, for it implies that young people move between two intact, coherent and homogeneous societies (Castles et al., 1987); and given the range of influences that affect youth cultures in Britain, it is evidently more appropriate to conceptualise the identities of many young South Asians as demonstrating "multiple cultural competence" (Jackson and Nesbitt, 1993, p.175).

The argument that has been advanced about cultural conflict asserts that the view that the culture of the home is at odds with the culture at the school and elsewhere; which inevitably leads to young South Asians having to face stressful cultural dilemmas. The situation has been presented as particularly acute for young South Asian women, and has been used as part of the explanation for the apparent 'limited career aspirations' and/or 'over-ambition' of young South Asian women (Thornley and Siann, 1991). In contrast to the popular stereotypes, however, there is also evidence to suggest that many young South Asian women enjoy better relationships with their parents than those experienced by their white British peers (Brah and Minhas, 1985).

This raises an important issue, for the influence of 'generation' is more complex than it might, at first, appear. Recognition of the more widespread nature of inter-generational culture clash, and is explained more fully by Frith (1984, p.6) in his consideration of youth cultures:

> The importance of the term 'generation' (as used by sociologist Karl Mannheim) is to draw attention to the fact that people grow up at particular historical moments and may, therefore, share crucial historical experiences with fellow members of their age group - experiences which differentiate them, as a generation, from both older and younger generations... Such different experiences make for different assumptions and expectations about how society can and should work, and these differences may, in turn, be expressed in social conflicts, in a 'generation gap'. (Frith 1984, p.6)

More specifically, as Catherine Ballard observes:

> In dealing with the problems of young Asians it is easy to forget that a phase of rebellion is an almost universal phenomenon, a part of the process of self-discovery in the transition from childhood to adulthood. A period of conflict does not necessarily signify a real wish to break with the family for good: a proportion of all teenagers are temporarily driven to despair and need help with their problems. (Cited in CRC, 1976, p.7-8)

When generational conflict is discussed, it is not only dealt with in the tone and rhetoric of a minor moral panic, but also from an adultcentric perspective. As Roberts (1983, p.36) has remarked, "Most versions of the inter-generational conflict theory portray young people as the offensive party". In the same way that minority groups are dealt with as causing a 'problem', so too young people are identified as the 'youth problem'. Thus there are two real issues concerning generation: the different values and expectations of any youth group from their parents; and the particular difficulties that young South Asians face in reconciling two contrasting forces of socialisation that may, on the face of it, be in direct opposition to each other. Some groups of Muslims in Britain provide perhaps the most vivid examples of this for the reasons already outlined (i.e., clearly evident Muslim cultural distinctiveness); and Bangladeshis who have emigrated to Britain from rural Sylhet are among the most distinct:

They [young Sylhettis] feel that parental values are being imposed on them and that it is difficult for them to live in two worlds... The causes of conflict with parents relate to parental pressures on children to go off to work (boys) or get married (girls) at a very young age. They are also restrained from going out, speaking English or mixing with English people, especially of the opposite sex. (Murshid 1990: 14-15)

Thus for some first-generation Sylhettis inter-generational conflict is a fact of life, though it need not necessarily be so. Malik (1989, p.25) explains that some South Asians have rejected the central plank of the traditional culture - religion - and have adopted a very Westernised lifestyle:

On Saturday afternoons they can be found at Valley Parade cheering on Bradford City, on Saturday nights at the Palace nightclub, jiving to Peter Singh, 'Punjab's only rock and roll king'. Whatever their cultural roots, the young Asians have more in common with their white peers than with their parents.

The important point, though, is that such conflict is, as Craft (1989, p.137) remarks, "a well-recognised feature of all **rapidly-changing** societies" [emphasis added]. As migrants to a new and different culture, many South Asian communities have found themselves in a process of rapid change, and either have experienced, or are still experiencing, these sorts of cultural clashes.

Generational differences have had an impact on the leisure lifestyles of South Asians in Britain; but the ways in which they impact are not fully understood, and are characterised by the vagueness of the comment from Verma et al. (1991, p.3):

Those who are first-generation settlers are probably still inspired by their up-bringing in the Indian sub-Continent which remains more significant in their everyday lives than their more recent British experience.

It is not explicit, but it is at least implied that second and third generation South Asians will become increasingly more and more influenced by 'British experience', and therefore less and less by the traditional culture of the sub-continent. That being so, it would be expected that young second-, and particularly third-generation South Asians would adopt the lifestyle and cultural characteristics of typically Western youth. Their attitudes to sport and leisure would be broadly similar, and these would be reflected in comparable patterns of participation.

The model of generational affiliation to traditional culture of origin that is based solely on a 'dilution' of traditional culture from one generation to the next, has an underlying logic of assimilation. There is evidence, however, of continuity as well as change in the behaviour and culture of second-generation South Asian teenagers (Iqbal, 1981). The experiences of some second and third generation South Asians are a product of both the traditional values of the Indian sub-continent and Westernised social mores (Brah, 1978; Weinreich, 1979). The reality for many young people of South Asian origin is that they are not faced with an either/or situation in relation to culture, but rather that they adopt a synthesis of the two

31

(Ballard, 1976) - what Ghuman (1991b, p.345) has called a "bicultural identity". The point is illustrated well by Pilkington (1986):

> While a growing individualism indicates some acceptance of British values, an emerging militancy points to a fierce rejection of these values and vehement pride in their separate cultural identity. (p.148)

Indeed Roger Ballard has gone further and argued that whilst there are generational conflicts, these occur because the "interest of [younger people] is primarily in reforming and changing Indian society, rather than simply becoming English" (Ballard 1973, p.38).

It is clear that sweeping generalisations about all South Asians can not be made (Craft, 1989), for whilst culture clashes have existed, and indeed still do, inter-generational conflict is not a uniquely South Asian phenomenon. Furthermore, for many other South Asians, a synthesis of cultures has provided an avenue for the adoption of certain Western values whilst retaining certain aspects of ethnic identity and cultural pride (Thompson, 1974; Lovell, 1991).

Class

During the 1960s and 1970s there was a tendency amongst researchers to generalise about the employment patterns of groups of South Asian men (though, significantly, not, until recently, about South Asian women). Broadly speaking, it became apparent that there was a concentration in the manual working categories, with a greater proportion of semi-skilled than skilled or unskilled. As research became increasingly sophisticated, regional patterns emerged; but as Taylor and Hegarty (1985, p.63) commented: "Generalisations may mask considerable differences, between sub-groups of Asian workers and between the same sub-groups in different geographical locations". The critical point that impacts upon sport and leisure participation is that although South Asians collectively were involved across the full range of socio-economic groups (see table 4.1), it is the clear and disproportionate concentration in manual employment that renders them vulnerable to downswings in the economy (Holmes, 1991). The direct implications for South Asians' involvement in sport and leisure are important, for it is clear from John Hargreaves' (1986) exposition of the hegemonic structure of sport in Britain, that class is a central factor in the understanding of participation in sport and leisure.

Predictably there have been debates on the definition, theory and analytical utility of social class as a variable in defining patterns of participation in sport and leisure (Coalter et al., 1995); and more specific concerns about the use of occupation as an indicator of class - principally because: "It reduces class to one dimension, the nature of work, whereas classes are constructed politically and culturally as well" (Hargreaves, 1986, p.96). Yet, as Anthony Giddens (1989, p.724) suggests: "Most sociologists use the term to refer to socio-economic differences between groups of individuals which create differences in the material prosperity and power"; and given

Table 4.1 Socio-economic status of South Asians and 'whites' in Britain, aged 16 and over, in employment, 1981

Occupational group (%)	whites male	whites female	Indians male	Indians female	Pakistanis & Bangladeshis male	Pakistanis & Bangladeshis female
A & B	22.3	7.7	19.5	7.1	19.6	9.0
C1	17.9	53.0	16.9	41.1	7.9	39.9
C2	38.0	7.4	36.7	13.0	31.7	14.1
D	20.4	31.5	26.6	38.7	40.4	14.1
Inadequately described	1.4	0.3	0.3	0.0	0.4	2.7
Nos. (1,000s)	13,325	8,945	174	93	69	10

(Source: Adapted from OPCS, 1982b - cited in Taylor and Hegarty, 1985, p.64; using occupational groupings from Reynolds, 1990)

the very positive correlations between occupation and other variables that might help to provide a multi-dimensional approach to understanding class, it does seem that socio-economic group - as defined by occupation - is a useful basic reference point for a class-based analysis of sport and leisure participation.

On the most obvious level, financial considerations associated with socio-economic position, inhibit the purchase of, or access to equipment and facilities for sport (DES, 1983). One attempt to place class as one of the key factors at the heart of an understanding of individual leisure lifestyles was undertaken by the Bradford Youth Research Team (1988), and by adopting what Reid (1989, p.43) describes as the "'money' model" for understanding social class, the main theme to emerge from the data gathered was the straightforward link between socioeconomic status, disposable income and financial barriers to sports participation. For example, "'I like badminton and cricket but I can't afford the cost of the kit'" (BYRT, 1988, p.77). This was accentuated by the experiences of the long-term unemployed: "'Unwanted, useless, out of things and short of money'" (BYRT, 1988, p.68).

But the importance of class as a factor in sports participation in Britain is well established in terms of both type of activity, and frequency of participation. The pattern to emerge from various participation surveys indicates that:

> Participation was generally higher among people in non-manual than manual socio-economic groups, those in the professional group having the highest rate of participating in at least one sport ... and those in the unskilled manual group the lowest. (Matheson, 1991, p.2)

33

Importantly too, of late, the increasing emphasis placed on individualism in the political ideology of Thatcherism in the 1980s, has coincided with what Bramham (1990) has identified as an increased individualism in sport and leisure in Britain. Tony Mason (1988) suggests that that this is a characteristic of the middle-class, which is manifest in the boom in jogging and squash. More specifically, Alan Tomlinson (1986b, p.45) suggests that the sort of person who might be playing squash is typically a: "White, suburban, middle-class professional male", reflecting what John Bale describes as "part of a lifestyle which defines an 'outer metropolitan popular culture'" (cited in Mason, 1989, p.6).

Through the maintenance and perpetuation of patterns of class-based social interaction through sports participation, and contrary to the popular functionalist perspective of sport as an integrative force in society, sport, like other leisure pursuits, actually reflects and reinforces patterns of social division and social inequality. For though it has been claimed that opportunities do exist in sport and leisure, working-class leisure is characterised by constraints rather than choices (Tomlinson, 1988). The reality is that the range of actual choices is not as wide as the range of facilities offered. Put simply, "Just because the resources or facilities are there is no guarantee that they are accessible to all" (A. Tomlinson 1986b, p.56).

South Asians, work and leisure

The centrality of class in an understanding of the sport and leisure participation of South Asians in Britain is directly affected by the work-leisure relation, for it is not possible to divorce the socio-economic position from those attitudes that are popularly perceived as being typically South Asian, which are reflected in the attitudes to work, and also leisure and sport. The full complexity of the socio-economic position of South Asians in Britain needs, of course, to be historically and socially contextualised; and for South Asians in Britain in the 1990s, the main economic factors that influence the work-leisure relation have been shaped by the post-war period.

The 1950s were characterised by a period of post-war reconstruction and economic boom. There was a shortage of labour, and it was in what Pryce (1986, p.56) has called "shit-work" that the shortage of labour was particularly acute. Employers were finding difficulty in recruiting to jobs that were hard and/or dirty and/or poorly paid; so too in the public services like the transport system and hospitals where hours and working conditions were unattractive. The black workforce was exploited, deskilled, segregated, and kept in low pay (Sivanandan, 1976). The classic remedy of capitalist societies in this sort of situation is to draw upon the pool of unemployed people to fill vacancies. But at this time of economic prosperity and low unemployment, there was no such supply, and employers were forced to turn their attentions overseas. Under the 1948 Nationality Act citizens of former British colonies were granted United Kingdom citizenship, which meant that workers from India and Pakistan could come to Britain and stay for an indefinite period (Bourke, 1994).

It is also important to recall that conditions in the Indian sub-continent provided strong encouragement for some to emigrate: British rule had created widespread and persistent impoverishment; the upheaval of the partition into India and Pakistan deprived millions of their jobs and their homes; and natural catastrophes as well as unnatural disasters - such as religious massacres - made the prospect of emigration especially attractive (Socialist Party, 1988). Hence United Kingdom citizens from India and Pakistan, 95% of whom were of rural origin (Dahya, 1973), migrated to Britain during the 1950s. Some did so in the realistic hope of finding work on arrival; others had been actively recruited before leaving (Todd, 1991). Britain encouraged immigration from former colonies as a matter of economic expediency, to meet the labour demands that would not otherwise have been met (Khan, 1985). Since then, in what Kapo (1981, p.20) has described as "the quick-change artistry of British morality", and what Stuart Hall has referred to as 'historical amnesia' (BBC TV, 1977), South Asians in Britain have been subjected to humiliation and discrimination in the jobs market of a predominantly white society (Forester, 1978; Wrench, 1989).

These experiences have undoubtedly influenced South Asians in their attitudes towards work, and therefore their perceptions of leisure and sport. Malik (1988) captures the crux of the matter in her observation that the South Asian communities in Britain are socially and economically disadvantaged, and culturally isolated; and that for them: "exercise and sport may not rank as a priority" (Malik, 1988, p.5). Indeed it has been asserted that not only is play in the most general sense unimportant to South Asian communities (Child, 1983), but also that there are moral implications associated with the concept of leisure that affect South Asians' participation patterns (Michaelson, 1979a).

A synthesis of some of the key pieces of published research on South Asian lifestyles indicates that in the clearly defined and separate gender-roles in many South Asian families (Taylor and Hegarty, 1985), it is well established that men have the responsibility for being the family provider (Hiro, 1973). Many South Asian men in Britain, particularly first-generation, have sought upward social mobility (Dove, 1975) and have adopted a very instrumental attitude to work. Work has often been seen as a means to fulfil economic needs (Lloyd, 1986), and became a central priority for many. In this way the commitment to the work ethic has fundamentally shaped participation in sport and leisure both directly - the availability of disposable leisure time; and indirectly - the positive attitude to work which implies a distinctly negative attitude to non-work. For example, there has been a view amongst some that leisure activities were a "money wasting drain on the family budget" (Michaelson, 1979a, p.66).

When working for an employer outside the kinship network, there is evidence that South Asian employees were often very willing to work overtime (Kew, 1979; Lloyd, 1986), thereby choosing to sacrifice leisure time; and were tolerant of shifts at unsociable hours (Verma, 1983; Taylor and Hegarty, 1985), suggesting an acceptance of restricted leisure choices. Furthermore, having sought the independence, security, respect and recognition that discrimination in the white-controlled jobs market denies them, many South Asians have turned to self-employment and entrepreneurial experimentation. The success of many such businesses has been indicative of the lifestyle choices that South Asian entrepreneurs and their families have been prepared to make (Forester, 1978). Many businesses have relied on long hours from workers just to remain solvent; and a large and increasing number of South Asian women have been employed as

35

subcontracted 'homeworkers' - for which they have been grossly underpaid (Mitter, 1987).

Whilst work has provided one highly-valued avenue for upward social mobility amongst adult South Asians, for their children education has offered an alternative (Tomlinson, 1983; Verma, 1983). Among the South Asian communities many parents have had high aspirations for their children (Lewis, 1979), and education is traditionally held in high regard (Dove, 1975; Bowen, 1981) - not necessarily as an end in itself, but in the hope that better academic performance will lead to improved employment prospects (Hiro, 1973). Hence many South Asian children received great encouragement from their parents to achieve academically (Taylor, 1973), and to use any available leisure time for educational purposes (John, 1971). Young South Asians have been disproportionately over-represented in private sector (fee-paying) education (Gidoomal and Fearon, 1993); and many often demonstrated a very favourable attitude to school (Dove, 1975), expecting to gain educational qualifications or a practical skill from their schooling (CRC, 1977). As Thomas (1990, p.42) explains: "Education is used instrumentally, then, as a weapon to—⟹ fight racial discrimination and gain status within the wider community and host society".

Examination achievements and practical skills are very clearly associated with prospects in the employment market by many South Asian parents, and anything perceived not to be directly concerned with the attainment of either or both of these has often been seen as a 'frill activity' (Hiro, 1973). School sport in the form of PE, has often been regarded by many parents as one such frill activity (Lashley, 1980a; White, 1990) - especially amongst first generation settlers in Britain. In spite of the status that Physical Education now has as a 'foundation subject' within the National Curriculum (DES and WO, 1991), and the increasingly academic focus of the subject with examination qualifications at GCSE and 'A' level in PE and Sports Studies, it seems likely that many South Asian parents still view PE as a marginal subject area (Leaman, 1984a; Carrington and Williams, 1988). Craft and Klein (1986, p.70) have suggested that, "Some Asian families are not convinced of the educational potential of physical activities and of 'play'"; and it can be inferred from the observations of the CRC (1977), that some South Asian parents may disapprove of their children's involvement in PE, seeing it as 'just playing around'. The argument that has been presented is that PE is degrading and not academic enough, and complaints have been made about school time-tables for their excessive stress on play and games (Hiro, 1969). It is likely that this view has been reinforced when South Asian parents have had, and in some instances have accepted the opportunity to withdraw their children from this element of the secular curriculum.

Reported involvement in extra-curricular clubs and out-of-school activities has also supported the proposition that young South Asians are disinclined to participate in frill activities. Hiro (1973), referring to a study conducted by David Beetham in Handsworth during the mid-1960s, speculates that South Asians have failed to grasp the meaning or usefulness of many such activities; but:

> Uniformed organizations - namely Brownies, Scouts, Girl-Guides, etc. - are the exception, because Asian parents consider these to be a 'legitimate'

part of school activities. Indeed Asians join these enthusiastically. (Hiro, 1973, p.166)

There is further evidence to suggest that different groups of South Asians have engaged in the activities of uniformed organisations (Colson, 1991), and that single-sex groups have appealed to the South Asian communities (DoE, 1977); yet recent surveys of the leisure patterns of young South Asians suggest the opposite (Carrington et al., 1987; BYRT, 1988). The important point, however, is that uniformed organisations, in spite of their religious associations have often been perceived more favourably by many South Asian parents because of their educational worthiness. A career in sport, by contrast, does not conform to a positive educational orientation, and as Jimmy Khan, a professional football coach succinctly put it, "The boys in the family are thought to be the bread winners, and it's like a taboo profession - football" (BBC TV, 1991d).

Sport, 'race' and perceptions of South Asians

An understanding of the participation in sport and leisure by people from the Indian sub-continent clearly requires a religious and cultural contextualisation, and explanations of sports participation that are advanced without acknowledging these influences are fundamentally flawed. Yet some commentators have done precisely that, and in a superficial analysis have referred to some quasi-causal link between 'race' and sports performance. Imran Khan, for example, suggests the sociologically discredited concept of nationally or 'racially' determined innate ability as an explanation for the sporting success that some Pakistanis have enjoyed in certain games:

> There is an extraordinary amount of talent in ball games in Pakistan... When I play in club games at home, I see young batsmen playing some remarkable shots that stem from natural ability, far more impressive than their counterparts in England. (Khan and Murphy, 1983, p.127)

Former Indian tennis star, Vijay Amritraj, is even more explicit:

> As a race, we are also handsomely endowed with hand-to-eye co-ordination, which is why so many of our youngsters excel naturally at ball sports like cricket, squash and tennis. (Amritraj and Evans, 1990, p.116)

Quite apart from the problems that have been identified by sociologists and anthropologists concerning the validity and usefulness of 'race' as an analytical tool (Husband, 1982 Cashmore, 1988; Miles, 1989; Solomos, 1989), the association of 'race' with natural sporting ability has also been very effectively discredited in relation to the claims made about people of Afro-Caribbean descent (see, for example, Cashmore, 1982, pp.43-56; and 1990, pp.86-88).

One important issue is that claims about natural ability and superiority in some particular areas, imply inability and inferiority in others. Thus, the sports in which South Asians have excelled are identified as those in which they have natural

37

ability, and those in which they have not excelled are identified as those for which they naturally unsuited. Apparent inability has been acknowledged and dismissed as an "hereditary problem that may take a generation or two to overcome" (Amritraj and Evans 1990, p.117). The factual accuracy of this claim for the geneticist is largely immaterial, for it is this emphasis on assumed suitability for certain sports that is a more pervasive. Such logic becomes the basis of stereotypes.

South Asians, sport and stereotypes

It was not until the mid-to-late 1980s that some of the established wisdom about the sporting and leisure preferences of South Asians were subjected to any sort of scrutiny; typically, such wisdom was couched in the form of stereotypes. Prior to that a prevalent perception of young South Asians was of the academic achiever, and this has become, what Gillian Klein (1993) has referred to as a 'benign stereotype'. Significantly, though, when set in juxtaposition with other stereotypes about the positive attributes associated with the physicality of other groups, the implication is that young South Asians are perceived negatively with regard to sports participation. Horace Lashley (1980a) has commented that: "Asio-black children are not expected to succeed in sports and PE... Asio-blacks are thought of as more highly motivated and successful academically" (p.5), and the belief that young South Asians were physically less able than their peers from other ethno-cultural groups became very widespread, especially in educational discourse. Stereotypic rumours, myths and assumptions about South Asian children became the norm amongst the physical education profession, emphasising negative characteristics. Some were generalisations about the physiological and anatomical capacities of young South Asians:

"Asian children have low ball skills, low coordination and are weak", "Asian and West Indian children dislike the cold" (cited in Bayliss, 1983, pp.6-7);
"Asian girls have great difficulties in PE" (cited in Cherrington, 1975, p.34);
"[South Asian girls] have difficulty in reproducing some simple body postures" (Cherrington, 1975, p.41);
"Where stamina is required, Asian girls are often at a disadvantage as they are usually small and quite frail" (Lewis, 1979, p.132);
"Asians are too frail for contact sports" (cited in Bayliss, 1989, p.20).

Others reflected the stereotypic perceptions of the aptitude of South Asians for certain sporting activities rather than others:

"Asians are poor swimmers", "Asian children dislike contact sports but excel in individual skill sports such as badminton", "Asian children are good at hockey (cited in Bayliss, 1983, p.6);
"Asians can only play hockey" (cited in Bayliss, 1989, p.20);
"Pakistani boys are exceptionally good at Badminton at an earlier age than most other groups", "Indian boys are excellent at hockey and running",

38

"Asian boys generally prefer non-contact games" (cited in Cherrington 1975, p.34);
"Sikh children not liking rugby" (cited in Coventry LEA, 1980, p.28)

There have also been attempts to explain the phenomenon of South Asians' perceived under-achievement in physical activities that have drawn upon psychological factors and the forces of socialisation during the formative years:

"[South Asian girls are] Not encouraged to play with toys, balls or ropes, but the daily household chores are stressed as important" (Lewis, 1979, p.132);
"Asian children are not encouraged to play with toys, balls, ropes, and this effects [sic] their ability to play games" (cited in Bayliss, 1983, p.6)
"Asian players are too excitable and they're too undisciplined [for football]. And maybe they haven't got the character, and maybe they haven't got the build" (cited on BBC TV, 1991d)

It is unlikely that these are merely blind prejudices. Lewis (1979), for example, confirms some of the prevalent views based on her own empirical evidence - albeit subjective and anecdotal; and for some of the reasons already discussed, it is not surprising to discover comments indicating that some South Asians are negatively disposed to certain contact sports. It is also unsurprising to find evidence of South Asians demonstrating competence in such sports as hockey and badminton; there is, after all, something of a tradition for these sports in the sub-continent, and they are the sorts of activities that first-generation South Asians are most likely to have experienced before migrating to Britain.

The real danger that existed and was perpetuated was of perceived South Asian physical inability which was explained by some quasi-scientific argument, despite the clear absence of objective physiological evidence to support physiologically based stereotypes (LCSR, 1989). As a consequence, a substantive critique and deconstruction of stereotypes does not start with the scientific efficacy of the explanations (which have been most convincingly discredited), but, as Small (1994) indicates, with the widespread attitudes and belief systems that have become entrenched. A common outcome is that:

The Asian pupil is typically seen as physically frail, lacking in stamina and likely to underachieve in physical education, in contrast to their stereotype as quiet, hardworking and intelligent in the classroom. (Williams, 1989b, p.167)

More alarming is the manner in which such views become established as 'folklore', and young South Asians are verbally abused using this bogus information; for example, "The white boys tell me they can run faster than me because they are white and I am a 'chocolate face'" (cited in MacDonald et al., 1989, p.134). These views even become elements of 'popular' sports coaching wisdom. For instance, among the reasons offered by Premiership football clubs in England for the failure of South Asians to break into the professional ranks, there are some fallacious arguments that border on the absurd:

Their diet is unsuitable - "all that vegetarian food". "They don't like open changing rooms." "They have to interrupt training to say their prayers." "Some of them refuse to take off their turbans". (cited by Rowbottom, 1995)

"The Asian build is not that of a footballer ... It may well be that Asian ingredients in food, or their nutrition that they take, [is] not ideal for building up a physical frame" - Dave Bassett [manager of Sheffield United Football Club] (BBC TV 1995)

It is clear that for <u>some</u> South Asians in Britain, each of these factors may, indeed, be relevant. But there is no good reason to suppose that a well balanced and nutritionally appropriate diet for intensive sports participation can not be developed from traditional ingredients from the culture of the Indian sub-continent. And it is both ignorant and unreasonable to suppose that all South Asians (or even all Muslims) would have to interrupt their training for prayers, or that all South Asians (or even all Sikhs) refuse to take off their turbans.

Perceived aptitude for particular sports became the basis on which many schools focused their PE curricula to accommodate a large South Asian population in the school. That is to say, an emphasis was placed on those activities that were considered popular with South Asian and other ethno-cultural groups, invariably cricket and hockey (Townsend and Brittan, 1973). Indeed assertions based on racially linked 'natural ability', which have been overwhelmingly rejected elsewhere, have become prominent as an expedient rationalisation of the situation. Some South Asians have internalised the self image, and even 'swallowed the myth' themselves.

The concept of channelling young people into those areas in which they are perceived to have particular competence has been applied to the way in which young Afro-Caribbeans have been pushed into a sporting career at the expense of academic study (Cashmore, 1982a; Carrington, 1983). It would seem reasonable to assume that the same is true - in reverse - for young South Asians (see Mac an Ghaill, 1988). The perception of South Asians as under-achievers in PE and sport inevitably influenced the behaviour of teachers towards them. As Anne Williams (1989b, p.167) explains: "Stereotyping Asian pupils as physically weak is just as likely to become a self-fulfilling prophecy as is the stereotyping of Afro-Caribbeans as academically inferior". It is not surprising to discover, therefore, that 'a lack of expertise' was identified by Carrington et al. (1987), as an important inhibiting factor in the leisure choices made by young South Asian women.

South Asians, sport and role models

The absence of high-profile South Asian sports stars in Britain has been remarked upon (Cashmore, 1982a; Rex, 1982; Datar, 1989; Lovell, 1991), though it is true, of course, that some of the world's top performers in certain sports are South Asians. But they are from cricket and squash in particular, and also tennis, hockey, wrestling and weight lifting. These reinforce the stereotypic notions of the activities at which South Asians more generally excel. Indeed by identifying those sports at which South Asians have achieved success, Craft and Klein (1986, p.70) may have unwittingly further reinforced them further still:

Stereotypes of Asian pupils being below par at PE exist in some schools, despite the fact that they excel in volleyball, hockey, badminton, cricket, lacrosse, squash, table tennis, tennis, polo and a variety of other sports.

For whilst they eschew the stereotypes of physical inability, they then highlight activities at which South Asians have excelled. Interestingly too, Pirani (1974) has suggested that South Asians do not even identify with typical role models - for example footballers and pop stars - in the same way as their white peers, and have more realistic aspirations. This is not insignificant, as there is a general view that more South Asian men will emerge in elite level sport in Britain once one player or athlete has made a real breakthrough - for example in football (c.f. BBC TV 1995); and hence mirror the emergence and development of elite African-Caribbean sportsmen and sportswomen. But that would seem to be a serious over-simplification for it ignores two main factors: first, the central significance of racism in the leisure lifestyles and sports participation of minority ethnic groups; and second, that sport is experienced and perceived differently in different ethno-cultural groups. There is an implicit assumption that sport occupies the same place in South Asian cultures that it does in African-Caribbean cultures, and that attitudes and motives for participation would be similar. This does not stand up to critical examination.

Sport and racism

During the last decade there has been a growth in the level of interest in sport and ethnicity. The reasons for this, Jarvie (1991a; 1991b) suggests, include the disproportionate number of successful black sportsmen and sportswomen, and the view that these successes indicate that sport is one area of society that is free of racism, thus providing real opportunities for minority groups (Freeman, 1986). The inescapable fact, however, is that sport is one institution within a racist society, and is itself inherently racist.

Abercrombie et al. (1984, p.173) define racism as "The determination of actions, attitudes or policies by beliefs about racial characteristics", and go on to outline two levels on which it operates:

Racism may be (1) overt and individual, involving individual acts of oppression against subordinate racial groups or individuals, and (2) covert and institutional, involving structural relations of subordination and oppression between social groups.

This definition does not embrace all elements of an ontological and epistemological analysis of racism (as, for example, Skillen, 1993, begins to); and does not catalogue in detail the specific types of racism (as Figueroa, 1993, attempts to). But it is, nevertheless, useful, as it does assist in framing an informed, but not restrictive, analysis of the sport-racism relation in Britain.

Grant Jarvie (1991b) raises further concerns about definitions of racism arguing that 'Afro-Caribbeans' and 'South Asians' are not monolithic terms, that they are not homogeneous groups of people, and that racism affects different groups in different ways. He suggests therefore that: "It is more realistic to talk in terms of racisms since the histories, ideologies and practices which contribute to each form of racism are as different as they are alike" (Jarvie, 1991b, p.21). This is an important distinction, and the way in which language is used is significant. But, at the same time, for our purposes here, it is a distraction from the substantive point that the experiences of racism in sport are experienced differently by different ethno-cultural groups, and they respond to it in different ways. Indeed there is even evidence that the ways in which an individual might experience racism in sport are modified by local and regional reference points (Burley, 1994).

It is inappropriate, therefore, to transplant the experiences of African-Caribbeans in sport directly onto South Asian. They do, however, provide an illustration of the pervasiveness of racism; and this is central to an understanding of the sport-ethnicity dynamic (Kew, 1979; Pote-Hunt, 1987; LCSR, 1989; Jarvie, 1991a; Lashley, 1991). The themes that apply to Afro-Caribbeans can therefore act as point of departure for the analysis of South Asians' experiences of Sport and racism.

Cashmore (1982a) has examined the experiences of Afro-Caribbean men in sport in his book Black Sportsmen, and in other published work (Cashmore, 1981; 1982b; 1983; 1986; 1990). His research is not without its critics, especially with regard to some methodological flaws (see Carrington, 1986), but his work gave impetus to the subsequent interest in this area. This ranges from the tabloidesque (Hamilton, 1982; Woolnough, 1982), through the empirical academic (Wood and Carrington, 1982; Carrington and Wood, 1983), to the theoretical (Carrington, 1983; 1986). Biographical and autobiographical accounts of leading Afro-Caribbean sportsmen and sportswomen also provide further anecdotal, and sometimes rather subjective, sources of evidence (Hill, 1987; 1989; Longmore, 1988). Indeed the subject of racism in sport has become so topical that the mass media has entered the debate with increasing frequency: television documentaries have proliferated (BBC TV, 1990a; 1991a; 1991b; 1991c; 1991d; 1992; 1995; Channel 4 TV 1991b), and journalistic descriptions and analyses of the documentaries and other relevant issues have reached a wide audience (Freeman, 1986; Hughes, 1989; Cashmore, 1990a; Glanville, 1990; Terrill, 1990; S. Wilson, 1990; P. Wilson 1991; Crooks, 1991; Hill, 1991; Mitchell, 1991; Walsh, 1991).

The research has focused predominantly on Afro-Caribbean males, but there is some evidence that Afro-Caribbean females are affected in some similar ways - as well as others. The broad conclusions to emerge are basically threefold. First, Afro-Caribbeans have suffered acutely from overt and individual racism (Pote-Hunt, 1987; LCSR, 1989). There are numerous examples that include abuse from team-mates, opponents, spectators, coaches and managers, all of which are well documented and from different sports (in addition to those already referred to above, see, for example, Greenidge and Symes, 1980; Sanderson and Hickman, 1986; Vitale, 1990; Harrison, 1991; Maguire, 1991; Mott, 1992).

Second, the fact that many Afro-Caribbeans have achieved national and international success in sport does not suggest that sport is free of racism. Rather, the sporting successes of Afro-Caribbeans indicate that they are being denied access to opportunities in other spheres of life in a racist society. As Cashmore (1990a) remarks, and with the benefit of hindsight the argument is unexceptional, quite simply:

> There is a relationship between blacks' persistently high achievement in sport and their rock-bottom status in society generally. Their sports success is attributable in large part to the fact that they have been - and still are - excluded from many other occupations. (p.10)

Moreover to achieve success it is "twice as hard for blacks" (Cashmore, 1982a; Regis, 1990). That is, as former professional footballer Danny Thomas explained to Cashmore:

> Initially, to make the breakthrough, it's very difficult for black people. It's the same as the rest of society, if there are two people of equal ability, the white person will usually be given the opportunity; he'll progress whereas a black man won't. (Cashmore 1982a, p.193)

Third, in spite of the successes that Afro-Caribbeans have achieved as performers, they are still being denied access to power on an institutional level. Afro-Caribbeans are seriously under-represented in the management, administration, officiating, governing and ownership of sport (Lashley, 1990; Liston, 1993).

Hence, as Jarvie (1991b, p.20) has observed, contrary to the view of some liberal-minded sports enthusiasts, academics and other aficionados - that sport "more than any other aspect of society, enjoys a certain degree of democratisation and equality" - the reality is that racism is rife in sport.

The reaction of the sports establishment when presented with this seemingly overwhelming evidence is that "there ain't no problem here" (Jarvie, 1991b); and although this view is argued with conviction, it is unconvincing. The response from Tom McNab (1990) to the television documentary 'Inside Story: The Race Game' (BBC TV, 1990b) is illustrative. He refutes the thrust of the programme remarking that, "I believe that Inside Story represents a gross calumny of our sport [athletics]"; and argues further that: "Nobody said life was fair, but that doesn't mean that any such unfairness is necessarily due to race" (McNab 1990, p.12). His criticisms of the evidence provided were that such evidence was atypical and anecdotal. The point is, though, that it was concerned almost exclusively with institutional racism - covert and structural discrimination that denied access to positions of power. Such evidence can be challenged, but there comes a point when the body of evidence becomes so large that its accumulative impact is far from atypical and anecdotal.

In the second point of contention, McNab suggested that as the evidence of racism lay outside his own personal experience, its existence could therefore be questioned. He remarks:

> Perhaps it [racism] is being experienced daily in sport by Afro-Caribbeans, Indians and Pakistanis on our tracks and on our games fields. If so, then I will duly apologise when the evidence is presented to me. (McNab, 1990, p.12)

What this myopic attitude fails to acknowledge is the typicality of McNab's own experience; as an elite coach he works with top-level athletes who have often succeeded in spite of the racism rather than because of its absence. Moreover, it fails to account for the Afro-Caribbeans and South Asians who never actually get to the track or games field because of their fear of racism. As Kriss Akabusi revealed in a television interview (ITV, 1995), experiences of racism in track and field athletics per se are perhaps not as blatant as in other sports, but his experiences as a black track athlete are significant because they reveal a certain acceptance of the place of racism in British society:

> Akabusi: "Athletes have a better sense of people and the world around them."
> Interviewer: "What about your mail-bag?"
> Akabusi: "In that I get the **normal sort** of hate mail. I've got letters - 'who do you think you're representing?' and 'go back to your own country'". [Emphasis added]

South Asians and racism in sport

With fewer South Asians involved in high-profile sport in Britain there is considerably less evidence of racism directed towards, or experienced by them. Much of it is anecdotal, but no less valid for that; and the big question then is the extent to which the phenomenon is commonplace.

Overt and individual racism directed at South Asians in sport has not been extensively documented, but from certain sources - even those in which its existence is denied - it is clearly apparent that it does exist. Ikram Butt, who made his debut for the England Rugby League team in early 1995, makes some direct and scathing comments about his own experiences of racism:

> There's a lot of racism in sport, and Rugby League is no different. You'll find you get a lot of racism from spectators and fellow professionals - most of it coming from opposing players. From the spectators point of view, you get comments like 'get back to your corner shop' - which I find amusing because I haven't got a corner shop. From fellow professionals I get comments like 'black git' and comments like being a 'Paki'. These comments and these jibes - you tolerate them; but I can never accept them. (ITV, 1995)

To further illustrate the point:

> Hitendra Tejura, a Hammersmith and Fulham Council Action Sport worker, who organised the football tournaments, has experienced it [racism]: "I used to play in Dagenham, and that's where we had most aggravation. I've been chased, and I've been beaten up in the car park afterwards. (Bhandari, 1991, p.24)
> Bouldering started positively with low level scrambles and tricky problems, but interest waned leading to high jinks and abusive confrontations with other outdoor enthusiasts in the car park. The

positive effects of Asians **'staying where they belong'** were expressed, serving only to inflame an already heated situation. (Oldfield, 1991, p.22, emphasis added).

Racism is part of life if you are young and Asian and living in Bradford... "If anybody says anything to me, I just have a go back," [the Alfalah Cricket Club] spin bowler said. (White, 1990, p.29)

Football spectator racism has been identified for some time (Robins, 1984; Williams et al., 1984; Hill, 1987; 1989; Taylor, 1994), but the absence of South Asian players has meant that Afro-Caribbeans have been the focus for offensive chanting and other abuse. Recently, however, with South Asians' issues becoming more to the forefront of public awareness, South Asians have also become targets: "At Elland Road, home of Leeds United, the racists on the terraces sing 'Rushdie is a Leeds fan'" (Malik, 1989, p.24).

One important factor in the recognition of racist abuse of South Asians is the manner in which spectator behaviour is treated as 'humorous' and therefore effectively condoned. In this way offensive verbal abuse can be explained away as crowd banter:

Last year whilst namesake Saddam was still testing the waters of international opinion, some boundaryside Derbyshire wit blurted ... "Give us our kids back you bastard", which even brought a lopsided grin to Nasser's normally cool countenance. He can probably expect a lot more where that came from. (Pringle, 1991a, p.35)

Another part of the difficulty in identifying the prevalence of this type of verbal and physical racist abuse is that sporting institutions are inclined to deny its existence, to refute allegations of racist practice, and adopt the "there ain't no problem here" stance. This is not, of course, some kind of elaborate conspiracy theory propagated by sports administrators concerned with the maintenance of the status quo. Rather, this position is often sincerely and genuinely advanced (for example, McNab, 1990; Dunnett, 1991), in spite of the overwhelming evidence to the contrary.

Rod Dunnett (1991) asserts that there is open access and equal opportunity in hockey in England, and cites the successes of individual South Asian players, umpires and teams with a South Asian representation as evidence. Yet he goes on to comment that:

Although racial taunts from spectators who ought to know better are not unknown even at small children's events, the vast majority of those involved in the sport bridge the apparent racial divide with ease. (Dunnett 1991, p.24)

Herein lie the fundamental flaws of this position. South Asians (and other easily identifiable minority ethnic groups) are subjected to racial taunts as a part of their experience in hockey. Players' experiences are influenced by skin colour, and opportunities are therefore not equal. Furthermore, Dunnett implies that there is a small minority involved in the game who do not cross the apparent racial divide with ease; and that there are also some who are not involved in the game who are unable to do so. Access may be open, but it would seem to be more open for some than for others.

When individual racism and institutional racism are experienced jointly, as they often are, the structural inequality is much more profound. The issues then are not solely concerned with personal abuse, but also with the allocation of power (Alexander, 1987). For example, the failure of a Yorkshire-born South Asian cricketer to make an impact at Yorkshire County Cricket Club is well documented, and illustrates the general phenomenon faced by minority groups when confronted by prejudicial attitudes, personal abuse and structural powerlessness.

Yorkshire CCC has been the venue of well-publicised racist abuse directed at leading Afro-Caribbean players (Richards and Foot, 1982; Marshall, 1987; Mitchell, 1991), and both Hopps (1989) and Henderson (1992) describe how the club has been criticised by minority groups and accused of racial discrimination. The allegation has been rejected by the club, but the attitudes manifested by some officials suggested the opposite. The following well publicised comments were made by the then-'Chairman' Brian Close:

> Bloody Pakistanis didn't know the damn thing [cricket]... If I went to another country I wouldn't expect people to fall over backwards. It'd be up to me to meet them more than half way. And I'll tell you something: the biggest community in this area - Yorkshire - is the Asian community, who are the poorer people. They hadn't bloody jobs over there, came over here to come into the textile trade - low wages. Did you know that over in Pakistan and India, the poorer people didn't even know cricket existed?... (BBC TV, 1990b)

Close was not alone in making such remarks, other club officials were heard at different times to express similar sentiments:

> At a trial match, Wasim Raja struck a quick and flamboyant score in the thirties before being caught on the boundary. As he walked off, he heard one Yorkshire official say to the other: "Typical Paki, never get their heads down". (White, 1990, p.29)

Such attitudes are manifestly racist and prejudicial, and it is not difficult to understand why the perception among the South Asian communities is that they are discriminated against. One South Asian player, Talij Butt, expressed a commonly held opinion:

> Being Asian definitely made it more difficult, and I got where I was just on hard work - I had no coaching. Other lads I know went along for nets at Headingley but felt there was a definite racial bias. It was a case of don't ring us, we'll ring you. (Holmes, 1990, p.20)

He elaborated elsewhere, quite simply that, "I think there is definitely a prejudice" (BBC TV, 1990b).

Consequently in 1983 the South Asian communities in Bradford formed the all-Asian *Qa'id-e-A'zam* League as a direct result of the frustration resulting from Yorkshire's apparent failure to recognise anything but white talent (BBC TV, 1990b). More recently, attempts supported at governmental level have sought to dispel the reputation that Yorkshire CCC has acquired (Hopps, 1992), but only the emergence of a Yorkshire-born South Asian cricketer in the Yorkshire CCC first team will begin to do that. Inevitably, the first South Asian to play for Yorkshire was likely to be the target for accusations of tokenism (Holmes, 1990), but the signing of Indian test batsman Sachin Tendulkar for 1992 may have provided a convenient 'window of opportunity' for Yorkshire CCC. In abandoning the necessary requirement that players representing the club must be Yorkshire-born, and by signing a player of proven international status, accusations of tokenism are less credible. Furthermore, a Yorkshire CCC official has indicated the 'public relations' importance of the signing: "Tendulkar's arrival will help persuade 'our Asian friends' that Yorkshire is committed to building bridges" (Henderson, 1992, p. 21). Importantly too in this regard, the 'Devon Malcolm Cricket Centre' is responding to the cultural strength of the South Asian communities in Sheffield by providing an outlet for the competitive talents of young South Asian cricketers in the area (K. Mitchell, 1995).

The existence of institutional racism has also been identified in much of the voluntary sector (London RCSR, 1989), and the response of the South Asian community in Bradford to racial discrimination has become the typical reaction of the South Asians elsewhere. Without the power to effect any structural change in inherently racist institutions, South Asian communities have remained in kinship and community organisations, and may even have withdrawn further into them. Opportunities for sport have been provided through a process of cultural segregation (Hoggett and Bishop, 1984). The annual Hindu Half-Marathon is a good example (Asian Times, 25/9/1990), so too the Leicester Navana Cricket Club (BBC TV, 1991b), and the National Asian Sporting Association acts as a policy-making governing body for the developments in 'all-Asian' sport - the All England Asian Five-a-Side Football Tournament and similar developments in cricket, badminton, table tennis, athletics and netball (Bhandari, 1991). As Hitendra Tejura, a Hammersmith and Fulham Council Action Sport worker explained:

"You've got open events in which Asians can't participate because of the racial aggravation, so we're just balancing things out. This is a national event where Asian people know they will be safe" (Bhandari, 1991, p.24).

Other South Asians have expressed the view that they have suffered from institutional racism, not necessarily in the form of this kind of overt racist practice, but rather in subtle forms that often go unnoticed by white people (Pote-Hunt, 1987). Rashid Mama has commented on the failure of football talent scouts to 'spot' young South Asians (BBC TV, 1991d); Kulbir Bhaura (1989) has remarked on selectorial bias in representative hockey; and the Pakistan Test batsman Younis Ahmed feels that he has been unreasonably overlooked when he has applied for coaching jobs. These are subjective judgements, and it could be argued that they are isolated and unrepresentative. The point however, is that when a substantial body of isolated bits of evidence indicating institutional racism is built up, the issue ceases to be of concern only to the individuals concerned, it becomes a much broader issue; and one for which the 'sociological imagination', emphasising the links between individual ills and public issues, provides an important conceptual framework.

South Asians, sport and leisure participation

Detailed analyses of South Asians' patterns of participation in sport and leisure are, as already explained, very limited. Projects have become increasingly ambitious, and it is almost a quantum leap to move from Lewis' (1979) small-scale analysis of a class of pupils of which a minority were South Asian, to the large-scale survey conducted by Verma et al. (1991). In terms of the scale of the work, somewhere between these two are the surveys by Livingstone (1977), Carrington et al. (1987), and the Bradford Youth Research Team (1988); and together these provide a useful, if incomplete picture of South Asian involvement in sport and leisure.

Amongst these studies, Livingstone's (1977) survey of young South Asian males might seem to have most relevance. The sample of 432 South Asian males aged 8-14 included large representations of Hindus (21%), Muslim (25%) and Sikh (41%); and the purpose of that investigation was to ascertain leisure involvement and needs. However its focus on uniformed organisations - particularly the scout movement - gave the survey an emphasis that was rather too focused for the construction of the broader picture of South Asian lifestyles. More recently, a survey of young people in Bradford provides more contemporary data of South Asian youth (BYRT 1988). Yet with a sub-sample size of only 32 South Asians (11% of the total sample), drawing meaningful conclusions about South Asian youth lifestyles is not possible. In this regard, the two more valuable investigations were those carried out by Carrington et al. (1987) and Verma et al. (1991). The former had a sample of 114 South Asians; and the latter a total of 952 respondents - of whom 282 were Muslim, 71 were Hindu and 51 were Sikh.

These, together with Beetham (1968), Botholo et al. (1986) and Lloyd (1986), indicate certain commonalties of experience that can contribute to an overall understanding of the issues relating to South Asians and sports participation. The sporting and leisure habits conform to the patterns, trend and stereotypes identified above. For example Beetham's (1968) study of school-leavers indicated that South Asians were generally reluctant to join out-of-school clubs, but when they did join, the clubs were most commonly sports clubs - hockey, cricket or football - which involved regular weekly commitment to practice and competitive matches.

This perception, which became the professional wisdom of physical educators during the late 1960s and 1970s, conceals a fundamental misconception, for assumptions based on stereotypes of South Asians as a single homogeneous group have further ramifications. Failure to acknowledge the religious and cultural variances that exist resulted in greater misunderstandings. For instance, Parmar (1981) describes how teachers assumed that all South Asian girls were unwilling or unable to participate in extra-curricular sporting activities. Neither the parents nor the girls are consulted about their wishes, and so they were automatically excluded.

South Asian youth has become the focus of increased interest from leisure researchers since the mid-1980s, and there has been some evidence to suggest that the participation of South Asians in sporting activities was less than that for other ethno-cultural groups. For example, South Asians were found to be proportionally under-represented as sports-centre users (Botholo et al., 1986; Carrington et al., 1987); and like other ethno-cultural groups, participation in sport by South Asian women has been identified as being less than South Asian men (Botholo et al., 1986; Lloyd, 1986; Carrington et al., 1987; BYRT, 1988; Verma et al., 1991). The important theme addressed by Carrington et al. (1987) is the extent to which gender differences in sports participation are more pronounced amongst young South Asians than whites. They concluded that:

... Gender differences, both in opportunity and behaviour, may be especially pronounced within South Asian culture. In this ethnic group, as in others, the leisure of adolescent girls and young women tends to be less extensive, varied and active than that of their male peers; it is more likely to be appropriated by other members of their family and is subject to greater parental control, particularly where out-of-home activities are concerned. (Carrington et al., 1987, p.276)

One of the key differences between South Asian males and females has been found to be the propensity for South Asian females to participate in home-based leisure (Carrington et al., 1987; BYRT, 1988). South Asian males, in contrast, engaged in much more out-of-home leisure; for example, 'going out', using a sports centre, cinema or youth club, visiting cafes, pubs, discos and clubs (DES, 1983; Carey and Shukur, 1985; Carrington et al., 1987). That is not to suggest that South Asian males do not engage in home-based leisure activities. On the contrary, leisure time is often spent resting or relaxing in the company of family and friends at home (Lloyd, 1986; Karmi, 1988). Watching television and video is also very popular (Carey and Shukur, 1985; BYRT, 1988). The leisure activities of the extended family are central to South Asian lifestyle (Kew, 1979); and weddings, birthdays and anniversaries are of major significance to South Asian communities (Kew, 1979). In this way, and through other specifically South Asian cultural rituals, leisure pursuits and entertainment, there is clear cultural transmission and continuity through leisure experiences (Michaelson, 1979a; Jackson and Nesbitt, 1993). Lloyd (1986) additionally offers some interesting insights into the ways that South Asian men budget their time, suggesting that more time is devoted to 'personal care - eating and sleeping'. She also referred to evidence that meals in South Asians' households were more prolonged, which is explained, in part, by the assertion that food is the key element in the preservation of cultural tradition (Taylor and Hegarty, 1985).

Of the specific sporting activity choices that were made, Botholo et al. (1986) reported squash, weight training, badminton, and table tennis as being popular. These findings demonstrated fairly close alignment with those of Carrington et al (1987), who additionally identified football, cricket, martial arts, and pool/snooker as sporting activities popular with young South Asian males. The traditional indigenous South Asian sporting activity of *kabaddi* has been identified as popular in certain areas of high South Asian population density - Leicester, Southall, the West Midlands; so-much-so that the claims by Malik (1988) that such activities are traditionally marginalised within South Asian communities can not be sustained.

The key point to emphasise here is that until the mid-1980s sports provision for South Asians was based either on the assimilationist model of race relations - the "they've got to make the effort" attitude, or on stereotypes about the sorts of activities that were perceived to be popular with South Asians. In both cases 'false universalism' about South Asian groups as being homogeneous was very much in evidence (see Raval, 1989; Fleming, 1994). For example, the Sports Council (1982, p.36) identified "ethnic minorities" as one of its target groups, and one part of the strategy aimed at achieving 'Sport for All' was to attract under-represented minority groups to: "existing facilities for sports of **direct interest**" [emphasis added].

Yet in spite of this paternalistic attitude of sports providers in general, the South Asian communities have not been inactive as providers, and the implications reach beyond the scope of just sport:

> In just one example, a primarily Asian cricket club explicitly saw one of its purposes as the development of community activities unrelated to cricket, to the extent that social activities almost outnumbered matches. There was a congruence between individual, group and general community values, no doubt influenced by the primarily Hindu religion of members, which argues for a sense of spiritual purpose in all of life's activities. (Hoggett and Bishop, 1985, p.31)

More recently there has been a change of emphasis from sports providers, not only is ethnicity located as a central factor that influences leisure and sporting participation patterns (Kew, 1979), it is now also recognised that different provision is needed for different ethno-cultural groups. The Sports Council in particular has initiated schemes to increase participation in sporting activity - particularly amongst South Asian women - and has done so by engaging the help and co-operation of existing community groups (Sports Council, 1994). Successful schemes have benefited from single-sex groups, creche provision, the eradication of racial harassment, female staff supervision, and the presence of an interpreter (David, 1991); and this blueprint is an example of the maxim of 'equal opportunity requiring unequal effort'.

One of the interesting aspects about the work that began with the Fairfax Community School project (Dixey, 1982), is that provision has moved away from those activities associated with the stereotypes of the South Asians in sport. For though work in the development of provision for South Asians in cricket, badminton and hockey has continued (Dunnett, 1991; Bhandari 1991; Sports Council, 1994), other activities have become the focus for particular attention. In addition to the Fairfax project, others have been concerned with 'keep-fit' and swimming (Thanki, 1989); and other recent initiatives include adventure activities (Oldfield, 1991), football, athletics and netball (Bhandari, 1991). The implications are becoming increasingly clear: participation levels between South Asians and other ethno-cultural groups may vary, but the sorts of activities that South Asians engage in are not restricted to those stereotypic assumptions about cricket, hockey, and the racket sports.

5 'Sorting it out': the research strategy

From the traditional culture of origin in the Indian sub-continent, and from the lifestyles of South Asians in Britain, there would seem to be a number of important factors that affect participation in sport. These are complex, inter-related and not easily teased apart. The general paucity of literature in this area inevitably creates certain difficulties and problems for researchers engaging in substantive investigation. This was especially so at the start of the research in 1988, and the project was of a very exploratory kind. It was intended that the research would help to provide a greater understanding for the role of sport in South Asian cultures, and have some practical application. In order to accomplish this, the data required were necessarily of a high-quality, in-depth and valid kind. For it is only when there is real understanding of particular phenomena that reasoned and purposeful action can be taken by policy-makers. In the proven and well-established case-study paradigm in the sociology of education, an ethnographic method was employed for this study.

Ethnography is, as Yates (1986, p.61) suggests: "the study of the world of people". It is well suited to exploratory research because, it permits the study of social phenomena through the greatest possible number of valid channels of enquiry (Willis, 1978), and it allows the ethnographer to participate:

> Overtly or covertly, in people's daily lives for an extended period of time, watching what happens, listening to what is said, asking questions; in fact collecting whatever data are available to throw light on the issues with which he or she is concerned. (Hammersley and Atkinson, 1983, p.2)

This method has not only been used to good effect in the study of ethnicity, minority cultural groups and 'race relations' (e.g., Pryce, 1986), and the lifestyles of young people (e.g., Willis, 1977); but also for investigating racism in the classroom (e.g., Wright, 1992), the leisure patterns of South Asians (e.g., Michaelson, 1979a), and also the influences of ethnicity and youth in the secondary school (e.g., Mac an Ghaill, 1991; Wade and Souter, 1992).

Social science research has often failed to provide a full account of the research experience. For whilst there are often descriptive accounts of the mechanisms involved in gathering data, the element of critical reflection - so important in ethnographic studies (Hammersley and Atkinson, 1983) - is often absent. Paul Corrigan's (1979) 'Schooling the Smash Street Kids' is a notable exception to this trend, as, in his own words, "What it portrays is the actual process of sociological research" (p.2). The benefits of such an approach are threefold. First, it allows the researcher to engage in a process of systematic reflexivity; second, it allows the researcher's interpretivist stance to be made clear from the outset; and third, it also enables the researcher to 'come clean' about the way in which the research was conducted, and make the nature of the creative process explicit.

The researcher is a part of the research situation, and therefore both affects it, and is affected by it. As a result, there are certain features of the researcher's persona that inevitably impact on the way in which the process of research is experienced. With specific regard to school-based studies, age, gender and class are important variables; and for studies that locate ethnicity centrally in their analysis, the ethnic identity of the researcher is also of critical importance (this is a theme to which the discussion will return). Indeed, John Solomos (1988, p.14) has argued that in the study of black youth, for ethical and political reasons: "It is incumbent on researchers to make public the methods, values and assumptions on which their work is based".

My background was one of relative material comfort based on white working-class sensibilities and socialist politics. Throughout my schooling, I was concerned more with sporting success than academic achievement, but I was able to pursue both through a Sport Studies degree at Newcastle and Sunderland Polytechnics. It was there that I first encountered the academic discipline of sport sociology and became particularly interested in the entrenched institutional racism and personal bigotry in sport. Later whilst undertaking a Post Graduate Certificate of Education at Loughborough University, I had to do an extended essay on an aspect of secondary school life that interested me. I wrote about the need for tolerance and understanding of Muslim communities, especially in relation to Physical Education and Sport (Fleming, 1987). The piece was well received by my Education Studies tutor, but the PE Course Leader was less enthusiastic. She remarked that:

> From the early days of absorption of Muslims considerable concessions have been made by integrating ethnic groups and the schools. He paints a rather negative picture - I think in PE that most problems have been resolved on an equitable basis.

At the time, I believed this to be simply untrue, and I privately bemoaned blinkered academics in ivory towers. Interestingly too, in retrospect, it is not insignificant that the language of her response evidenced an integrationist stance on 'race relations', and was also symptomatic of the complacent attitude of the PE profession.

With an interest in sport and ethnicity there was, it seemed, an infinite number of research problems that could have been investigated; and on my arrival at Brighton Polytechnic in October 1987, the research problem had not been crystallised. I did, however, know that it was going to be concerned with sport and ethnicity, so I attended an undergraduate course on 'Racism in Society'. I was immediately impressed and profoundly influenced by the work of Miles (1982) and Sivanandan (1982), and the anti-racist philosophy advocated by Mike Cole (1986a; 1987; 1989). It was with this anti-racist perspective that I undertook the research.

Choosing the role - a raison d'être

The final focus of the project was decided in collaboration with the Greater London and South East Regional Sports Council, which had acknowledged that there was a lack of information about the sports participation of South Asians in Britain. Gaining access to a subject group that was perceived as being both 'problematic' and under-represented in sports participation, however, was a practical difficulty; but it was resolved by adopting a secondary school as a central focus for the research. This was, after all, one place where young South Asians would be present, and they would have some experience of sport through physical education.

When engaged in ethnographic research which includes participant observation, the role adopted by the researcher takes on critical importance. It is evident that in the school situation, the adult researcher is visibly not a member of the group being studied, and other roles have to be sought. The most obvious role for the adult researcher is as a teacher, and this has been used extensively (e.g., Pollard, 1985; Mac an Ghaill, 1991). This gives the researcher the opportunity for interaction with potential subject groups, but can create genuine researcher-teacher role conflict, and can pose a major dilemma for successful research may require a lessening commitment to teaching (Peeke, 1984). Moreover, although the role of the teacher gives the opportunity for interaction, due to the authority structure in schools and the power relation of the teacher *vis-à-vis* the pupil, the quality of that interaction - the openness and frankness of respondents - is questionable (Corrigan, 1979). In spite of this concern, the role that I intended for this research was that of the 'PE teacher/sports coach doing research about young South Asians'. This enabled me to interact with the members of my subject groups, and there was also the strategic reason of being able to offer my services as a qualified PE teacher and sports coach as a bargaining tool with the school in exchange for the opportunity to interact with my subject groups. This functional role that I was able to offer was *quid pro quo* to the school and clubs, and in view of the sensitive nature of the study, I was aware that a researcher studying ethnicity and racism might not otherwise be made particularly welcome.

Negotiating an entrée

It was initially intended that data would be gathered from two main sources: an appropriate secondary school, and the local sports clubs. My contact at the Sports Council acted as a 'gate-keeper' and negotiated access for me with the Physical Education Adviser in a particular north London borough. The borough served the purpose very satisfactorily: it had a diverse ethnic mix; it was run by a council that

53

was favourably disposed towards sport and the social services; and it had a number of high-profile sporting institutions. After a discussion with him about the various merits and demerits of the appropriateness of a number of schools, I then wandered round the borough on foot - 'A to Z' in hand - doing some preliminary reconnaissance. As it turned out the final choice of school was left to me, but it seemed clear that there were certain expectations from the Sports Council about the clubs with which I would associate. My choice reflected these expectations, in part because of arguments presented to me that certain institutions would be important sites for data collection; and in part too because I felt under some sort of implicit obligation to the gate-keepers to act upon the recommendations that I received. More important than these expectations, though, were my own concerns based on the logistics of transport (the proximity of the Underground Station). The PE adviser gave me a point of contact at the school - one of the Deputy Heads - and she granted me an entrée into the PE department, and introduced me to the Head of PE. As Lacey (1970) had discovered in his use of the Chief Education Officer to legitimise his presence in the school, my path was smoothed by this recognised and sympathetic authority figure. Thus, in April 1988, fieldwork at Parkview School - a large, well situated, multi-ethnic secondary comprehensive school - commenced, and this became the focus for the year-long period of field-work.

My contact at the Sports Council also introduced me to a number of local sports clubs so that I could get a more complete picture of the sports participation patterns of South Asians in the borough. Of the twelve sports clubs that were included in the research, all but three were contacted through the Sports Council, and/or with the use of the Sports Council name, and/or by the use of the name of the Sports Council gate-keeper. (It was interesting, though not very surprising, to discover the number of doors that could be opened by this form of 'name-dropping'.)

At the same time I was concerned about 'labelling' and self-fulfilling prophecies, for it did seem that the kind of sports clubs to which the Sports Council could act as an effective gate-keeper, were the very sports clubs where there were fewest 'race relations' problems, and where 'good practice' was well established. (The reality was that minority groups were under-represented in many sports clubs - to the point of being totally absent in some, and so there were few, if any, 'racial problems'.)

Of the other sports clubs that were included in the study, two posed very real difficulties and frustrations. The first, a boxing club, was advertised in the school, though not through the PE department, and seemed a good place to pursue the relevant lines of enquiry. As a somewhat 'green' apprentice researcher at the start of the fieldwork I did not handle the initial contact well. I did not fully appreciate the sensitivity of the issues (which became much clearer to me when I gleaned some specific local knowledge), and without the legitimisation of my presence by a credible figure, I was what Kemp and Ellen (1984, p.229) describe as: "The newly-arrived fieldworker, labouring hesitantly and painfully in a very alien and difficult environment". I was guilty of "blunders of interaction" (Moore, 1977), and as I had been rather too explicit about the nature of the work I was engaged in, it was almost inevitable that defensive barriers would be erected and hostile suspicions aroused.

The biggest single blunder was to refer directly to "racism". Not surprisingly, this caused concern amongst those who had agreed to allow me to visit their club. Chivers (1990) makes the point that the topicality and sensitivity of 'race relations issues', and racism in particular, makes people defensive - especially when they feel that they are being threatened or accused. It was not until later that I discovered exactly how sensitive this topic had been. One of the boxers explained:

Paddy McMahon: "We were in the paper [a national Sunday newspaper] and all that. Why couldn't they go to a big club - Northbridge, or somewhere like that? I'll tell you why, you know Northbridge, they'll train anyone white, and that's the end of the story. If you're black they don't wanna know. At the moment it's like that anyway, the trainers don't like blacks. We've got a lot; there's four black geezers here. We don't say "You're black, you're white"; if you're good at boxing and you wanna learn, Stan'll teach you. It's all the same, we have a joke, always winding each other up. I mean they tell racist jokes, but they know how to take it. It's silly what they say about racism an' all that. They give as good as they get. Stan doesn't give two tosses what anyone's like, an' we don't neither. If you're good, and you get on with people - good as gold".
SF: "When I started coming down [to the club], I felt a bit uneasy. I thought people were suspicious about why I was there..."
Paddy McMahon: "Yeah, because - how can I say - they were wondering if you were saying "Are these racist?" 'Cos did you know that they [Northbridge ABC] were saying about us, that our club's racist? They were trying to close us down. Everyone thought you were doing something on racism an' that. Northbridge were accusing us of being racist".

(What is also apparent from this interview is that after about three months of visiting the club, I had become trusted and accepted - for had I not been, this sort of open dialogue would not have been established.)

At the outset, I was asked to assure the club coach/organiser that I was neither a teacher nor from the Sports Council; both of which I was able to do, but about which I felt somewhat uneasy. As it transpired there were no South Asian boxers at the club, and so my blunders did not affect data-collection. It was a club to which a Sports Council gate-keeper did not have access; and without a gate-keeper of any description I was perceived to be an intrusive threat.

The sensitivity of the subject matter of the research was made abundantly clear to me much later in the project during my visits to Elm Park Swimming Club. By this time I was sensitised to my own use of language, and wary of the interpretations attached to what I said. My gate-keeper in this instance was a one of the students at Parkview School who had commented to me in conversation that this particular swimming club had two South Asian swimmers. Through him I sent a letter of introduction/explanation to the club's coach. At my first visit to the club it became clear that I was unwelcome, and was threatened with physical violence:

18/1/1989 I was introduced to the club coach but he was busy. A few minutes later he returned and demanded to know precisely what I was doing. I explained in the briefest and most general way, and he seemed placated. He even suggested that if there was anything I needed to know I only had to ask... At the end of the session I asked him if I could arrange a chat with the South Asian swimmer, to which he replied: "I'll ask him, and you won't talk to him unless I'm there". I was taken aback by the aggressive tone he adopted, and that I was clearly perceived as a threat... I explained what I wanted to talk about, and he made it clear that I was not to talk about anything other than swimming: "And if you do talk about anything else, I'll punch yer lights out, and you'll be on yer bike - understood?" (Field-notes)

The threats of violence did not particularly alarm me, and I was certainly not intimidated by them, but the tone for the interaction was set. I was permitted to talk with one of the two South Asian swimmers, but only in the presence of his father and the club coach; and then I was only permitted to ask questions specifically about swimming (i.e.,. stroke technique, favourite swimmers, best times, etc.), I was asked to send a transcript of the interview, and treat the data confidentially and anonymously.

With hindsight, it was perhaps not an unsurprising reaction to my interest in the club; particularly when the coach's view of research of this kind was placed in some sort of context:

"I think it's people like you, on their soap-boxes who spout on about it that cause all the trouble. Kids come here, and whether they're black or white, no-one cares. It's only when attention's drawn to it that there's a problem. I went through Higher Education, so I know". (Field-notes)

Yet at the time my emotions went through a range that included despondency, frustration, anger, and amusement. It all took place at a relatively advanced point in the fieldwork, and there was insufficient time to gain acceptance in the ways that I had been able to previously.

Acceptance, access and field relations

Having established the specific location for the research at Parkview School, the conditions of my presence were negotiated. The deal was, quite simply, that in exchange for the school granting me the opportunity to gain access to the subject group, the PE department would have the use of an additional qualified member of staff. The members of the PE department that I joined were welcoming, though I suspect a little apprehensive about my presence. I discovered afterwards that they had not been briefed about what I was doing (as I had assumed they had) except that it was concerned with the subject of ethnicity. Initially, my role was not unlike that of the student teacher on 'teaching practice'; I would be a part of what was going on, but only in a peripheral sense. At the time this was irritating as I was anxious to establish some sort of identity, particularly amongst the young people at the school. When asked if I was a new PE teacher, as I frequently was in the first weeks, I replied somewhat weakly, "Sort of". This seemed at the time like a reasonable strategy that justified my presence and indicated that I was in some way different from other teachers, without the necessity for a lengthy explanation. As it turned out, although deliberate vagueness had served a useful purpose for Corrigan (1979), it caused real uncertainty about my role in the school. It soon became clear that the young people at Parkview had sought information about me from other sources - especially other teachers and the caretaker - and had been given a misleading impression. A colleague in the PE department told me, for example, that he had heard me referred to as, "the tall geezer that's here to make sure we react proper!"

Before long, though, I gained acceptance from the staff on a professional level - largely through their recognition of my competence as a teacher - and the perception of me changed from research student to colleague:

> 14/9/1988 I spoke with Stuart Dennison [member of the PE department] today, and he is quite happy for me to be involved in his lessons in the quasi-formal way that I had with others last term. He has to teach the GCSE PE group this term, and has to cover pole vault. He asked me if I would do this for him: "You coach at the athletics club don't you? You'd be able to do pole vault better than I can. What do you think?" (Field-notes)

Socially, however, I sensed a degree of wariness. At times it was very clear that my presence inhibited their normal patterns of behaviour, especially with regard to racist jokes:

> 12/7/1988 Mr Jenkins: "I've got a joke. It's a bit racist, but it's a good one".
> Ms Taylor engaged me in eye-contact, and looked embarrassed.
> Ms Taylor: "No, we've probably heard it. And I bet it wasn't funny in the first place". I think she was very conscious of my presence - partly because it might have provided me with some data that I could use; and partly because I think she sensed my uneasiness. (Field-notes)

This resolved a potentially knotty dilemma for me, as I was not put in the position of compromising my convictions to avoid offending my hosts.

In time, the social distance disappeared, and there were some important indications that I was actually trusted too:

> 17/11/1988 Slowly, I have gained acceptance among the PE staff. I have been invited to departmental meetings, gone on departmental visits to the pub, have been included in the departmental 'clothing budget' and am even taken into the confidence of some colleagues - especially those who want a sympathetic ear to moan and whinge. Even the non-PE staff no longer treat me as an outsider. (Field-notes)

My role became an intriguing mixture of researcher, colleague, friend, and go-fer (errand-runner). The working relationships with my hosts could be viewed as incidental to the data-gathering process; it was, after all, not the teachers that I was intending to study. Yet establishing some degree of acceptance in the department was important for allaying my own insecurities, as well as developing the trust necessary for gaining co-operation and collecting other important background information.

Locating respondents from within the subject group was relatively easy, they were a 'captive audience'. But gaining access to them was less easy. As Hammersley and Atkinson (1983, p.56) explain: "Access is not merely a matter of physical presence or absence. It is far more than a matter of the granting or withholding of permission for research to be conducted". More specifically, being in close proximity to subjects does not mean that they will necessarily be trusting and/or co-operate (Fine and Sandstrom, 1988). After the confusion and misinformation that surrounded my arrival at the school, I settled on the explanation that I was "working at the school and doing some research into 'kids' and sport". In addition to this loosely defined raison d'être, I also behaved in a way that was akin to the "least-adult" role adopted by Mandell (1991); though in my case it was more of a 'least authoritative' role. The purpose was to negate the effects of the power position that adults occupy in the school situation, and thereby gain valid and trustworthy data from respondents with whom I spoke and interacted.

Field relations were therefore concerned, especially at the outset, with 'impression management' (Hammersley and Atkinson, 1983), and minimising social distance (Mandell, 1991); and in this sense Ball (1990) is quite right in the view that social skills are worthy of greater emphasis than technical competence. Being identified as relatively young was an advantage, one of the students at Parkview described me as: "The one that looks young, but who's only got as much hair as Mr. Thomas [who had very little] - but at least you can talk to him". It also seemed that there was a direct correlation between age and perceived power and status.

The importance of personal appearance has also been identified as a central concern, for if the ethnographic researcher gets it wrong, it can jeopardise the work (Hammersley and Atkinson, 1983); for, quite simply: "A consistent disregard or lack of concern for the group's basic cultural values will severely impede research progress" (Fetterman, 1989, p.55). My role in the school as a member of the PE department necessarily required that I adopt the appropriate clothing - a tracksuit; and as it turned out this was the garb worn by many of the young people at the school. In my general demeanour and behaviour I also found myself slipping easily and naturally into conversations with them about football and music. These conversations gave way to very informal good-natured banter when they found out that I came from the Midlands (which they immediately labelled "the North"), and that I was a fan of the Nottingham Forest manager, Brian Clough. There was plenty of common ground for informal interaction, and there was an almost inevitable trading in good-humoured comments about the 'EastEnders' and 'Grange Hill' television programmes in exchange for remarks about flat-caps and whippet-racing!

Communication skills were central to the 'least authoritative' role, for there were potential problems associated with the language and speech of youth subcultures (Mandell, 1991). It was clear, for example, that 'street-language' had been significantly influenced by African-Caribbean and African-American entertainers (particularly Michael Jackson and Lenny Henry). Words such as "bad", "wicked" and "safe" were in common use, and their interpretations were very different from their dictionary definitions. Had I attempted to use this language, it would have not only sounded incongruous, but also unnecessary. As Fetterman (1989, p.56)

58

elaborates: "Being natural is much more effective than any performance. Acting like an adolescent does not win the confidence of adolescents, it only makes them suspicious". What was much more important was that I, as the researcher, understood what was being communicated to me.

There were other strategies that were adopted when talking to the South Asians specifically that further helped to minimise social distance. The choice of venue for interviewing was often in 'neutral territory', with the PE changing rooms a preferred location. There were other instances when the PE office was used, and there was seldom any indication that this was an intimidating environment. My own behaviour was intended to make the respondent feel at ease, and involved, amongst other things, slouching, sitting on the floor, and chewing gum. The two most productive means of minimising social distance, however, were the unprofessional behaviours of swearing (when it was judged that respondents would not be offended), and joking about members of staff (with comments about personal appearance being especially valuable). The effect was that as the interviewer, I was able to take the interviewee into my confidence, demonstrate my trust in him by sharing in a non-deferential climate of scepticism towards authority, and break down barriers by sharing the normal language of the interviewee as the mode of communication. It also meant a degree of normality about my own behaviour which Fetterman (1989) values so highly. In the role of researcher, I also tolerated nick-names and jokes at my expense - for example, "Beam me up Scottie" - that I would have considered unacceptable had I been concerned about my 'professionalism' as a teacher.

Away form the school in the local sports clubs, with the exceptions of the boxing club and one of the swimming clubs, acceptance was almost immediate, and I soon became a familiar face. The boxing club was different in that I did not adopt the role of the coach, but rather that of the coached. I experienced a lot of difficulty gaining acceptance in the boxing club (some of the reasons for which have already been described), but after a number of weeks there was a point at which I felt that I had gained the trust of many club members. I had been asked if I wanted to go to Canvey Island to support two of the boys who were competing in a 'Gym Show'. I drove over to Canvey Island more out of interest in the event than any desire to allay any fears about me, and found that my arrival was very unexpected. As I discovered later, by demonstrating my enthusiasm to the members in this way, I had created a very favourable impression, and I perceived an immediate change in attitude towards me:

> Paddy McMahon: "Yeah, well, none of us expected you to turn up. And when you did, it showed that you was interested. And if you can be bothered, Stan's [club coach] got a lot of time for you".

At the next training session in the gym I was made the butt of some good-natured jokes about being 'a teacher', and was even entrusted with charge of the younger boys sparring - previously my main utility had been in hanging the punch-bags from the ceiling at the start of the evening, (I was the only one present who was tall enough to accomplish this with only the assistance of a table!)

Gathering and recording data

The ethnographic method draws upon many sources for the collection of data. Willis (1978), for example, lists the techniques he used in his research for 'Profane Culture' as: "Participant observation, observation, just being around, group discussions, recorded discussions, informal interview, use of existing surveys" (p.196). Some researchers have also used quantitative survey methods in addition to their qualitative fieldwork, others have drawn upon other documentary evidence such as local newspapers, census data, official documents/confidential reports , and others still have talked to 'significant others' - teachers and parents (c.f., Pryce, 1979; Ball, 1981; Boneham, 1989; Gillborn, 1990).

This eclectic approach to data-collection provides opportunities for some methodological triangulation through mutual empirical verification (Hammersley and Atkinson, 1983; Blease and Bryman, 1986); enables the combination of the strengths of different methods (McNeil, 1985); and creates an overall picture of the phenomena under investigation (Bryman, 1988). These reasons constituted the rationale for the range of techniques employed in the study at Parkview School, which included all of those above. As Gillborn (1990, p.13) comments of his own ethnographic research at City Road Comprehensive: "None [of the research techniques] is sufficient in isolation, but together they can reveal a detailed and critical picture of the processes at work in a school".

In the qualitative thrust of the research, the main data-gathering technique can be described as 'talking to respondents' in many different ways - alone and in groups; structured, semi-structured and unstructured - but always informal. In many ways the interviews could best be described as "focused conversations" (Acland and Siriwardena, 1989, p.565). Initially the first interviews were based on a checklist of what, at the time, was considered directly relevant. This list was little more than a cue card designed to prompt, so that no issues were omitted through my failure to remember them. The first informants were those with whom I had already developed the best rapport. Some of the interviews were conducted during PE lesson time, and time was not a major constraint when the particular individuals were not taking part. On other occasions, respondents were giving up their free time to talk to me, either during breaks or after school, and maintaining their goodwill was of paramount importance. As Fetterman (1989, p.55) remarks, "the individual's time is precious". On average these first interviews lasted between 20 and 30 minutes.

Having guaranteed confidentiality and anonymity, most respondents were willing to talk openly and honestly, particularly when they were convinced about my genuine interest. The first interview with any individual was essentially a fact-gathering exercise, and it became fairly structured. It was often a means of setting the agenda for subsequent follow-up interviews. In these the format became progressively more and more unstructured, and by the third or fourth occasion the plan was, at most, only very loose. The manner was more conversational, and the discussion was not only more interesting, but actually making a contribution to my understanding of the issues of the research project. Some of these discussions lasted as long as an hour at a time.

At the outset observational data were recorded in a hardback bound notebook, and took the three forms that Burgess (1982) has identified:

Substantive field notes, giving details of major observations and conversations; methodological field notes, consisting mainly of details about the circumstances of collecting data and the techniques used; and analytical field notes, in which hypotheses are developed and theories explored. (Cited in Morison, 1986, p.53)

I thought this preferable to a loose leaf binder on the basis that I was less likely to lose a notebook. I made a back-up copy of the notes every few days, and this working copy was ultimately used in the analysis as notes were scribbled, and cross-references made. I persisted with the notebook throughout the fieldwork, and by the end there was a good deal of background data that supplemented interview material. (It was also a useful cathartic outlet for frustrations and irritations during the research.)

Interviews were recorded in one of three ways. First, some were recorded on tape, and later transcribed. The clear advantage of this was that quotations were recorded verbatim, and as the researcher I had nothing to distract me from the interview itself, and interpretation and analysis could be conducted over and over again (Fetterman, 1989). Some respondents seemed to enjoy being recorded, and there were instances when a respondent would make a point of emphasising that I should note/record what they had said: "Put that in your book, and my name's spelt with two Ts". On other occasions some people appeared to feel snubbed when the tape recorder was not being used - as though their contribution was, in some way, less valuable or important than someone else's. There was also the suggestion that a small number of respondents were 'performing' for the recorder, but these tended to be the younger subjects, and were in the local sports clubs rather than the school.

Another consideration associated with data gathered in this way was the mind-numbing process of transcription, and while I was seldom bored during an interview in the way that Newby (1977) reported, the transcribing was especially monotonous. Hence his comments are apposite:

The novelty began to wear off. Respondents began to settle into a pattern, and interviewing became a routine. Eventually a certain tedium set in; enthusiasm could only be raised with an effort, and asking the same question for the two-hundredth time became a hard slog. One longed for an eccentric respondent to disrupt the established pattern. (Newby, 1977, p.117)

Second, some interviews were recorded on paper during the interview, and later written up in full. As the researcher, it was my judgement which of the respondents would be intimidated by the tape recorder, and it was not used in these instances. Furthermore, every subject was asked at the start of the interview if he objected to its use; on very rare occasions some respondents did, and it was not used. When full notes were being made during the interview, the main problem was both appearing to be, and actually being distracted from the conversation whilst writing. It was also unsatisfactory in terms of the researcher-interviewee dialogue. To alleviate this difficulty I adopted the principle outlined by Schatzman and Strauss (1973, p.148), that:

A single word, even one merely descriptive of the dress of a person, or a particular word uttered by someone usually is enough to 'trip off' a string of images that afford substantial reconstruction of the observed scene.

Third, other interviews were written up retrospectively. Like Robert Moore (1977), rough notes were made including as many quotations as I could remember, as soon after the event as possible. Powers of recall were trained and became very effective (Pryce, 1979). Whilst at school, the immediate notes were most often done at lunchtime or at the end of the school day; and after visits to local sports clubs, it was done in buses, on trains or under lamp posts on street corners. I then wrote up full notes as soon as time permitted. This usually took place on the following day. As Ken Pryce (1986, p.229) explains of his own project:

My method was to write down these observations as soon as possible after hearing or observing them. The rule of thumb I constantly exercised was to record them while they were still fresh in my mind, generally the same day. It was my practice never to record anything, especially conversations, after three days.

Further to these, I also tried, as far as possible, to get something down on paper from one interview before conducting another.

In addition to fieldwork and qualitative interviewing, my role as a member of the PE department enabled me to administer the questionnaire during PE lessons. But there were implications of doing so that I should have anticipated, but had not. Most of the students at Parkview School seemed to enjoy PE, or at the very least found it a welcome diversion from 'pen-pushing' in the classroom. Not unnaturally they were unimpressed to discover that their time for doing PE was being eroded at the expense of more of what they perceived to be something akin to 'school-work'. Fortunately the first group who completed the questionnaire was in the first year, and though they expressed their dissatisfaction at having to do the task, the did do it.

As a result, the coping strategy was to attempt to use non-PE time for the questionnaire, which in turn necessitated the co-operation of other members of the Parkview staff. In the event, and in spite of all the pressures that the teachers were working under, all of those that were approached were very helpful. Indeed the manner in which PE was seen as 'precious' worked positively in the non-PE situation, as respondents seemed to be enthused by the content of the questionnaire. There were two points of contact: English, and Personal and Social Education (PSE); and the questionnaire was introduced under the auspices of developing "communication skills" in English, and as both a useful form-filling exercise and a means of conceptualising sport as leisure in PSE. In both instances the different sets of respondents almost always reacted positively to something that was perceived to be more interesting than what they would otherwise have been doing; as one respondent, whose English lesson had been disturbed, remarked: "I'd rather be doing that thing about sport than shitty poetry".

Only very rarely did respondents react unfavourably to the questionnaire, and the number of instances was so few that the overall validity of the data, and the statistical significance of the findings were not affected. Typically, this manifested itself in a rejection of the authority structure inherent in the school, and reflected some role conflict that some of the principal informants were experiencing:

> 20/3/1989 Marjorie Saunders allowed me to use 4th year PSE time for the questionnaire with her group, and she was present throughout. She seems to have no rapport with the group, and it was as though they only did what she asked very begrudgingly; and they made their irritation audible and obvious - I found it all very embarrassing. Jayant [a Street-kid] was a case in point: when we had spoken previously, he had been co-operative, frank - an ideal interviewee; in this different environment, he was the opposite - awkward, obnoxious and objectionable. In front of an audience, he adopted his anti-authority mode of behaviour - which included his responses to me. Later, when he was alone he met me in the corridor, we shared a joke and he apologised for the way that he had behaved earlier, he explained: "I was a pain in the arse, wasn't I; but you've gotta do it, haven't you?". I asked him if he would complete the questionnaire again, doing it properly this time. After checking to make sure no-one was around (in a way rather reminiscent of a comic double-agent) he agreed and took a copy [which he completed and returned the next day]. (Field-notes)

The school provided a 'captive audience' of respondents, but there was still a number who did not complete the questionnaire. Hence the explanation for a response rate of only about 75% of the male population. Different reasons for this included a burst water pipe that meant closure for the day; careers interviews; 'red-nose' day events; negotiated timetables - students who had a poor attendance/behaviour record were permitted to attend only particular lessons during the week; and truancy. Yet in spite of these, all the South Asians at Parkview were included, because a specific point was made of contacting them all.

A comment on ethics

There are, of course, some key ethical concerns in the collection of data through researcher interaction, and I have addressed these in rather more detail elsewhere (Fleming 1995). They are, however, sufficiently important to the research process to warrant some brief remarks here.

By the very nature of the research in which they are engaged, ethnographers adopt certain strategies to minimise social distance. In this particular instance explicit attempts to disabuse respondents of their natural reluctance to 'open-up' to an almost complete stranger. Such techniques have the primary function of making respondents adopt abnormal modes of behaviour. By attempting to break down barriers, Homan (1990, p.125) contends that social scientists "design schemes to put them [subjects] in a more co-operative mood". He further asserts that it is also unethical to "probe around issues that respondents are reluctant to talk about" (Homan, 1991, p.58). Yet in this study it became very evident that not only were these strategies necessary, they were, in fact, the only means by which these important data could be gathered. Indeed, had they not been gathered, the analysis would have been simplistic and meaningless to the point of futility.

A more sinister criticism that has been levelled at researchers engaged in participant observation is that the method often involves deceit and subterfuge (Morison, 1986). To avoid this, the principle adopted throughout was not to tell lies, but it certainly was true that a certain amount of selective concealment and/or distortion of the whole truth was occasionally practised. The purpose was solely concerned with minimising social distance, and to reduce barriers and inhibitions. But it was a practice that I was particularly uneasy about, and avoided when it was possible to do so without affecting the process of data collection.

The debate about 'open' or 'covert' methods of enquiry is particularly fascinating when dealing with the research of potentially sensitive issues. The argument Homan presents, and it is very compelling, is that:

> Open procedures are desirable not merely because human subjects are entitled to know what is going on but because the research community will suffer and have less constructive relationships in the long term if it is noised abroad that sociologists are lurking in disguise. (Homan, 1991, p.3)

There are two issues here. The first is concerned with the basic human right to know, and is in a very real sense part of a wider moral and philosophical argument. The pragmatic response to that sort of criticism is clear. In order to glean the sort of data that will actually inform people about the views, perceptions, opinions and attitudes of particular groups of people, as well as reveal insights into lifestyles, these techniques are not only appropriate, but also necessary. Given that researchers are seldom able to truly immerse themselves in the culture and lifestyle of the researched, the role of the researcher is to act as a mouthpiece for the subject groups. Indeed it could be argued that while data are gathered from individuals in this way, the groups of which they are a part are actually empowered, by giving a voice to those that would not otherwise be heard.

The second issue that Homan raises is more of a 'professional' concern for the social researcher. On reflection, it is this that causes me the greater pangs of conscience. If the guiding principle for researchers is not to 'muddy the waters' for future research, then my own feeling is that I have been guilty, to some extent, of doing precisely that. There are clear directions that have emerged for future research, but some of the clubs that I visited might be rather more reluctant to act as host to a researcher in the future than they were to me. One of the great difficulties was in severing links with people who had become not only subjects of the study, but also friends; and it was hard to escape the conclusion that not only did I exploit them, but also that they probably felt that they were exploited and manipulated by me.

There were other issues that presented themselves in the research process that were knotty ethical problems: to act on information that was given in confidence, and so risk a breach of trust; how to handle verbal abuse directed at me in my role as a "sort-of teacher" without prejudicing the way in which I was perceived by subjects; how to respond to flagrant disregard for the school rules. In each of these I allowed my conscience to dictate my actions, and where possible I attempted to avoid affecting life in the school by my presence. In the end, however, there were certain instances that had to be acted on, and with the considerable benefit of hindsight, I believe that I did the 'right thing'.

In the less subtle ethical issues, for example anonymity and confidentiality, I have ensured that the school, and individuals within it remain unidentifiable. No purpose would be served by disclosing an individual's identity, and I had also assured the school that anonymity would be maintained. Hence, pseudonyms have been used throughout, and all identifying descriptors have been omitted.

"A white man studying blacks, the very idea!"

Of the researchers that have written about black youth and sport in Britain, Ellis Cashmore has been one of the most prolific, and the issue of being white and studying blacks has not escaped him. He considers the matter in the opening chapter of 'Black Youth in Crisis' (1982c), which is entitled 'Black Youth for Whites', and from which the sub-title above has been borrowed (p.12). For the reasons that I will explain in the discussion that follows, I initially found the general thrust of what he said then to be weak and unconvincing, and still do; but I now find myself much more closely aligned to the position he adopts - though not for the same reasons.

From the early stages of the work, the fact that I was a white researcher studying young South Asians had been at the forefront of my consciousness. People who became significant figures in the development of the research made various enquiries that caused me to indulge in considerable introspective self-examination. By re-visiting Cashmore's (1982c) analysis, it is possible to address this and other pertinent issues.

White researchers in crisis

Social researchers often exploit their subject groups; and PhD students in particular can often, quite reasonably, be accused of "carpet-bagging" (Corrigan, 1979, p.9). Cashmore's first point relates to the final product of his research, and concerns the intended audience for it. He was of the opinion that "it would be read by a wide span of people" (p.10). My view of my own research about South Asians was that it would principally be for whites and white-dominated institutions; I concurred with the reasoning that had been pointed out to Cashmore: "They [the subjects of the research] know what it's all about without reading [the] book. They know 'cause they're black and know what it's like to live as a black person" (p.11). It seemed to me that South Asians would know what it's like to be South Asian in Britain, and wouldn't need to be told what role sport played in their culture and lifestyle. Having conducted the research, my view on that has changed. The important consideration that such a view ignores is the heterogeneity of South Asians in Britain; for though there may be some commonalties among the South Asian populations, there are still very important differences that other groups of South Asians do not fully understand. Indeed some of the findings of Verma et al. (1991) suggest that the levels of understanding across the South Asian religious groups and sub-groups are only slightly more sophisticated (or less ignorant) than the stereotypes and assumptions that permeate the perceptions about South Asians generally amongst other ethno-cultural groups. So, in its humble and very finite way, the research could inform the subjects as well as others.

The second strand of Cashmore's argument was that "if we wait for [the subjects to write about themselves], we'll be waiting forever" (p.12). Initially I found this to be weak to the point of inadequacy. There was, I thought, no reason why South Asians should not study sport and South Asian culture, and just as importantly, no reason why they should not want to. After all, sport and physical activity play an important part in the lifestyles of many people in the Indian sub-continent; and the general trend of the academic South Asian in Britain moving into the professions was well established. The reality, however, as indicated in the literature (for example, Cherrington, 1975), and as I later discovered, is that sport has a low status in many South Asian communities in Britain, and even the serious scientific study of sport is often seen as little more than 'play'. As one young Pakistani Muslim explained to me:

> Nah, I like sport, but I don't wanna be a PE teacher. That's a shit job innit; you ain't got no respect. If you're Asian, people think more highly of you if you're a bin-man than a PE teacher - no offence!

It is not at all surprising therefore, that sport has not provided the source of serious academic study for South Asians in Britain. There is a sense in which the emphasis placed on research of this type may be such a low priority that we might indeed be waiting for some time for a study of South Asians in sport to be conducted by South Asians themselves.

More profound than this though, is the implication of Cashmore's comment that the best research would be conducted by members of the relevant cultural group. This is a view that has also been advanced by Parekh (1986), and there are two responses to it. Firstly, the anthropological argument advanced by Iganski (1990) and Rhodes (1994), that the social distance of a 'cultural-outsider' enables description, analysis and understanding of a particular socio-cultural group that is not plagued by subjective 'insider' biases (Hammersley and Atkinson, 1983). Secondly, this underestimates the importance of the ethnographer's empathy. It was suggested to Cashmore that he was not a Rasta, did not experience the social world as a Rasta, and therefore he could not understand Rastas. It is a claim for which he provides no satisfactory answer; and this is a crucial point, for a failure to answer such a claim could be seen as tacit agreement for it.

Moreover, to demand that only people who actually experience the lifestyle of a particular group can conduct meaningful research on it, inevitably devalues much of the important and perceptive research done on all manner of disadvantaged, powerless and deviant groups, and on powerful or privileged groups - indeed, on any group or constituency other that/those of which the researcher is a member. In the situation where the researcher is necessarily outside of the subject group, the skill of the ethnographer is to act as a 'mouthpiece' for that group in a way that was otherwise unavailable to it: "It involves letting them speak for themselves - giving them a voice and then listening very hard" (Riley, 1985, p.63).

The underlying epistemological argument is that in order to understand a phenomenon and/or a group of people experiencing that phenomenon, the researcher must experience the phenomenon at first hand. That being the case, even the most thorough and in-depth ethnographies (e.g., Pryce, 1986) would not satisfy this demand for total immersion in the subject group, for the reality is that academic research is usually carried by academics who could, if they chose, leave the research project at any time for a relatively comfortable lifestyle. Cashmore's experiences are again illustrative, and he reflects on the sceptical comment of one white boxing coach: "When all's said and done, you're white, you're educated, you work in a university and your future is going to be a lot different from these guys here" (p.12).

Crisis, what crisis?

The answer, of course, is that it is not necessary to <u>experience</u> in order to understand, and perhaps the stark simplicity of those few words conceals their profound implications. The justification is that phenomena are clearly observable, and so do not have to be experienced at first hand; the sensitive reporting of the first-hand experiences of others can provide the information needed for understanding and empathy.

Perhaps the most compelling reason for research on blacks to be conducted by whites is that, in the final analysis, institutional and personal racism, though experienced by blacks, is a problem for whites (Cole, 1986a). Cashmore was one of the targets of Errol Lawrence's (1981) critique of much of the work in 'race relations' in the late 1970s and early 1980s. He accused Cashmore, amongst others, of being preoccupied with "'pathological' aspects of black family life" and "'alienated' black youth", and suggested that there was a "tendency to study black people rather than white racism" (p.7). In spite of the defence that he and Barry Troyna (1981) presented, Cashmore's crisis of conscience which re-surfaced later (1982c) may have been well-founded, for the arguments that he presents in defence of his epistemological and methodological stance do not stand up to close examination.

Thus I do not share the theoretical perspective that Cashmore advances. Instead I adopt the stance of the white anti-racist. At the core of the analysis is the notion that it is whites who must confront their prejudices and discriminatory practices, and work conducted by white anti-racists has an important contribution to make to that.

6 'In the field': life at Parkview School

Northbridge is one of London's inner-city boroughs. Since the 1950s it has become a settling ground for migrants from all over the world, but especially from the former British colonies and central Europe. There is now a very real 'multi-cultural' population with a rich ethnic mix. At the heart of Northbridge, the Elm Park ward is a sprawling residential estate. A large proportion of the terraced houses and multi-storey tenement blocks were once, or are still council-owned, and there are a few owner-occupied semi-detached houses. But in the main the properties are from the cheaper end of the market, and a number of them are in a state of disrepair. These are the properties that the disadvantaged groups of society, particularly those that are discriminated against, are often forced to seek for their housing. Consequently, it has become an area of concentration for a number of minority groups within the borough.

The architectural symmetry and structural squareness of the buildings create a sense of environmental claustrophobia; but this is eased by expanses of urban greenery. At the centre of the estate, one such expanse of greenery provides the playing fields and parkland that surround the two-storey buildings of Parkview School. Close by, this predominantly working-class catchment area is served by a large, modern 'show piece' sports centre, and a youth club that is frequented by the Parkview students. The immediate scene is a mixture of breezeblock and red brick, fenced playgrounds and grassy verges, open spaces and quiet corners. Around the school there is evidence of use and of the users: an ice-cream van in the car park, discarded cigarette-ends behind the bike sheds, wire fences distorted from being climbed over or scrambled under, and the ubiquitous hieroglyphic 'tags' - graffiti in the form of the personalised insignia of an individual or group.

Between March 1988 and May 1989, Parkview School catered for around 1,000 pupils - which included a small sixth form. Males and females were represented in approximately equal numbers, and not surprisingly, the demographic profile of the school reflected the ethnic and cultural diversity of the Elm Park ward. The place of family origin was spread amongst 27 countries, though in addition to Britain, the four geographical regions of most heavily represented were Africa, the Caribbean, central southern Europe, and the Indian sub-continent. In total, there were 56 young South Asian males at Parkview School, and in terms of nationality and religion (two important defining characteristics concerned with ethnicity of South Asians), most were either Bangladeshi Muslims (n=18), or Indian Hindus (n=16), or Indian Sikhs (n=11). Just as important, many of them had received exposure of the influence of the traditional culture of the Indian sub-continent at first hand: 27 were South Asian by birth (i.e., first generation); 26 were the British-born sons of South Asian-born parents (i.e., second generation); and three had to trace their lineage back to grandparents to find their last South Asian-born ancestors (i.e., third generation). By these criteria alone, therefore, there was considerable ethnic heterogeneity.

Parkview School: lifestyle and sub-culture

The factors that influence South Asian lifestyles that have already been identified in previous chapters provide a complicated and multiplex framework for the analysis of the sport and leisure participation of young South Asians. But these variables were not necessarily the important features of the social order at Parkview School. They did not provide the primary basis for social interaction, and they were not the features that the South Asians themselves identified as important to their school-life. Rather, the approach adopted here, like that used in other school-based studies, is concerned with a typology of the young people at Parkview School as "a means of making the world of everyday life 'cognitively manageable'" (Wright, 1992, p.28).

There were four groups of young South Asian males that could be easily identified. They were not strictly defined according to any specific national, religious or cultural parameters; but most individuals, most of the time, could be identified as a member of one of them from his behaviour and general demeanour (see figure 6.1).

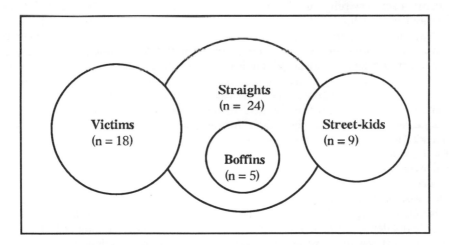

Figure 6.1. Typology of South Asian males at Parkview School

The Victims, Boffins, and Street-kids were mutually exclusive groups. That is to say, whenever there was any ambiguity about the group in which an individual could be categorised, the ambiguity was never about any overlap amongst these three. The Straights were the single group which had certain shared characteristics with the others, including its sub-group the Boffins. Yet that is not to suggest that the Straights were a 'common denominator' group, for they had distinctive characteristics of their own too.

The Victims - "everyone picks on us, I think they hate us"

In the day-to-day life of Parkview School, the most obvious group of young South Asian males was a very visible group of Bangladeshi Muslims. They were Victims because they were persecuted by their peers, and greatly misunderstood by everyone, including members of the school's staff. In one sense then, they could be defined according to national and religious criteria, but these were not the criteria that made them Victims. Rather, they were Victims because of they way that they were treated in the school, and it was the way that others behaved towards them that characterised their disadvantaged position within the social order of the school. Importantly too, the Victims perceived their disadvantaged position very acutely, and felt victimised; as 12 year-old Abdul explained: "I don't like this school because people are picking on me".

Like many Bangladeshi migrants to Britain, the Victims were, as a group, very rigid in their adherence to traditional Muslim norms and values (Carey and Shukur, 1985); though within the group there was a certain amount of variation in the levels of devotion to particular aspects of the Muslim lifestyle. Some, like Hussein were very conscientious about their commitment to the practicalities of devotion to Islam: "I am very religious, I pray in the school as well, every lunchtime. Every Friday I leave school early at lunchtime to go to the Mosque for special prayers". Others, like Abdul, interpreted the teachings of the *Qur'an* more loosely: "When you have to pray, you could pray anytime". This attitude was not unusual, and reflected the pragmatic and logistical difficulties of adhering strictly to the letter of the *Qur'an*. At Parkview though, provision had been made for young Muslims to engage in the mid-day prayer - a Deputy Head's office was available for that purpose; but few took advantage of the facility. It was outside the school where these young Bangladeshi Muslims received their instruction and guidance in Islam. Most attended the Mosque and supplementary classes in Arabic and the *Qur'an*. Though for the younger Muslims there is a sense in which some were subjected to coercion, and even fear of incurring the wrath of their fathers: "If I don't read the *Qur'an*, I get beaten. My dad says I have to pray" (Mahmood). There were also certain inconsistencies in the interpretation of Islamic teachings, and even some factual misunderstandings of the *Qur'an* (some of which will be discussed later); but these should not detract from their commitment to their own understanding of Islam, for it was this that was the most salient feature of their religious conviction.

Many of the Victims left rural Bangladesh as a result of one of the many natural disasters that have struck the country in recent years, in order to settle in Britain. This was not without problems of adjustment for some, and though most were agreed that they liked living in Britain where the material quality of their lifestyle was invariably better than it had been previously, they spoke affectionately of their former rural existence:

> Our country [Bangladesh] is a big country, very nice. There are many fields and when the wet weather comes, our fields get very wet - flood. I had a cow, and I go to the field with my cow. I want to go back to Bangladesh. (Mahmood)

Bangladeshis constitute the largest group of most recent migrants to Britain (S. Tomlinson, 1986a), and the rural background that characterises the experiences of many of them poses severe difficulties as they attempt to settle in an unfamiliar society. The additional multiple oppressions of poor and over-crowded housing, long-term unemployment and harassment mean that the Bangladeshi communities are amongst the most disadvantaged. At the same time, as Bains (1988) has also observed, "poorer families tend to be more traditionalistic in their orientation". The families of the Victims at Parkview were undoubtedly the most impoverished, and clearly the most committed to traditional lifestyle and culture.

In the Elm Park ward the process of 'ghettoisation' had not reached the crisis point for Bangladeshi communities that it had elsewhere in inner-city Britain (Boseley, 1990), but it was clear that here too, Bangladeshis inhabited the poorest housing in large extended families, and sought security from kinship and neighbourhood networks. But as one minority group among many in multi-ethnic Elm Park, the Bangladeshi community had not galvanised itself into the sort of political activity that is very much in evidence in mono-ethnic 'Bangla-Town' in the Brick Lane area of the East End of London. Described by Gaffar Choudhury as: "culturally, linguistically and otherwise it is a part of Bengali culture and Bangladesh" (BBC TV, 1990a), the concentration of Bangladeshis in this area has enabled the community to draw strength from within and challenge some of the social injustices from which it perceives itself to be suffering. The Bangladeshi community in Elm Park had no such strength, and though there were some activists, in terms of political influence it was relatively impotent.

The far-reaching effects of long-term unemployment on the Bangladeshi community contribute to a vicious circle of poverty and deprivation. The fathers of many of the Victims at Parkview School were disproportionately and significantly over-represented among the unemployed, and even above the national average for unemployed Bangladeshis (Reid, 1989). Bangladeshis throughout Britain are subjected to harassment and abuse on a daily basis (Kerridge, 1989; Cook, 1991). There have been numerous attacks on South Asian families generally, and the frequency of them is increasing (Ruddock, 1993). Some of the most violent have been on Bangladeshis (see, for example, Carey and Shukur, 1985; Asian Times, 18/11/1988; Collins, 1988; Gordon, 1989; Muir, 1989). The experiences of the Victims at Parkview School were, in this sense, no different from any other Bangladeshi communities.

In the social environment of the school the Victims perceived themselves to be 'picked on', and the evidence they cite lends support to that view. Collins (1988) suggests that there are two main reasons why South Asians generally suffer from more harassment than other minority groups. The first reason is because of their adherence to their own culture and languages. This is certainly part of the explanation for the hostility directed at the Victims at Parkview, but it is the broader concept of 'differentness' that lies at the heart of the antagonism that they perceived from other groups. In addition to traditional culture and language, appearance and behaviour also contributed. Indeed in terms of day-to-day interaction, it was language, appearance and behaviour that shaped the responses to them more than traditional culture (though culture clearly influences each of these). For these are the most obvious manifestations of 'differentness' - both visible and audible. In 'The Logic of Racism', Cashmore (1987, p.23) explains the underlying principle:

> The retention of values, beliefs and behaviour patterns specific to an ethnic culture is regarded as somehow offensive, an affront to white culture. It is seen as part of a general reluctance to participate in society; ethnics [sic] are in society but not of it.

The apparent unwillingness of the Victims at Parkview to communicate with each other in English was clearly seen as just such an affront, and the sounds of the Bengali language were imitated by members of other ethno-cultural groups who were unimpressed, and even irritated by this example of ethnic insularity.

In their appearance the Victims were different; not merely in their phenotype, but also in their mode of dress. Parkview had no dress code (or at least none that was adhered to), and the clothes that were worn made some important statements about those wearing them; for, as Paul Willis and colleagues (1990) have observed, clothes, style and fashion are key elements of the expression and exploration of individual and collective identities. The clothing worn by the Victims was an outward demonstration of their impoverished lifestyle for it was often ill-fitting, poor quality and worst of all in terms of the way that they were perceived, unfashionable. In their behaviour too, the Victims followed the pattern that Collins (1988) considers to be typical of South Asians, in that they are traditionally seen as passive and meek and were often overtly submissive in the face of undisguised hostility from their non-Victim peers.

> They [the other pupils] call me "Paki" and "faggot". It's because they find me soft - they can pick on me. I don't talk a lot, so they think I can't fight. (Rashid)

The Victims were subjected to verbal abuse and physical bullying on a regular basis, and this significantly shaped their day-to-day school life. They lived in fear of it, and they felt the powerlessness of their situation very acutely. They referred to the other pupils, particularly those responsible for the abuse as "they" and "them":

> We don't like them because they say things to us, "Paki", "smelly-face", "fucking bastard". If we say them back, they hit us. If we do anything, they are going to hit us. (Akram)
> I am scared of them. Stewart started hitting me once, and everyone came and hit me. They don't like me. They hit me everyday, I don't know why. (Mukhtar)
> I tell Miss, but she didn't do anything. (Massur)

Not surprisingly, they were reluctant to seek popularity outside their immediate group of Bangladeshi friends, and this had been observed by members of the PE Department:

I'm a bit worried about them [the Bangladeshis] developing into little groups. It may be because some of them are quiet - 'cos some of them are. Not all, but some are very quiet. But they stick together, and they've developed some sort of protection racket, and that's just as bad as them being bullied. (Mr Jenkins)

The Bengalis are picked on. They are the bottom of the pile. I don't remember any other immigrant kids going through what these kids are going through now. (Mr Thomas)

In making these observations, Mr Jenkins and Mr Thomas revealed that this phenomenon had not escaped their attention. But whilst the reference to a 'protection racket' indicates an awareness of the Victims as a persecuted group, it also implies some sort of extortion which the Victims, in their powerless and disadvantaged position, would have found impossible to perpetrate. It further suggests a level of co-ordinated resistance that was not evident. Most alarming of all though, was the apparent failure to question the need for a 'protection racket' - whether real or imagined.

A small number of the Victims adopted their own tactics of resistance to their situation, and the indifference that they perceived amongst the School's teachers. It is a pattern of behaviour that has been observed by Brah and Minhas (1985) in their study of young South Asian women; and Mr Thomas was aware of it:

Some of them take advantage and don't attempt to integrate. Anil [a third year Victim] for example, he pretends he doesn't understand English, but Dr Malik [E2L teacher] says his English is quite good. He just doesn't co-operate and makes no attempt to integrate.

Unlike some of the anecdotal evidence from the Swann Report (DES, 1985) - 'Education for All' - which indicated that teachers were unaware of the attacks on young South Asians, the teachers at Parkview were cognisant of the symptoms, if not the causes; but did little to alleviate the plight of the Victims. Mr Thomas' attitude, like that of his colleague, indicated an overall lack of understanding of the causes of the social phenomena that they had observed.

The more frequent response by the Victims to the situation in which they found themselves was typical of what Levine and Nayar (1975, p.365) describe as the "defensive path" of immigrant adaptation. There was a tendency to retreat to the security of kinship networks and public spaces of relative safety, in a process of self-isolation, which ultimately served to alienate them further. Some of the other South Asians at Parkview had also observed this:

The Bengalis get a hard time in this school. They get picked on because they don't mix with the other kids, and they were a different colour... Because they're brown-skinned they wanted to hang around with other brown-skinned - all their own group. (Rajinder)

73

There was also a certain amount of sympathy from some, and even the suggestion that the Victims should be helped, but it was not clear what form the help should have taken, nor who should have been responsible for its implementation:

> They do talk pretty loudly and their voices speak out. People take the Mickey out of the food they eat, the way they speak. They don't realise that it's hard for these people as well to settle down. They come here and it's hard for them. People have got to try and help them along. (Suman)

For all of these reasons concerned with social disadvantage, the Victims at Parkview seemed destined to follow the well-established trend of educational low achievement among the Bangladeshi communities (St. John-Brooks and Greenwood, 1988; J. Murphy, 1989). Indeed the Swann Report comments of young Bangladeshis that: "Their degree of social and economic deprivation, not to mention racial harassment, is so high that we are not surprised at their marked level of underachievement" (DES, 1985, p.87). The notion of high academic achievement amongst Britain's South Asians has been challenged by Tanna (1990), and the performance levels of members of the Bangladeshi communities are in stark contrast to some of the research on the academic attainment levels of other South Asians (for extensive reviews of such research, see S. Tomlinson, 1986a; Keysel, 1988; Drew and Gray, 1990, 1991). As Robinson (cited in Tomlinson, 1983, p.386) explains:

> Asian under-achievement is restricted to ... the low status section of the community, characterised by Asians with little education, restricted aspirations and poorly-paid employment.

The Victims at Parkview School had received some schooling in Bangladesh, but only a very small number had studied seriously. None were fluent in English on arrival, and this has been seen as the biggest barrier to their educational progress (Murshid 1990), and exacerbates every difficulty where communication is important (Gidoomal and Fearon, 1993). For though the vast majority could communicate verbally to good effect, the quality of written English was often poor.

The Victims' experiences of sport were shaped by their culture - with all of its influences from both the Indian sub-continent and inner-city Britain - and the patterns of their lifestyle. Moreover their experiences reflected in microcosm their more general position in the social order, and the levels of misunderstanding and intolerance that they were subjected to in society at large. Sports participation was largely confined to the school environment, as opportunities to take part outside school were very limited. Often, there were important family, religious and cultural commitments to attend to: "I can't stay after school, I have to go home with my sisters and read *Qur'an*" (Mukhtar). The Victims were also frequently excluded from many of the informal playground activities of other young males. They were not invited to take part in playground games of football, and any games that they did play were disrupted. Consequently, they were forced to seek the refuge of the relative safety of the lawn in front of the staff common room. They used it to play the sorts of 'chasing' games that might have been more readily associated with much younger children:

They don't say "Come and play football with us", so we play on our own. In the first year we had two footballs. We don't want to play with them because they push us, and they don't pass it [the football] to us. Boys stole one of them and kicked it on the roof of the hall, and we say we aren't playing there because they nick the ball and kick it away. So we play on our own on the grass. We like it there. We play 'He' games - if you go off the grass you're out. (Akram)

There is a temptation here to see some of these 'play' activities as rather child-like, but that would, in part, be a failure to acknowledge the importance of the indigenous 'chasing' games of the Indian sub-continent (*Kabaddi*, *kho-kho*, etc.), and the effects of cultural continuity and percolation upon them. What is indisputable, however, is that their involvement in all types of play suffered, they had a deficient vocabulary of basic motor skills, and their sporting competence in many of the major team invasion games (particularly football and basketball) was clearly under-developed.

It was no coincidence that the lawn in front of the school buildings was so popular with the Victims, and the reason for it was less to do with its suitability as a venue for their play activities than its proximity to the staff room. As Abdul pointed out: "We go there [the grass] so we can be near Miss". This had been observed by at least one member of the teaching staff, but there was a real lack of sensitivity and understanding evident from the remarks that he made in relation to it: "Look at them all [the Bangladeshi Victims]. They've got a bloody playground, but they stand out there on the grass. It's stupid" (Mr Jenkins).

The opportunities that the Victims had for involvement in sport were therefore restricted to PE lessons; but PE was no different from any other aspect of their daily existence. Personal racist abuse - both verbal and physical - was as prevalent there as elsewhere:

I was tackling Mark and he didn't want me to take the ball off him, and by mistake I just pushed him, so he started swearing at me, very rude - "You 'Paki', bastard, idiot, get back to your own country". (Aslam)

Moreover, what they considered to be unprovoked physical violence directed against them was often legitimised through contact sports: "I like football, all the Bengalis do. But people think we are no good; we can't stop the ball. They have boots on and they kick us" (Akbar). Their own lack of understanding of the physicality of activities like football meant that they felt under physical threat; and coming from a culture that places less emphasis on the physical contact in team-game sporting encounters, the Victims felt even more 'picked on'. One particular incident helps to illustrate the point:

2/2/1989 During the first lesson the second years were taken onto the playground for a 5-a-side football tournament... In one particular game Rafiq found himself close to the wire fence that marked the edge of the pitch (the ball remained in play off the fence like a side-wall in indoor football). Facing towards his own goal line, Rafiq began to kick out wildly behind him 'donkey-fashion' in an attempt to kick the ball upfield.

Stuart was kicked by Rafiq, and retaliated by kicking him back. The situation, which was quickly quietened, was a consequence of Rafiq's very under-developed understanding of the nature of the game of football, allied to his own personal lack of skill. Rafiq explained later that the experience had left him with a very negative view, and that he thought that this was yet another unprovoked assault on him that had been ignored by the teacher. Furthermore, the episode also confirmed what the other kids already apparently believe - that Rafiq, and by association all the Bangladeshis, can't play football. Through incidents like this, which are unavoidable, the stereotypes are reinforced, the prejudices exacerbated; and the skill gap (as footballers) increases even further. (Field-notes)

In PE lessons too, the Victims actively sought the support of their Bangladeshi friends. When pupils selected teams themselves - as was the usual practice at Parkview - the Victims aggregated in all-Bangladeshi teams. Commitment to the friendship group was much greater than the desire to take part in a winning team, and some of them also changed classes for PE lessons so that they could join their friends. This was not done through the formal channels that may have existed, and caused the Head of the PE Department some annoyance. More worryingly, he did not seem to understand why they had done it: "All the Bengali kids stay together. I tried to, split them up, but they just go back to the same lesson. It's a real nuisance" (Mr Thomas).

The harsh reality is that for the Victims, sport through PE was not the 'great equaliser' that it is often claimed to be. On the contrary, the inequality was evident, even before lessons began, from the PE kit that was worn:

Those kids in the second year [a group of Victims], their parents are not rich, and they don't wear those kind of first-class clothes, and they don't wear good trainers like 'Reebok', 'Nike' and so on. So the other kids, they say "Oh look at him, he's got shit trainers", or "they're crap trainers", and they take the Mick. (Rashid)

Thus in sport, by their appearance alone, the Victims were isolated, marginalised and ridiculed. Rashid himself had experienced this before one particular PE lesson when he was wearing some new training shoes for the first time:

9/6/1988 Rashid seems to be picked on a lot. Today he had some new trainers, but these were not a recognised brand name (e.g., 'Adidas', 'Converse', 'New Balance', 'Patrick', 'Puma', 'Reebok', etc.). Rather, they were similar in appearance to cheap 'market-bought' trainers and had been designed to look like the 'Adidas' brand - but with 2 stripes instead of three. It was not clear whether Rashid had bought them thinking that they were Adidas (I doubt it), but he was unlikely to have anticipated the reaction that he received. He was humiliated in front of the whole PE group whilst getting changed:
John: [to the rest of the group] "Who's got some new trainers then? They look like Adidas, but they've only got two stripes" [laughs].
Rashid: [indignant] "They're just as good". [laughter from the rest]

John: "How much were they then ?"
Rashid: [with pride] "£14". [laughter from the rest]
John: [sarcastic amazement in tone] "£14. Fuckin 'ell, they must be good
then". [laughter from the rest] (Field-notes)

Rashid was persecuted in other ways too. Whilst changing for PE on another
occasion, he had his clothing hidden, and was made the butt of the 'jokes' in other
ways. His response was interesting:

14/6/1988 Rashid again bullied by his peers, but he is reluctant to admit it
when we talk, and he won't name names. His loyalty to a group in which
he is unpopular, and even ostracised, is fascinating. Sadly for him, his
unwillingness to 'grass' on his classmates does not seem to endear him to
them. If anything, the opposite may be true: he is sneered at and held in
contempt because of his failure to do anything about his situation. (Field-
notes)

As well as the footwear, the clothing used for PE was also important as a status
symbol. There was an itemised PE kit for all pupils at the school which was
functional and unattractive. The younger Victims (11 and 12 years old) seldom had
all of the correct kit, but had an acceptable variation on the theme. The clothing
was unfashionable and often ill-fitting. Some of the older Victims bought football
shirts to wear, but these were old styles. Rafiq, for example, bought an England
football shirt and wore it to school. But it had been out-of-date for some time
(though not long enough to have come back into fashion) and was the source of
some amusement amongst his peers. It was thought that Rafiq had got this shirt to
be trendy, but it had all back-fired on him because the shirt was obsolete (and not
yet old enough to have come back into fashion as a piece of football memorabilia).
Clothing therefore made some young South Asian males very conspicuous. Further
social stratification occurred as a result of apparent success or failure in sport. Low
sporting ability was very visible and frequently resulted in rejection by peers,
especially when it merely confirmed some of the stereotypic assumptions that were
held about South Asians in sport.

Even within PE lessons, then, some Victims were denied some of their
opportunities to take a fully active part in sport. Football is a high-status activity
among young working-class males, and could be the unique opportunity for
contributing to 'multi-racial' understanding and harmony that Townsend and Brittan
(1973) suggest. Yet the Victims started with little emphasis placed on their 'play
learning activities', they had little or no prestige in sport, and were invariably not
permitted the opportunity to gain any. Far from breaking down cultural barriers and
encouraging tolerance, sport served to maintain and fortify ethnic boundaries, and
was a source of discord and conflict.

In spite of this, the Victims' attitude to PE was very positive: "I love it. It keeps
me fit and I enjoy it" (Rashid). This was all the more surprising in view of the
religious and cultural considerations that undoubtedly influenced their perceptions of
PE and sport, and their participation in it. The approach that recognises the
problems faced by South Asians in relation to cultural diversity in PE has caused
concern (Bayliss, 1989), but certain South Asian lifestyles do militate against sports

participation (White, 1990) - because of the way that sport is widely practised and excperienced in Britain. The Victims are clearly affected by at least three of the so-called 'problems'. The first is concerned with "Clothing, Modesty, Privacy, Changing Facilities..." (Rotherham MBC, 1988, p.7), and influenced their behaviour during post-sport showering:

> After our PE when we shower, they take all their clothes off, I have to keep my pants on. And I have to keep my tracksuit on when I'm doing PE... If I can't do something in a tracksuit, I can wear shorts, but I have to wear a tracksuit mostly... It's my religion, I don't know why. (Aslam)
> When I take my shorts off, and I take my underpants off, I have to put my shorts on again to go in the showers. I shouldn't show to people... I'm allowed to go in, but not without my shorts. (Wasim)

Showering after PE, often identified as an important issue for South Asians generally, and Muslims in particular, caused some of the Victims some genuine anxiety. For Aslam and Wasim, the issue was clear, and they had adopted a mode of behaviour that enabled them to cope with the situation in which they found themselves: taking a full part in compulsory school PE lessons whilst not compromising their commitment to Islam. For other Victims though, the obligatory after-sport shower posed a significant threat, and it was not one that they could adequately resolve themselves. Their response was either to pretend to have showered, to hide in the toilets, or to feign illness to avoid doing active PE at all. On more than one occasion Akram (a 12 year-old Victim) chose not to take part in PE lessons, and in-so-doing incurred the usual sanction imposed on non-participants, writing lines. To Akram and some of his Victim friends, writing lines was a preferable alternative to taking part in the lesson. Reluctantly, he explained: "We don't like showers because it's cold and we are shy to take our clothes off. Muslims are supposed to be shy. That's why I don't do shower at school".

Second, involvement in dance as part of the PE curriculum posed another potential cultural dilemma for some of the Victims. The cross-cultural appeal of dance and its importance as a means of increasing community pride and multi-cultural awareness has been the focus of much discussion for a considerable time. Lashley (1980b) remarks on the cultural significance of dance to various groups of young South Asians, and Kansara (1984) describes the value of South Asian dance for fostering respect for a variety of cultures, yet it also caused a real moral and cultural predicament: "Our religion [Islam] says you don't dance, to music and that... Our holy book says if you dance, you get punishment" (Rafiq). The factual accuracy of this comment is, in one sense, immaterial. For though there is evidence that this is indeed a valid perception (Lewis, 1979), and that dance is 'undesirable' (Jeffrey, 1972; Sarwar, 1983); the precise under-pinning from the *Qur'an* has been questioned (Hedayatullah, 1977). The important point is that Rafiq, like other Victims, believed it to be true.

Third, the relative unimportance of sport for the Victims meant that it was often low on their list of priorities. Prayer was one important aspect of Muslim lifestyle that many 'strict' Muslims prioritised ahead of sport. Rashid commented on the difficulty encountered if the pattern of Muslim prayer is to be devoutly adhered to:

It's quite difficult for me. I have to pray five times a day. If I have to pray at 12 o'clock, and there's a match, I can't play... If it's a matter of life and death, you can pray afterwards. But sport doesn't count as a matter of life and death. (Rashid)

The Victims were caught in a vicious circle where the difference in sports skill level between them and their peers from other ethno-cultural groups was constantly increasing. Sport was becoming less and less attractive to them. They were suffering abuse in their sporting experiences - sometimes for their lack of sporting ability, sometimes taunts and bullying that were motivated by overt racism. Many of them were made 'uncomfortable' by the post-sport ritual of the communal shower, and for these reasons may have chosen not to take part in activities that they actually enjoyed. They had few opportunities to take part in sport, and these were diminishing.

The Straights - "Hindus aren't that good at football"

The Straights are so called because they were basically conformers, and had much in common with two of the case-study South Asian male youths described by the CRC (1976, pp.66-68). Most were second generation British-South Asians, but they were not defined according to their religion. Amongst the Straights, Hindus and Sikhs were well represented, and there were some of the South Asian Muslims too.

The Straights collectively all demonstrated the same level of commitment to the different religions and traditional cultures represented amongst them; but this was considerably less 'strict' than the Victims. One of the Straights was Farukh, and as a Muslim his level of commitment to Islam contrasted sharply with that of the Victims generally, and Akram in particular. His attitude might almost be considered irreverent:

SF: "So you pray every day then ?"
Farukh: "[laughs] Nah, I don't do none of that, don't do nothing. I occasionally go Mosque if it's a special festival, but the only reason I go there is for the food! [laughs]"

But even for the Straights who had the will to be more committed than they actually were, many were finding it practically difficult as they attempted to assimilate into a predominantly Western but nonetheless multi-ethnic society. Mr Patel faced the reality that his children were less committed to the family traditional culture and lifestyle than he and his generation were:

I'm sure our children don't read or write our own language [Gujerati], they can only speak that. We, my wife and me, we can read a little bit and write a little bit, but they can't. Religion is up to them when they grow up and what they feel. They can take it up. I'm not against any religion, they can adopt anything as long as they are happy.

The attitude of many Straights had been considerably influenced by their parents (and fathers in particular) and was that they were, to adopt Solomos' (1988) socio-political use of the terms, 'black immigrants' rather than 'black British'; and that it was therefore incumbent on them as 'guests in another country' to make compromises in order to gain acceptance. Mr Chandra articulated this perspective very cogently: "It doesn't matter if Asian kids don't keep some of their culture. If it matters to them, they shouldn't have come here in the first place. You've got to adapt to people here".

The Chandras were, in many ways, typical of Straight families more generally. They were the owner-occupiers of a small and neat, previously council-owned terraced house on the fringe of the Elm Park estate; and in it there were some of the trappings of relative material comfort: remote controlled television, video tape recorder, mini-stack hi-fi. The Chandra family was Hindu by denomination, but not strict in commitment. They adhered to certain Hindu codes of behaviour - those that were easiest to observe, but there were many others that they chose to ignore. Rajesh explained:

> My dad does not believe a lot. He goes to the pub. He drinks alcohol and he smokes. And he once won £85 on the pools. We speak Gujerati at home, but my dad sometimes makes us speak English at home, because it's necessary for jobs.

If any group of the South Asians males at Parkview were "caught between two cultures", it was the Straights. This concept has been something of an obsession in the research of South Asian female youth (Brah and Minhas, 1985), and it is typically couched in the following way:

> The Asian child is living in two cultures: the culture of his parents and the culture of the host community. For instance he [sic] goes to the local school where he speaks English, and he takes his meal in school. On his return home he speaks his own language and eats different food and conflicts are bound to arise. (Morrison, 1976, p.30)

The situation that many young blacks are faced with, Solomos (1988, p.68) asserts, "was thus compared to that of groups living on the margin of two cultures, and thus facing problems of 'integration' into both cultures". The implication is clearly that this situation is irresolvable, and therefore a source of inter-generational conflict. Indeed, there has been a good deal of reactionary rhetoric to this phenomenon, the tone of which is illustrated by a BBC television documentary about the Bangladeshis of London's East End:

> ... The new generation of young Bengalis find themselves in the middle of a potent collision between East and West. Every day of their lives they have to pick their way through the cultural minefield of Bangladesh and the East End: tradition, deep family respect and the laws of Islam, set into a world of pop music, videos, sex and race. (BBC TV, 1990a)

Based on the principle that young South Asians are neither totally South Asian nor fully Westernised, some of the Straights did express uncertainty about their individual cultural identity. But interestingly, neither the Straights themselves, nor their parents indicated that there had been any of the inter-generational conflict that has previously been considered symptomatic of the difficulties facing young South Asians in Britain (CRC, 1976). Most of the Straights seemed to have resolved the situation in their own minds, and were even able to express ethno-cultural ambiguity without any personal dilemmas of identity: "I think of myself as half British, half Indian - 'cos my mother and father were born in India, and I was born in England" (Sanjay).

The Straights were keen to achieve academically, and viewed education as their most accessible means of upward social mobility. Career aspirations were often directed toward the affluence, material rewards and prestige of the professions (Taylor and Hegarty, 1985). The reaction of Mr K. Singh to the suggestion that his son might become employed in a trade was particularly revealing about the importance of education, and status of professional occupations:

SF: "If your son had to choose between a career in sport and a profession or trade... [interrupted]"
Mr K. Singh: [adamant] "Not trade, but I would love it if he went into a profession. Trade is one thing which is very common, basically I would love for him to finish his education, go to the university and then he can decide what he wants to do on his own. That is one thing he must do - get his degree... This is the view of 99% of Asian families".

The status of sport, even professional sport is put into context by Ranjit, who observed that because professional sport is considered to require a negligible intellectual capacity, it is held in low esteem:

A lawyer, an accountant, or an engineer... Sikhs take the attitude that a lawyer or an accountant is better than sport. Parents want their children to be fit, clever and everything. But the attitude is that you don't have to be clever to be a sportsman, you can be really stupid. They'd rather you be clever.

Some, however, were realistic enough to appreciate that the academic success and qualifications required to enter the professions may have been beyond them:

I have chosen to do electronics engineer. First of all I wanted to be policeman, but you don't get much money at it. Then I chose mechanic, but it's not for me. Then I chose electronics engineer. I'll see how physics goes, if I'm no good at it I'll be a mechanic. I want to work for someone then get my own business. (Ravi)

Like the Victims, the Straights were also subjected to harassment and abuse, and while this angered many, they tended to succumb to the apparent futility of confrontation, and accepted it with self-imposed tolerance:

I don't like it when people call me "Paki" and so on. I feel like hitting them, but I don't like fighting, and you get into trouble. (Rajesh)

I get angry because I'm not really a "Paki", but I still get called it... If they're older than me I ignore them. If they're younger I tell them not to do it... I don't get into fights, I don't like fighting. (Ravi)

I hate the name - being called "Paki"... I'd just like to beat them up, but I just ignore them, 'cos they are bigger than me and they can beat me up. Even if they were weaker I wouldn't 'cos some of the weak boys have big brothers and sisters who might beat me up. I just wish I was big and strong. (Javinder)

As a consequence the Straights seemed to avoid conflict situations, and were cautious about where they went, when, and with whom:

I'm careful. I don't go down alleyways and stuff, and I don't go to some places. If I go out in the night I just walk along the main roads. I don't live far from the tube station, so it doesn't matter, and I just walk home; no problem. (Farukh)

They modified their behaviour to avoid confrontation and abuse. This took them away from a number of scenes of social interaction, which inevitably included leisure and sporting venues.

In general though, the Straights were not as unpopular as the Victims because, as many of them were second generation British-South Asians, they didn't demonstrate the same degree of 'differentness' from the dominant culture of the numerical majority. Some were also part of a positive spiral of being popular and being favourably perceived. Ravi was a case in point:

23/6/1988   Ravi is short, overweight and something of a figure of amusement in his class. He doesn't know the exact reasons for this, but thinks it may be to do with his ready smile. I think that part of the answer is also that he is a very likeable person - in a more general sense. This likeableness is greater than any hostility towards him based on racist stereotypes. If he were less popular there would be more hostility directed towards him, and the situation would be further exacerbated by his 'South Asian-ness', for this provides a very visible and obvious focal point for racist abuse and perpetuating the stereotypic notions. (Field-notes)

As a group the Straights seemed to have a relatively restricted range of leisure-time interests which was often home and/or family centred. One home-based sport that was relatively popular however, was snooker; and some of the Straights either had their own small-sized snooker tables, or access to one at a friend's or family member's house. A typical evening after school was described in the following way by Ranjit:

In the evenings I do my homework for about an hour, and I watch television - I do a lot of that. Sometimes I go upstairs and play on my

82

computer if there's nothing on television. And I don't have time for anything else.

For Ravi too, there was little evidence of residual leisure-time. The priority was homework and study, then assisting his parents in domestic and household chores: "If I get a bad report [from school] I am in big trouble. But when I've finished my homework, if mum needs help, I help her. Or I help my dad fix the car and things".

Although there was apparently little time for leisure activities, and in spite of the low status that sport had, the general attitude of the Straights to sport was favourable. In addition to the health-related benefits, there was recognition of the cognitive, social and enjoyable aspects of sport:

> Sport is good because it's a good way of keeping fit, because it's fun. Some people will do 20 press-ups for a good workout, but not everyone likes that. So you can run about in games like football. You're more active, and you use your brain more. You get to meet people as well. (Javinder)

In spite of this positive attitude towards the benefits of sport and physical activity, the Straights tended not to participate in sports clubs outside school that required regular attendance. Some did, however, take part in recreational physical activities as part of their family's leisure; and others became involved in sport through religious and cultural commitments. The local Sikh Temple hosted a number of low-key and non-serious sports clubs:

> It was announced at the Temple, and mum said "Why don't you go and see what it's like?" So I did. We play badminton, basketball and volleyball; and we're going to start playing hockey and football as well. (Javinder)

The Straights were also positively motivated to the principle of PE. They took part, and always wore the regulation kit, though some were more willing than others. This requires more elaboration because it is, in a sense, a manifestation of their conformity to the imposed social order of the school's rules and regulations. The Parkview regulation PE kit was:

> Plain navy blue, round-necked, long-sleeved acrylic sports shirt or
> Navy blue and white reversible rugby shirt;
> Navy blue or white nylon shorts;
> Navy blue knee-length sports socks;
> Footwear (as appropriate);
> Towel.

It was functional rather than decorative, and was disliked - particularly with those who had fashionable football strips or track suits. As the year cohorts progressed up the school, there was increasing resistance to the PE uniform; so that by the final year of compulsory PE (the third year), it had been rejected by most students. The notable exceptions to this were the Straights who continued to wear it because, as Naresh explained, "it's the rules".

Physical Education lessons were frequently seen as a welcome distraction from the classroom, and served a number of functions:

It's good. You get to do some exercise, so you're more fit and healthy. And it's enjoyable. (Naresh)
It's not like other lessons because the time passes quicker, and it's not so long till going home. (Sanjay)
If I do lots of sport, it helps me to be skinny. (Ravi)

But the experiences of sport of some of the Straights at Parkview also reflected racial tension and acrimony: "If I am a goalkeeper and I let in a goal, people say "Look you fucking 'Paki', you can't do anything" - that happens even at school" (Naresh).

Given that this was not an isolated or unusual incident, it is perhaps unsurprising that the Straights seldom involved themselves in extra-curricular sports teams or clubs. Naresh himself was something of an habitual 'skiver', and seldom took part in PE. On such occasions, he always observed the school's protocol of providing the staff with a note from his mother, but since she was unable to write English, the notes were written in Gujerati and Naresh would translate them!

Some of the Straights were evidently affected by various, sometimes conflicting, perceptions of South Asians in sport. Two seemingly contradictory views of Sikhs existed. On the one hand, there was an emphasis on musicality at the expense of sport in Sikh culture: "Most of the Sikh people are into music not sport... All sorts, pop and disco music" (Sanjay); but on the other, participation in sport may actually be valued by the Sikh religion: "If anything my religion probably encourages it" (Javinder). The latter view was supported by some quasi-historical evidence:

The last Guru was a fighter, and he used to race a lot and keep his body fit. The Sikhs were being terrorised by Muslims and people like that, so he fought them, and taught the other Sikhs to fight. And he said "You've got to be fit, you can't be fat and podgy". So he gave them exercises. (Javinder)

There was, understandably, a sense in which these views are somewhat self-serving. Javinder was very enthusiastic about sport, while Sanjay, by his own admission, would have preferred not to do sport: "It's tiring... I don't like exercise, it pains me".

Amongst the Straights generally, more common perceptions of South Asians in sport were many of the prevalent stereotypes, especially those concerning football and cricket.

Hindus aren't that good at football... They don't know how to play football, they only know how to play cricket... Cricket is a famous game in India. Their ancestors taught them how to play, so they still play. But they don't want to play football, they don't like it. (Rajesh)

Some of the Straights had clearly identified certain activities to which they felt well suited. That is, they had begun to swallow the myth of the generalisations and stereotypes themselves. The suspicion that some of the Straights had about the relative sporting abilities of South Asians more generally, were confirmed, for them, by the absence of South Asian footballers. They explain this absence with reference to the success and preoccupation with games and activities more extensively practised on the Indian sub-continent:

> I had a football book and there was no Indian playing for any team. They're probably no good. Well, some of them might be good, but the people who are good, they will have other jobs or something like that... They don't play football very much in India, they play loads of Indian games - marbles and *kabaddi*. (Arun)

This notion was reinforced by their own experiences of sport at the lowest level where South Asians were proportionally under-represented in participation statistics.

> I went to [the sports centre] with my dad, and I looked very carefully, and I saw that there weren't any Indians there... They must be scared of coming there as well... I don't know why, but I kept looking to see any Indians there. I was wondering why there weren't any Indians. We were the only ones and I was a bit scared... White people don't like us, and they might do something. I was embarrassed, I couldn't find any Indians doing anything. That's what my brother is scared of, no Indians there. (Rajesh)

The Straights were keen to assimilate into British society, and sport is one scene of social interaction that was perceived to be confrontational. Hence, they often chose to avoid it. Fourteen-year-old Rajesh explained how he thought even his allegiance to Indian sporting teams could pose difficulties for him, should the Indian teams become successful:

> I'll give you an example. Brian is an Arsenal fan and Stefan is a West Ham fan. Once West Ham won against Arsenal, and Brian was so angry he started to beat him up. And if there was an Indian team against someone, and if the Indian one won, they would beat me up. (Rajesh)

Sport, ultimately, was not an especially important part of the Straights' lifestyles, and for families that were socially and economically disadvantaged in particular, sport and exercise did not rank as a priority (Malik, 1988).

The Boffins - "Maybe we're just not interested in sport"

As a sub-group of the Straights, the Boffins had much in common with them; and as a group share many of the characteristics of Gillborn's (1990, p.87-89) other case-study of South Asian male youth - particularly those related to commitment and academic success. Like the Straights, they too were conformers, and were very 'respectable'. Most were very aware of their religion and traditional culture, but were more strongly committed to it. Their fathers, who greatly influenced the Boffins, aspired to the material rewards and comforts of the middle-classes, and were ambitious for their sons. The Boffins were very sensitive to this ambition, and were highly motivated to achieve at school, reflecting the high esteem in which education is held by many South Asian families (Dove, 1975; Cashmore, 1982a); not only, as Thomas (1990, p.42) suggests, as an end in itself, but also as "a weapon to fight racial discrimination and gain status within the wider community and host society". Achievement was equated to examination qualifications, and for these young South Asians, high educational achievement was a realistic expectation. Hence the Boffins were the young South Asians who best matched up to the educational-achievement criteria of "a society where the highest achievers are white middle- and upper-class males" (S. Tomlinson 1986b, p.181).

The Boffins encountered personal racist abuse in sport - particularly football - as in other spheres of life. The most common coping strategy was to question the appropriateness of the insults, and reason that if they did not apply, then they need not have caused offence:

> The sort of thing I get most often is "Paki" or something like that. But I'm not really all that bothered because I'm not a Pakistani. (Suman)
> Occasionally they call me "Paki" and stuff... I just ignore it, I don't come from that country, don't come from that part of the world. I just ignore it. (Paramjit)

Though Vitesh did also admit that:

> You get people taking the 'Mickey' out of other people. Stuff like "Paki", "Nigger", stuff like that. And sometimes I get the urge to call them names back or get into a fight, but that isn't the sensible thing to do.

Minority ethnic groups at Parkview constituted the majority of the school population (about 55%), and the school was seen as something of a cultural 'melting pot'. Different ethnic groups were striving to assert their cultural identity all the time, and occasionally this manifested itself in the abuse of other groups. It is this that seemed to cause the Boffins most unease and alarm:

> I find that very offensive. They're attacking a whole country, a body of people. If someone says anything to me, "Paki" or whatever, I don't take it personally. But if it's about my family, then that's when it hurts. (Suman)

Their leisure-time activities were all pursued with vigour and enthusiasm, and often included a wide range of interests: "Homework, TV, reading adventure and sci. fi. stories, going to the shops, playing the piano, judo, and going to the cinema" (Suman). These were pursued with parental encouragement, but on the condition that studies did not suffer as a result. Suman's father even believed that there were some additional benefits to be gained for study through participation in sport:

Sport is a very valuable activity in many ways for any child; whether he is Asian, or any child. it improves health and the mind. Apart from the culture of mixing with people. In that way it makes them better in their minds when they do other school lessons - well mannered and disciplined. Sports would take a good part in that. (Mr Abdullah)

The Boffins evidently enjoyed PE, but it could prove to be something of an inconvenience, as it was seen as an unnecessary and unwelcome distraction from the important business of being prepared for academic exams. Through PE there was also the opportunity for 'differentness' to be highlighted and ridiculed. Sohan, for example, took trouble to avoid drawing attention to the *Kusti*, a religious adornment that he, as a Zoroastrian, was supposed to wear at all times. He removed it either at home before going to school, or when he went home at lunchtime. The Kusti never actually posed a difficulty for him, he didn't allow it to. What is important though, is that he thought it might: "I was concerned that other people might make fun of the cord when they see me get changed, because they might find it unusual".

There was a real sense of the relevance of their qualifications, and GCSE PE, though a qualification like any other, was deemed by some older Boffins less 'valuable' than other subject areas: "If I choose PE, I can't do one of the other more important subjects"(Sohan). They also appreciated the instrumental values of sport for maintaining physical and mental fitness, acquiring specific skills, encouraging team spirit and 'sporting' behaviour, and engendering strict discipline. They tended to see sport in these terms rather than for any of its intrinsic rewards. Many chose sporting activities that they considered would have a 'useful' purpose for them, with self-defence and the martial arts being especially popular. Indeed some of their sporting interests were pursued because of the threat of physical attacks:

Doing Judo's good because I can defend myself if I ever get attacked... That's why I started it, I haven't been attacked yet, but if I was I think I could look after myself better. (Sohan)

The Boffins had an interest in sport, and a favourable attitude towards it, but tended not to consider it as a possible career. Their analysis of the functions of sport was more concerned with its health-related outcome, and value to whole communities. Suman commented: "Sport is important to the Zoroastrian community because it improves your health, body and mind". Their perception was shaped further by their own understandings of South Asian involvement in sport, and curiously these understandings were expressed in the 'third person':

Not many Asian people go into sport. They don't get recognised too much, it's mostly white people... There's hardly any Asian players in the football world. In the Asians there's less people going into football. They go on to other jobs, and do other things. They're just as good at sport but they do other things. (Paramjit)

An extended general knowledge that reflected their interest in sport, gave the Boffins, especially those in the sixth form, a heightened awareness of sportsmen (though not sportswomen) from the Indian sub-continent:

I know [of] Vijay Amritraj, and there's Ramesh Krishnan; and the squash players, they're Muslims, Jansher Khan, Jahangir Khan. I know [of] some of the cricketers as well, Imran Khan, Kapil Dev, Gavaskar... As sportsmen I think they're good, but I couldn't really say that they inspire me. (Suman)

South Asians were disproportionately under-represented in the high-profile media sports that influenced working-class South Asian youths - athletics, boxing and football. Though in Bradford where cricket is the central leisure-time pursuit of many young South Asian boys, the Pakistani all-rounder Wasim Akram is one sportsman with whom many of them do identify (White, 1990). The Boffins identified the absence of South Asian sporting role-models as being of considerable importance, and related this to the effects of discrimination. In doing so, they acknowledged the stereotypic academic South Asian:

English people see Asian doctors, and they just assume that all Asians are going to become doctors. So I would be glad to see some Asian people in football. (Paramjit)

The link between this perceived absence and the various mechanisms of discrimination was cautiously hypothesised:

I've never seen any Indian footballers. I don't know if it's the Indians being too shy to play football, or just being rejected - perhaps because of their ability or the colour of their skin. (Vitesh)

The more forthright opinion of the powerful forces of discrimination against South Asians was also expressed, and again Paramjit, a 14 year-old Boffin, speaks in the 'third person':

Their colour doesn't change their ability does it?... But the other people don't let them play. The blacks and whites don't let them play, and won't allow them to play. (Paramjit)

For the Boffins, sport was only a very peripheral 'life interest'. It was only one part of a very full programme of leisure-time activities. Their experiences of personal racism in sport reflected their day-to-day existence, but these did not deflect the Boffins from an interest in sport. Paradoxically, they may even have stimulated the interest in a functional sporting activity that some of the Boffins believed may have been used to combat racism.

The Street-kids - "If you're quiet and Asian, you're open to prejudism [sic]"

The young men in this group were very 'street-wise'. They were mostly British-born South Asians who had lost their strong commitment to traditional religious values and cultural mores; though they were very aware of their 'colour', and they took great pride in it:

> I can't get rid of my colour, I have to face up to my colour. I'm proud of it. It depends how you take it. If you think your colour's bad, then that's a bad thing. But if you think about your colour - you have to put up with it. You have to like it or lump it, and I like it. (Dinesh)

They formed part of a much larger multi-ethnic street gang that had an integrated sub-culture that was heavily influenced by popular youth culture as well as Caribbean street culture; and did not encounter some of the barriers to social interaction that Carey and Shukur (1985) identified as being associated with skin colour and negative perceptions of South Asians. Occasional deviant behaviour, and a general reluctance to accept the authority of the dominant culture - teachers and the school establishment - had led to some of them being viewed with suspicion by members of the school's staff. Indeed for Street-kids, there was a good deal of 'sport' to be had in the high-status activity of giving the school's teachers a 'hard time' by being generally uncooperative and disruptive. In this way, the Street-kids behaved in ways that contradicted the established stereotypic teacher perception of the passive, meek and quiet South Asian (Bagley, 1976; Gillborn, 1990), and had more in common with the anti-school South Asian group 'the Warriors' identified by Mac an Ghaill (1988) in an analysis of pupil sub-culture, and based on the pro-school/anti-school model.

Ramdin (1987) has reported a teacher in another school commenting that pupil sub-culture is concerned with image projection:

> It's a matter of style... In the eyes of the children, West Indians have it and Asians don't. When a West Indian boy walks in, the girls look up; they don't do that for an Asian. In our school there is no doubt there is a hierarchy - the West Indians at the top, the Asians at the bottom. (p.464)

For the South Asians at Parkview, this was broadly true. But the Street-kids had their own 'style' in and around the school which was largely influenced by African-Caribbean youth street culture. In appearance and behaviour the Street-kids were influenced more by sub-cultural values than by ethnicity; and there was a general conformity to some of the characteristics identified by Roberts (1983) as typical of working-class gangs more generally, for example the use of peers as "reference points for tastes in dress, music, hairstyles and argot" (p.75).

The clothes they wore constituted the 'uniform' of the street: loose-fitting shirt; baggy jeans; a jacket of leather, pseudo-leather, or denim, or a ski-jacket; running shoes or basketball boots (with laces left untied); and personal stereo. All of it fashionable, and there was appreciable kudos to be gained by wearing new and expensive training shoes with a recognised brand name. As 15 year-old Ranjit explained: "It's the way people dress. In this school there's Jayant in the fifth year, and the way he dresses, they all like him, he's trendy. So he doesn't have a problem". At Parkview they were respected, though not necessarily admired by the other South Asians, and enjoyed high social status amongst their peers. They considered themselves to be adult, and the assertion of independence from adults was clearly important to them.

The Street-kids were hostile to any remarks made with racist intent, and used to get into numerous fights over this. They had all acquired a reputation as fighters, and hence did not get insulted with the frequency that they used to - thereby supporting the suggestion that attacks on Asians decrease as the ability to fight increases (CARF, 1981). Within this street gang, the group members often addressed each other by terms of racist abuse: "Sometimes my friends - Tony, Virendra - say stuff like 'Paki' or 'Nigger', and I suppose it's kind of racist, but they don't really mean it. It's a joke" (Ranjit).

If, however, the comment had not been made as 'a joke', the reaction would have been somewhat different:

> Someone once called me "Paki" in the street. He didn't know me, so me and my mates went and beat him up... If I know someone says something as a joke, it'd be different. But if he was serious I'd go and kick his head in. (Dinesh)

At break-times during the school day the Street-kids could often be found kicking a football around, or playing either 'pool' or table-football at the local youth club with the gang. A good deal of time was also spent "doing nothing" or "hanging around" (Corrigan, 1979; Roberts, 1983; Oakley and Carey, 1986; Sugden, 1987), which Jitendra described as: "Going out with my mates, having a few laughs, walking around the streets, smoking a few fags, and having a couple of drinks". In this way in public spaces where there was little interference, the Street-kids often appropriated their own space, and access to this was denied to people outside their immediate group.

Generally the Street-kids were positively motivated towards PE, but tended to 'vote with their feet' by excluding themselves from activities that they did not enjoy:

> It depends what sport. I don't like things like badminton, it's boring. I don't like volleyball, it's boring too, and dance and gym... I find football interesting, I like it, and play it a lot. I like hockey as well. (Ranjit)

They opted to continue with it beyond the Third Year when it ceased to be compulsory, seeing it as preferable to sitting in a classroom. Some took the GCSE - PE option: "I decided I was going to do PE; it's better than proper lessons 'innit! And I thought I might as well do the GCSE to get a qualification out of it" (Dinesh). More opted to do Recreation PE: "GCSE wouldn't help me as a mechanic... I wanted one lesson when I didn't have to think about school, and I could mess about. And I like PE, it keeps you fit" (Suresh).

For the younger Street-kids, PE was an opportunity for them to assert their individuality, and also their status amongst their peers. The PE uniform was unpopular, and for these image-conscious young South Asians, it was important to look trendy. Clothing for PE was also an issue for the older Street-kids. For those not engaged on the GCSE option, PE also enabled them to express their dissatisfaction with the authority structure of the school. By not wearing correct PE kit, or even bothering to change out of their 'everyday' clothes, they were able, in a very clear and visible way, to 'buck the system'. Fifteen year-old Suresh explained:

> I just can't be bothered to bring all the kit. And if Mr Taylor [PE teacher] is saying that we've got to bring all our kit, we'll leave it in the classroom. Never wash it, just bring it out, and never have a shower. Or most probably, we'll go in the shower and use the same smelly towel every week. It's a waste of time really. But it's Mr Taylor's new rules, and we're laying down a new way to get out of it.

The intention was that Suresh would cause members of the Parkview staff considerable irritation. He had evidently achieved this objective, for Mr Taylor remarked later that same day: "Suresh is turning out to be a right pain in the arse - just like the rest, always whinging".

Sport, or more specifically football, played an important part in the lifestyle of Asian Street-kids, though they were seldom sufficiently motivated or committed to join and remain a member of a sports club or team: "If they wanted me to play for the school team, I would; but I'm not interested in all the training and going to away games and that" (Salim). They played a lot of informal, non-serious 'pick-up' games in parks, in playgrounds, or on the streets. Football was characterised not by 11-a-side teams, goal posts, nets, corner flags, and referees, but by a non-competitive informal 'kick-about' that enabled them to show off their skills - many of which would have had little value in the full game, but which looked impressive. They described themselves as supporters of one of the local First Division [now Premiership] football teams, but this seldom extended to attending live games. For this, they are often accused, in a good-humoured way, of being 'armchair supporters' by other members of the street gang.

Despite their interest in football, though, the Street-kids did not dream of becoming professional players, and had more realistic and attainable career goals: "I'm only interested in it [football] as a hobby. I want to be an electrician" (Dinesh). The implication is that football and paid employment are perceived as mutually exclusive: "Asians aren't really interested as much in football as getting a job" (Salim). Thus, while there may be unrestricted and multiplex avenues for a young South Asian to achieve wealth, status and feeling of self-adequacy (Cashmore 1982a), sport was not seen as one of them: "I never thought of doing it [sport] and earning money... They [South Asians] see it like me. They don't see it as a money-making prospect" (Jitendra).

The processes identified by Cashmore (1990b, pp.79-93) that make sport seem like an attractive 'way out' for young blacks (by which he means African-Caribbeans), did not, therefore, apply to the Street-kids and to young South Asians in general. Unlike the African-Caribbeans to whom Cashmore refers, the Street-kids did not see sport as a mechanism through which they could escape the limits imposed on them because of their ethnicity and because of racism. Moreover, membership of the street gang was almost incompatible with both the acquiescence to authority that representing school teams implies, and the acceptance of the work-ethic associated with committed sports participation. Thus peer group pressure might, indirectly, have restricted involvement in a number of sporting activities.

Perceived parental attitudes also reflected the esteem in which sport is held by older South Asians: "I doubt my dad wants me to take up sports. He says 'Try to get a good job, and don't waste your time on sport'. Dad would rather I got a real job" (Suresh). Such attitudes were strengthened by the absence of sporting role-models which confirmed the marginal status of sport as a career outlet: "They don't really see Indian people doing sports, they think no-one does it really" (Salim). Yet somewhat incongruously, the Street-kids were aware of the stereotypic view of South Asians' involvement in sport, and curiously Jitendra, a Street-kid, also talks of this view of South Asians in the 'third person':

> They only play certain types of sport. There's cricket, badminton, squash... Hmm, I think that's it. They're the most publicised with Asians in it. They don't play the others. (Jitendra)

Their experiences of sport had not been without personal racist abuse being directed at them, but this was accepted as part of normal existence:

> Now and then when I go down the park to play football, they [people at the park] say things like "Get back to your own country 'Paki', What are you doing here? Your lot can't play football". At the time you just swear back: "Fuck off! You don't know what you're talking about". Or sometimes I just lose my temper and say "OK, if you want to fight, let's fight now". Sometimes they back off, but sometimes they start fighting; I've had lots of fights. I used to get called a lot - a couple of years ago, but not so much now. (Dinesh)

Despite this coping strategy, the influence of personal racism was an important factor in an analysis of South Asians' sports participation: "Asians can't be bothered. Either that or they're scared. If they get called racist names and that, they'll lose confidence" (Jayant).

A common denominator: personal racism

The young South Asian males at Parkview School comprised a heterogeneous population. They came from a range of ethno-cultural backgrounds, and their lifestyles were clearly affected by a myriad of complex inter-related socio-cultural variables. Yet their shared perceptions and experiences of daily life generally, and sport in particular, enable them to be identified in terms of a four-category typology. The common denominator across the Victims, the Straights, the Boffins and the Street-kids was their experience of the effects of personal racism (see page 41).

Behaviour that is inherently racist has been described as 'racialism', but this is a term that is more popular in everyday use than in academic discourse. As Robert Miles (cited in Cashmore, 1988) comments:

> Where used in the latter, it is rarely explicitly defined, but tends to be used to denote the practices which embody or express racism. These practices

are more commonly referred to by the concept of racial discrimination. (p.245)

The following list is what ILEA (1986, p.36) described as "manifestations of racialist and discriminatory behaviour":

(1) Physical assault against a person or group because of colour or ethnicity.
(2) Derogatory name-calling, insults and racist jokes.
(3) Racist graffiti or any other written insult.
(4) Provocative behaviour such as wearing racist badges or insignia.
(5) Bringing racist material such as leaflets, comics or magazines into the school or college.
(6) Making threats against a person or group because of colour or ethnicity.
(7) Racist comment in the course of discussion in lessons.
(8) Attempts to recruit other pupils and students to racist organisations and groups.

It was certainly not the case that all of these practices were evident at Parkview. A key point in this regard was the multi-ethnic composition of the school itself; for manifestations of racism directed generally against all minority ethnic groups would not have been tolerated. (The concept of racism was a 'buzz' issue in and around the school, and some pupils would often misuse the word, especially when it was used rather threateningly against members of the school's staff). Rather it was racism directed specifically at South Asians that was more apparent. There were, for example, few if any incidents of recruitment to racist organisations, or of the wearing of offensive racist badges and insignia. But the other forms of behaviour made an impact on the lifestyles of the South Asians very directly.

The Victims were, as already outlined, subjected to physical assault on a daily basis. Akbar outlined one particular incident, and his more general view of the situation:

> I don't like to fight, but they hit us. Like yesterday, the black guys in the 5th year - they are six, and we are three only - they punch my friend Grushan, and we did fight... I don't know the reason. they don't have a reason to fight with us. But they don't like brown people.

Jim Murphy (1989) observes that "Asians are much more likely to suffer racial abuse than any other racial groups", and he goes on to cite some evidence from a study conducted by Eggleston et al. (1986), which found people of South Asian origin to be 50 times more likely to be subjected to racial attack than white Britons, and also more likely to be attacked than Caribbeans. At Parkview School, the Victims were not the only South Asians to suffer from this sort of attack. The Straights did too, but on a less frequent, less intense and less systematic basis. Tejpal explained: "Peter is very rude. He hits me. But the only trouble is, he only tries to go for weak people; he doesn't go for the big ones".

Racist graffiti, if not common-place, did exist:

> People make fun out of the food of ours - Indian food. They start making fun. I saw in a religious book, it said "have a hot curry". People wrote "Fuck off Paki" underneath on the book. (Ravi)

So too racist comment in lessons, and verbal threats. But the most frequent manifestations of racism are the derogatory names that many of the South Asians are called on a regular and frequent basis.

Verbal abuse of South Asians has been recognised as a feature of their daily lifestyle (Brah and Minhas, 1985; Thomas, 1990; Matthews, 1992). Specific instances of racist name-calling have been analysed by Kelly and Cohn (1988), and the findings of their studies are supported by the experiences of the Victims, the Straights and the Boffins. Typical among the terms of abuse is "Paki" - all the South Asians seemed to get called that, regardless of their nationality of ethnicity. That, however, did not cause as much offence as insults that were directed more broadly against an individual's family:

> One of them did call me names just now. She's in my class. She said I was a "tramp" and a "Paki bastard", and the whole of my generation is as well. I try to ignore it, but that makes me very angry, [especially] when all the people around say it. (Ashok)

Verbal abuse that was concerned with sex or gender was also considered offensive (Kelly 1988, Ruthven 1991), but the most insulting form of abuse was undoubtedly that which combined sex or gender with female family member:

> Mahmood: "They say things like 'smelly Paki' and 'fucking bastard'"
> SF: "And do you get into fights about that ?"
> Mahmood: "No, never. I am scared".
> SF: "You've never been in a fight ?"
> Mahmood: "Err... Yea, I was last year."
> SF: "What was that about ?"
> Mahmood: "Jason said something about my mum".
> SF: "What ?"
> Mahmood: "He said to me to 'fuck her'. I get angry about that and I lose my temper".

Clearly then, personal racism was a central feature of the daily lifestyles of all the South Asians at Parkview. It was the different responses to it that determined the position of each group in the social order. Indeed these responses help to illustrate some of the existing analyses of South Asian youth. For example, Wilson (1983) sees the responses to personal racism lying somewhere along an assimilation-conflict continuum, but then suggests that many young South Asians are caught in a position of unfortunate compromise, rather akin to that of the Straights:

> For an Asian child growing up in Britain there is a choice. Either you stand outside your own community and see yourself as non-Asians see you, which often means identifying with racist opinion, or you learn to hate people who say racist things. Many children are caught in between. They

lead a double life, on the surface passive, even servile, but inside they suffer. (p. 14)

That is, in itself something of an over-simplification, but certain elements of it did apply to the South Asians at Parkview. It was clear that the Victims suffered most. They retreated submissively, and consequently were denied opportunities to participate in sport. The Straights were both cautious and tolerant, and tried to avoid the conflict of sport and the hostility - either real or imagined - of sporting venues. Boffins responded by rationalising the nature of the abuse, and developed a coping strategy that in some instances included the pursuit of sporting activities that were considered valuable for self-defence. The Street-kids confronted racism directly, and it would appear that their sporting behaviour was not significantly altered by it.

What was interesting about the Street-kids is that they would often use racist language to each other (Kelly 1990). Virendra attempted to justify this, and in so-doing indicated the norms and expectations that surrounded their daily interaction:

It's just like when two black guys call each other "Nigger". That's what we do, me, Tony, Warren, we do it all the time. We call each other "Niggers", "Monkeys" and "Pakis" and all this. It's a joke. (Virendra)

If, on the other hand, the comment had not been made 'as a joke', his reaction would have been very different. The important factor here in defining the response to the use of such language, was perceived intent. If racist remarks were perceived to have been made 'as a joke' then that is how they were taken. If, on the other hand, the intent was hostile, then the response would have been at least as hostile too.

As Wilson (1983, p.14) remarks: "Schooldays are said to be the best days of your life, but for Asian children in Britain they are often the harshest". Life in school was, for some, a relentless battle against racial antagonism. Sport was clearly affected. But it is also true that for many of the Asian males at Parkview, sport was not high on their list of priorities. As Javinder (a Straight) commented: "I play for fun. I don't want to be really serious about it", and it became apparent that formal organised sport is only a peripheral life interest for the South Asian youths at Parkview.

In the final analysis, sport, popularly conceived of as providing minority groups with equal opportunity, is not only failing to integrate them, but is a vehicle for the expression of ethnic antagonism and racial tension, and is consolidating and even exacerbating social division.

7 'Taking each game as it comes': patterns of participation

The recognition of heterogeneity amongst young South Asians is of paramount importance to an understanding of the role that sport plays in South Asian youth cultures. Yet there are certain shared characteristics of South Asians generally that differentiate them, as a collection of ethno-cultural groups, from the others in British society (Beckerlegge 1991). At the most obvious level, as Ballard (1990) notes, because of the use of skin colour as a 'social marker', they all share the experience of social exclusion to some degree; and as already discussed in chapter six, various experiences of racism could be seen to act as a common denominator amongst all the young South Asians at Parkview School. But more than this, there are also certain shared cultural commonalties. Aware of the risk of over-generalising, Rex (1982) asserts that:

> Asian families, be they Sikh, Hindu or Muslim, Pakistani, Indian or Bangladeshi, are all, compared with English families tight-knit and all attached more or less strongly to a culture pattern far more sharply differentiated from English culture than working-class English culture is differentiated from the middle-class culture of the schools. (Rex, 1982, p.59)

With regard to lifestyle preferences, different groups of young South Asians are influenced both by their traditional culture from the Indian sub-continent, and by their experiences in Britain (Ballard 1990).

Participating in sport

The sporting participation patterns of young South Asian males have been, and are still difficult to ascertain with any real confidence; but very preliminary evidence has pointed to the existence of South Asian under-representation in sport and physical activity (Botholo et al., 1986; Sports Council, 1982). For the young South Asians at Parkview School, participation in sport took four different forms: formal PE lessons, extra-curricular school activities, out-of-school teams and clubs, and informal sport played in locations such as playgrounds, parks, gardens, and the streets.

The first of these, formal PE lessons, were extremely influential in shaping their opinions and attitudes to sport and physical activity. The syllabus, as in many other schools, included games (invasion, striking and fielding, net), gymnastics, athletics, dance and swimming; though there was a clear imbalance in the time allocation to each of the broad categories, with, not surprisingly, the major team games receiving the lion's share of the time. As such, PE lessons provided a source of some common understandings about the nature of sport and physical activity. Rather than formal and compulsory PE lessons, however, it was voluntary involvement in sporting activity that revealed more about the role of sport in South Asian male youth cultures, for this was 'freely' chosen.

The school-based extra-curricular sporting activities have been the focus of research concerned with minority groups (particularly, for example, Carrington and Wood, 1983; Cashmore, 1982b; Sargent, 1972; Wood and Carrington, 1982). This has, without exception, been concerned with African-Caribbean youth; though this preoccupation is perhaps unsurprising given the use of extra-curricular sport as a means of social control for disaffected black youth (Carrington, 1983). Yet as Carrington (1986, p.8) also points out:

> The potential of sport as a mechanism of social control and a **context for celebrating the official ideology of schooling**, has long been recognised by educationalists on both sides of the Atlantic, who have variously depicted it as: a medium for 'character building' and **disseminating favourable attitudes towards authority; an appropriate vehicle for enhancing the unity and solidarity of schools** and channelling the interests and energies of 'problem' children; and a means of fostering a competitive ethic. [Emphasis added]

In view of the stereotypic 'pro-school and deferential' attitude of many South Asian students, it is more surprising that there have been no studies of the extra-curricular involvement of South Asians in school teams. (Indeed, the 'problems approach' adopted by many physical educationalists to South Asian female students, actually identifies extra-curricular activities as a cause of special concern.)

At Parkview School the extra-curricular sports teams and clubs included athletics, basketball, cross-country, football; and also sports that conform more readily to the stereotypic South Asian sportsman, badminton and cricket. Collectively, the young South Asians were disproportionately under-represented in these, as they were in out-of-school teams and clubs too. Though interestingly, there were more South Asians involved away from the school context and environment than at Parkview itself. This is an important comment on the way that school sport was perceived by them. For it is clear that in most instances, school sport was more accessible than out-of-school clubs; yet a relatively large number of South Asians were prepared to pursue the latter with all the additional problems of access, travel and erosion of residual leisure time that this entailed.

An additional related issue was the general lack of awareness amongst the South Asians of the local sporting facilities (i.e., within the borough). Mr Ahmed, a local community leader, explained that this lack of awareness was wider than being merely restricted to the South Asians at Parkview School, but it affected them most acutely:

> Now there should be enough publicity and enthusiasm to try and get the Asian communities involved in it [sport]. And I would suggest that there should be a sports liaison officer in every sports institution or organisation where they could send that representative to the various Asian organisations and community groups and inform them what sorts of activities Asians can participate in, and what facilities they have got for them; to try and get them into it. It would get them interested in it. But there's not much publicity. I've never seen any publicity. Parkview Sports Centre are never putting out any publicity about what they are doing, what sort of things. There's not enough information filtering out.

Superficially, some of these findings might seem to indicate South Asian under-representation in organised sport. Yet closer examination of actual participation patterns indicated that in many cases it was the situational context of the participation that influenced involvement in sport. For example, of those who participated in out-of-school sport, some did so as a direct consequence of their involvement in cultural and religious groups. Javinder (a Straight) explained in chapter five that the Sikh Temple was a centre for an expanding involvement in sport for those who attended regularly. But as his father indicated, these Sikhs were providing sporting opportunities for themselves in the same way that other South Asian groups had in other parts of Britain (e.g., Bradford, Leicester, Southall):

> In the temple we go to every Sunday, they do about four hours of sports there. They hire a hall - badminton, volleyball. I think what they're trying to do, because there aren't many [Sikh] people around here, they're trying to organise a Sikh society of sports. They want to organise more hockey and other things. (Mr Singh)

The intention from the outset was not necessarily to increase levels of participation in sporting activities, but there was evidently a demand for it. Unlike the mechanism for the increasing participation in sport among South Asian women described by Dixey (1982) in which sport was 'smuggled' in alongside something more acceptable - education; in this instance a religious and cultural orientation provided the focal point for the social interaction which spawned participation in sport. Mr Singh explained how the two were able to co-exist:

> It's getting Indian, Asian kids to start coming into sports, it's another way of pulling them into sports. At the end of the year they have a tournament and they give prizes and shields. At the same time they also teach Indian language, our own language - Punjabi. At the end of the year they have an evening for the kids when the Mayor, and the kids get the prizes. The same way they do it for the sports. One day they do everything; the two of them, they come together.

In this sort of environment, unthreatening and with a measure of shared cultural homogeneity, sports participation amongst young South Asian males was undertaken with eagerness.

Stereotypes, the self-fulfilling prophecy and role-models

The stereotype of the 'racket-sport South Asian' is prevalent in discussions of South Asians and sports participation (Cherrington, 1975; Williams, 1989b). One of the Victims, 14 yea-old Aslam, described the popularity of badminton in urban areas of Bangladesh where adequate facilities existed for participation in the game:

> When I was in Bangladesh I lived in a big town and I played badminton a lot in school. My teacher in PE in Bangladesh said "You're good at badminton and football". I've got medals for badminton, but I left them in Bangladesh.

Consequently, the stereotype is perpetuated further still by young Bangladeshis and others settling in Britain, attending British schools and demonstrating not only greater expertise in badminton than in other sports, but also greater competence than their peers from other ethnic groups. On the face of it, therefore, there would seem to be some empirical base for their reinforcement and perpetuation of such stereotypes, albeit anecdotal and subjective, and based on 'argument by example'. The danger arises when a causal link is established between, for example, prowess on the badminton court and 'being South Asian' that has physiological and even psychological under-pinnings. As Cashmore has observed (1990a), once that line of reasoning is followed, the implications are much more profound than a mere explanation of sporting behaviour. Of African-Caribbeans, he elaborates:

> If we accept as proof of the natural ability argument the outstanding results recorded by blacks sports performers then what are we to infer from the 'underachievement' of blacks in formal education? That they are naturally limited intellectually? (p.88)

A similar sort of argument could be advanced in relation to South Asians: if we accept as proof of the natural ability argument the outstanding academic examination performances of some South Asian youngsters, what are we to infer from their apparent under-representation in sports participation? That they are naturally limited physically?

South Asians do, of course, have something of a tradition for success in hockey, squash and tennis (Craft and Klein, 1986; Williams, 1989b); but these are activities that are not as easily accessible for working-class minority groups in inner-city Britain. Hence young working-class South Asians have fewer avenues for the expression of ethnic pride that other groups enjoy. The 'knock-on' effect of this is that cricket, which was relatively accessible, offered the only real opportunity for the demonstration of sporting prowess in an activity in which there was an expectation of competence - and even elite performance - from both outside the South Asian communities and within them.

These activities, and hockey in particular, have provided the basis for the development to 'stardom' of the South Asian sports<u>man</u>. For Sikhs especially, their involvement has been central to the international success of the Indian national team. By their physical appearance alone, many Sikhs are immediately identifiable by their turban or patka; and are constantly asserting their religious and ethnic identity in a very visible and overt way. The Sikh presence in Indian hockey has, in a sense, set an expectation of Sikh prowess; and it is an expectation that is handed down through the generations. So much so, that some of the Sikhs at Parkview, who had not themselves experienced the culture of the sub-continent at first hand, believed it: "We ain't no good at football an' that. But Sikhs have always played hockey good, it's in our history innit?" (Jitendra).

In cricket there is even the sense of a self-fulfilling prophecy of crude stereotypes. The view that South Asians are especially good at cricket is well entrenched, and there are even some fallacious physiological arguments for this analysis that are held by practising physical educators: "ethnic minority kids are more useful at cricket - their body-type is more conducive to this activity" (cited in Carrington and Williams, 1988, p.88). Significantly too, some of the South Asians at Parkview School had the sort of background in cricket that they did not have in other sports, and had been socialised into it by the influence of significant others. Mr Kumar explained further:

> I don't think he's capable of being a kind of good footballer. Some of it is passed down - inherited, and I basically feel that if he show a little of that, then to encourage. Let's put it this way, if tomorrow my youngest son came to me and said "come on, let's go and play football", I wouldn't go and play with him. I'd say he was out of his mind; I can't kick a football. But if he said "let's go and play cricket" - Yes, because I can play, and I'd be able to teach him to play as well.

Many young South Asians also believed that this was a sporting activity in which they could compete on an equal footing with their peers from other ethno-cultural groups, and at which they could excel.

There are numerous Indian tennis stars (all men) who have succeeded at International level, and some successes have been as relatively recent as reaching the Davis Cup final in 1987. Yet these successes, and others in cricket and squash, have been experienced and enjoyed by people who - on one level - have very little in common with working-class South Asian male youth from the inner-cities of Britain. There may have been some association with 'skin colour' and nationality (see below), but in the main, the lifestyles and socio-economic background of South Asian sports stars were so different from those of young people at Parkview School as to make them largely irrelevant. There were some Indian, Pakistani and Sri Lankan cricketers who earned their living in Britain, and some of the Pakistani squash players lived in Britain, these were not the people with the young South Asians at Parkview truly identified.

The whole concept of sporting role-models is something that John Rex (1982) has touched on, though he merely pointed to the absence of South Asian sports-stars. Over ten years after Rex made this observation, there are, of course, many South Asian sports-stars, and some of them are widely-known in Britain; but most are not British-born. Rather they are from the sub-continent, and have made or are still making a professional sporting career in Britain. Even the British-born South Asian cricketers are not typical of working-class South Asians in Britain, having a comfortable middle-class family background (and in some cases a University education) as part of their sporting development (Pringle, 1991b). Mr Singh explained:

> SF: Do you think that Asians generally identify with the cricketers on the telly - the famous ones: Imran and Kapil Dev?
> Mr Singh: Not in this country, no. In their own countries, yes. They are mini-gods. But here, no-one has got that kind of time to bother about them.
> SF: Asian kids here don't recognise Imran Khan in the same way?
> Mr Singh: I think the kids here, they recognise Michael Jackson more than they recognise Imran Khan [laughs].

Like other aspects of the perceptions of sport that they shared with their peers from other ethnic groups, South Asians could identify footballers and other sports-stars that they admired. Other than the Victims, most were easily able to report on their favourite footballer or cricketer or athlete; and they spoke most readily of non-Asian sports-stars as their heroes (though not heroines). Some reported Imran Khan or Kapil Dev as their favourite cricketer, but there was no distinct ethnic association with them, and a lot of confusion was expressed about their respective nationalities and religions. The implication being that this was, at most, an identification with 'skin colour' rather than national, religious or ethnic consciousness. The wider picture showed that the people with whom the young South Asians identified were from a range of ethnic backgrounds and a range of sports; but the reasons for their popularity were concerned with perceived ability and success achieved (e.g., Daley Thompson), 'style' (e.g., Ian Botham), their 'closeness to home' (e.g., Tony Adams), or a combination of them all (e.g., Gary Lineker).

Understanding non-participation patterns

In contrast to some of the stereotypes about culturally oriented preferences for sporting and leisure activities, the young South Asians at Parkview demonstrated a favourable attitude towards a whole range of sports and physical activities. Indeed, the sporting preferences expressed by all of the young males at Parkview School were broadly similar, and there were considerably more commonalties than differences. That is to say, not only were the stereotypes about South Asians' sporting preferences too narrow to accommodate the full range of sporting interests; but the assumption of difference based on cultural criteria was also flawed, for some sporting interests transcended ethno-cultural barriers.

Of the activities that were less popular, however, there were some, like dance, gymnastics and aerobics, that were generally not liked amongst all young males at Parkview. Others, by contrast, were only unpopular amongst the young South Asians, for example, boxing, rugby and American Football. There are two important themes that begin to account for these: first, gender-specific associations; and second, cultural perceptions of violence. Additionally, there were certain levels of involvement that could be explained, at least in part, by some general perceptions of the nature of the sporting venue, and by some cultural experiences of participation.

"Dance is for Girls" (Ranjit)... and so is aerobics!

Dance has often been cited as a vehicle for increasing multi-cultural awareness and understanding (e.g., Kansara, 1984; Todryk, 1988; Gajadhar, 1990). This is true enough, but, as there is also a very real danger of multi-cultural tokenism, which is potentially very damaging. BAALPE (1990) advances the view that the inclusion of Gujerati folk dance in the PE curriculum will develop awareness of South Asian culture. Yet this is fraught with difficulties, some of which are concerned with the inherent problems of multi-cultural education, and some of which became apparent from the situation at Parkview School.

First, the projection of Gujerati folk dance as representative of South Asian cultural dance makes an assumption about the homogeneity of South Asian cultures that cannot be sustained logically. There is a rich mixture of traditional cultural dance forms from the Indian sub-continent, but the practicalities and logistics of the school curriculum prevent them all from being studied. A focus on one form of cultural dance not only misrepresents South Asian dance forms, but can also cause offence to South Asians from other ethno-cultural groups.

Second, the multi-cultural approach to dance seldom acknowledges the cultural concerns that some Muslims have about dance. Daley (1991, p.31) has commented on the varying degrees of 'strictness' amongst different Muslim groups; and herein lies a cause for concern, for it is clear that dance is considered culturally taboo for some Muslims, and no amount of "replacement [of the word 'dance'] by more acceptable wording (e.g., creative movement)" (Daley, 1991, p.32) is going to alter some of these fundamental objections. At Parkview different groups of Muslims demonstrated a whole gamut of responses to the 'strictness' of Islam: the Bangladeshi Victims were extremely committed, while the Turkish Muslims were a good deal less so. For the latter, dance was no different from any other part of the PE curriculum; but for some of the Victims, participation in dance created a real moral and religious dilemma.

Third, there is a more general problem about the way that dance is experienced and perceived by all students. Dance was almost universally unpopular amongst the males at Parkview. The syllabus was exclusively Eurocentric, and took the form of a very brief introduction to British social and country dancing in the first year only. It was taught by the female members of the PE department only, which reinforced the gender stereotyping associated with the activity. Evidently, working-class adolescent males were less concerned with engaging in activities that may be educationally, socially and emotionally valuable, than they were in asserting their masculinity through other activities that they perceived to be more 'macho'. Hence the comments:

"Dance is for Girls" (Farukh),
"The dance you do in PE is 'poncey'" (Jayant),
"Why do we have to do it? It's OK for the girls - they like it, but we don't. Why can't we do what we wanna do - football an' that ?" (Ramesh).

In this regard, the South Asian males were no different from the other ethno-cultural groups at Parkview. The reality is that little [ ] had either in the content of the dance syllabus, or in the manner throu[ ] was taught.

That is not to say, though, that dance does not feature prominently lifestyles of young South Asians generally. On the contrary, a unique hybr[ ] Western popular music and traditional Indian music - *Bhangra* - and the dance cra[ ] associated with it are both very popular; and though there are indications that *Bhangra* has greater appeal for Hindus and Sikhs than Muslims (Ghuman, 1991a; Nesbitt, 1991), there is still, nevertheless, widespread interest in it, and a clearly articulated wish for participation in it (Asian Times, 2/4/1991). Amongst the South Asians at Parkview, however, only 16 year-old Jayant had been involved, and he was one of the Street-kids who explained that he had been to a *Bhangra* club once or twice, and was intending to make a habit of it: "Well it's good 'cos the music's like when you go out clubbin', but it's for us [South Asians], and we can appreciate it, innit. And 'cos it's for us, there ain't no other people there". For Jayant, at least, the implication was that the hybrid musical form that combined traditional Indian with popular Western influences had direct appeal to him as a young South Asian in Britain. Equally, the absence of other non-Asian ethnic groups was as important as any opportunity to assert cultural solidarity and ethnic identity.

Fourth, and perhaps most important of all, there are 'racist dangers of tokenism' (McFee, 1994). The sort of tokenistic South Asian dance practised in some schools merely serves to confirm and reinforce racist stereotypes; and exacerbates ethnic antagonism. In an environment like Parkview School, the mechanism for this is clear: adolescent males preferred not to be doing dance of any kind, and being forced by the PE syllabus to engage in South Asian cultural dance would have caused resentment and ultimately hostility that would have been directed not only at the activity, but at people associated with it. Jayant speculated on the hypothetical situation of South Asian dance becoming part of the PE syllabus that he had to engage in:

> All that Asian dancin' and that, it's OK, but most kids here think it's a load of shit. Can you imagine if Joel 'n' Anton had to do it, they'd really take the piss out of us [South Asians]. If you wanna teach us dance, teach us 'moonwalking' an' that.

In short, far from increasing multi-cultural tolerance and understanding, South Asian dance was perceived as an activity that would draw attention to ethno-cultural differentness, and would make some of the South Asians subject of further vilification. It would be very difficult to argue that dance plays an important part in the day-to-day lifestyle of these young South Asians; and given this apparent level of antipathy, it would also be hard to argue its value in the enhancement of self-esteem.

The position of BAALPE (1990), amongst others, indicates a lack of understanding of the complexity of the social relations in a secondary school like Parkview, and a failure to acknowledge the generational issues surrounding South Asians in Britain, for there is a fundamental flaw in the proposition that traditional South Asian dance is a central part of the cultural activities of many South Asians

already indicated above that contemporary dance forms - in
of black American street-culture, and popularised amongst
on - had more interest and relevance for him than traditional
om the Indian sub-continent. Vitesh (a Boffin) put it very
does about as much traditional Indian dancing as the average
rris dancing".

young males at Parkview had about keep fit/aerobics were
types of gender-specific activities for women, and were
dia hype that surrounded Jane Fonda, 'Mad Lizzie' (the
nd others. Aerobics in particular, was an activity that was
unpopular with young working-class males for these reasons. In spite of this,
however, many of the South Asians expressed the positive attitudes they had
towards health and fitness:

> Jayant: "I like sport because it can make you fit".
> Jitendra: [written] "Sport is important because Sikhs are required to have a
> fit body".
> Vitesh: "Sport is good for exercise and keeping fit".
> Mahmood: [written] "Physical Education is a sort of exercise and it is very
> good for our body and it can make us strong".
> Anil: "PE is good. You get to do some exercise, so you're more fit and
> healthy... And it's enjoyable".
> Akram: [written] "The thing I like about PE is that it keeps me feet [sic]
> and I enjoy it".
> Abdul: "I like to train for exercising, I like to be fit and good and healthy".

Sport and PE were seen as a means of improving physical fitness, and as such were
seen in a very positive light. Yet activities that have this end as their raison d'être
were negatively perceived. The gender-laden images that surround aerobics in
particular, and the entire fitness chic more generally, were important contributory
factors.

"Asians tend to go for less physical contact which is violent" (Mr Choudhury)

Three sporting activities that were perceived unfavourably by the South Asian
respondents were violent contact sports - American football, boxing, and rugby
football. From this evidence it would be easy to conclude that these expressed
attitudes are a reflection of one of the common stereotypes that exist: that "Asian
boys generally prefer non-contact games" (cited in Cherrington, 1974, p.34); or that
"Asians are too frail for contact sports" (cited in Bayliss, 1989, p.20). Moreover,
this view is so pervasive that some South Asians themselves were convinced by it.
Mr Patel elaborates: "Indoor sports are the only things that we take up. I haven't
seen any Asians playing football - soccer, over here; neither rugby. These are
'harsh' sports, too harsh for us". The view that South Asians are naturally gifted at
certain physical activities, and therefore by implication, less naturally gifted at
others, is also a prevalent notion; and becomes a self-fulfilling prophecy as some
South Asians believe themselves to be less competent at these violent contact

sports, and better suited to the 'skilful' demands of striking games such as hockey, cricket, and the racket sports.]

This concept of South Asian ineptitude in violent sporting activities requires further consideration, for there is a cultural dimension to it too. As already explained in chapter three, Hindu culture, influenced by Jainism, places great value on *Ahimsa* - non injury, and this has been offered as a partial explanation for the apparent reluctance of Hindus to engage in contact sports. Yet in spite of this, Hindus participate in certain contact sports that are potentially violent with great vigour. In *kabaddi*, for example, Hindu participants practise what could be described as a mixture of rugby, wrestling, karate and 'tag', and seek divine intervention from their gods as part of a pre-match ritual (C4 TV, 1991a). Here, then, is an apparent contradiction; but it is one that demonstrates the complexity of cultural concerns in defining sporting and leisure activities.

The cultural concerns about participation in violent sporting activities also include a consideration of the way in which violence is perceived. For Wasim (a Victim), it was the association with violence that he anticipated would not have pleased his parents:

> My father does not like it if I do something like boxing. It is too dangerous and too rough. He says people will say bad things about us if we do these things; he doesn't want them to say bad things about us.

But it also seems that physical violence is valued much more in other religious and cultural groups. Ravinder provided more quasi-historical evidence:

> That's where the sentence "we must be soldiers as well as saints" - or something like that [came from]. That's where the word 'Sikh' comes from, it means 'lion'.

"I like swimming, but ... " (Sanjay)

Swimming and leisure pools are the venues for many forms of social interaction for young people, providing cheap and enjoyable recreational family entertainment. But with fashion consciousness to the fore in the public consumption of leisure bathing (Standeven, 1991), swimming pools also provide an opportunity for the public assertion of adolescent sexuality. Nixon (1986) has acknowledged the maintenance of social order in swimming pools, and the respect for the privacy of others was identified as a central aspect of that; but concerns among South Asian parents remain about the suitability of these places for their children. Of greater alarm however, is the threat of racial harassment, and this seems to have been largely ignored. For example, Standeven (1991) remarks upon the social benefits to be gained from the use of swimming pools, but fails to address the concerns of disadvantaged minority groups about potential conflict:

> These leisure activities [the various leisure pursuits that are located at a swimming pool] are social out-of-home experiences. They have the potential to offer an antidote to the increasingly passive, plastic and private lifestyles which dominate our social world, and the possibility of

strengthening family and community ties, emphasizing sociability as the key to happiness. (p.305)

Mr Chandra articulates his concerns, not so much in terms of the swimming pool, but rather the additional features of the swimming pool complex, and more importantly, the type of person that he believed was attracted to them:

I think they're a bit scared to get into the environment, where you see a sporting facility in this country is to a certain area, and specified - a place, a sport centre or so. I don't see the Indian families coming there. That's a big problem with them. I mean, don't know what they feel: if they feel a bit odd or something like that. You see, these kinds of things will happen at certain places - not everywhere. I mean if I went to a 'theme park', no-one would bother me. You'd be one of those who's come to have a day out in the country. But like the sports centres, there would be comments made. And you see, we go to [our local sports centre], and if you go really and see what it is, and where you have these gambling machines - fruit machines - you shouldn't have those things in the space in the sporting facilities. People go there to play, and that is one thing, and they should take them out of there. And that kind of environment attracts undesirable people.

The outcome was that in order to ensure the safety of his family, and also engage in active leisurely pursuits for the whole family, Mr Patel took his family en masse to the swimming pool every week. For other South Asian families, though, this was not so easy.

A common perception of South Asians and swimming, and one that has its roots in the 'problems approach' to South Asians in PE, is the notion of 'South Asian modesty'. It is one that is grounded in cultural actuality, but the difficulty that surrounds it is that South Asians are often treated an homogeneous mass, and consequently the 'modest' label is attached to all South Asians without acknowledging the differences that do exist. The generational factor provides a part of the answer to the differences that occur amongst South Asians, for whilst a number of South Asian parents clearly wish to maintain cultural modesty amongst their children, many of the young South Asians themselves are less concerned by it, and particularly those who are second generation South Asians and less committed to some of the traditional cultural mores and codes of behaviour.

A more important issue, however, and one that is clearly not unconnected, is religion - and more specifically, differences within (as well as between) broadly defined denominational religions. The young Muslims at Parkview fell into two important groups in terms of their participation in swimming. First, those who did participate but only on an infrequent basis; many of whom were second generation South Asians, and had been more greatly exposed to Western influences, values and norms. Second, those who never participated, and who were the Victims for whom the whole concept of going swimming at a swimming or leisure pool was alien to their lifestyle and was fraught with difficulties and dilemmas. They were not familiar with the use of swimming pools in Bangladesh, and even though they had experienced swimming as part of the school PE curriculum, it was not generally perceived as a viable leisure activity option. As Mr Rokib explained, for unemployed Bangladeshis, swimming for their adolescent children was not only questionable on religious and cultural grounds, but did not rank as a priority for the use of whatever disposable income was available: "I not have job, don't have money to take Rahman [his son] to swimming. We have to do swimming separate from womens [sic] as well, where can I do this?" The clear danger of assuming homogeneity amongst all Muslims is that these different sub-groups are treated in a similar way.

There were surprisingly few swimming pools in and around the Elm Park area of north London, and those that were accessible were traditional swimming pools rather than leisure pools and were consequently less attractive to the non-swimmer. In addition there was the cultural aspect of nakedness that posed difficulties for these very committed Muslims with their traditional values and beliefs. For while the exposure of the female Muslim form is well documented and strategies have been suggested to minimise the practical difficulties encountered by this (Rotherham MBC, 1988; Coventry LEA, 1980), the exposure of the male body is also a cultural taboo.

There are suggested guidelines for the clothing that should be allowed for swimming lessons (Sarwar, 1983), but these are seen as huge concessions by those who subscribe to the 'assimilationist' model of race relations, and there are two wider issues associated with them. First, that clothing regulations for PE are particularly Eurocentric in their outlook, and the tendency in Western culture is to expose rather than conceal the body. Consequently it is important to acknowledge that some Muslims do not share these same cultural norms and values concerned with nakedness. Failure to do so forces unreasonable cultural and moral choices on some young Muslims. The communal changing before and after PE lessons, and the reluctance to shower also create some serious dilemmas for some Muslims; and as already explained, some chose to exclude themselves from lessons rather than subject themselves to this. The further paradox is that when 'special allowances' are made for some Muslims, enabling some of their dilemmas to be resolved, their differentness is highlighted and accentuated, which can, in itself, be divisive.

The very public demonstration of religious and cultural associations did not, however, seem to affect the Sikh participation in swimming, for the Sikhs were relatively well represented. Yet it is Sikhs who are probably the most easily identifiable religious group amongst South Asians. The turban or top-knot and for adult males the unshaven beard, are easily recognisable. But this did not affect the Sikhs at Parkview as none adopted these religious and cultural symbols. Sakhinder explained his own attitude and that of his family, which was typical of the other second generation South Asians at Parkview School:

If you want to wear a turban, you have to go through a ritual; and if you do that, you have to stop eating meat. Sikhs aren't supposed to drink or smoke, and I'm not going to do that anyway. But if you wear a turban you have to say prayers really early - about 5 a.m. - and then you have to wash your hair every day, oil it and comb it, and you have to keep a beard and not cut it off. If you wear a turban, you've also got to wear a dagger, and that's too much bother. My little brother [also at Parkview School] used to have a top-knot, but my mum had it cut off because all the kids were

107

taking the fun out of him... I never had a top-knot, mum said it wouldn't suit me!

Part of the explanation for the relative under-use of swimming pools by South Asians generally was also to do with the verbal and physical abuse that young South Asians are subjected to on a daily basis, or, just as important, the expectation of harassment:

> SF: "Why don't you go swimming in the pool down the road ?"
> Akbar: "Some boys, they will be bad manners [sic] to us. They will say rude things and hit us"
> SF: 'What have they said to you ?'
> Akbar: "Nothing. I don't do swimming".

The fact remains that even in an area of very high African-Caribbean and South Asian presence, the swimming pool was predominantly a white preserve.

"We like football, all the Bengalis do" (Rahman)

It comes as no great surprise to find that football was popular with the vast majority of South Asians at Parkview School. But as important as football was to young people in Bangladesh (Datar, 1989), and in spite of claims about its wide appeal amongst young South Asians in Britain (Thompson, 1974; BBC TV, 1991; G. Hodgson, 1995; Rowbottom, 1995), for many at Parkview it did not feature prominently on the list of leisure priorities. Football is, of course, a game that lends itself to unstructured and informal modes of participation as well as the more formal competitive versions, and as such, actual levels of involvement are difficult to gauge. Yet patterns of participation were uneven amongst different South Asian cultural groups, with a group of Hindus expressing a real dislike for it.   It is tempting to attribute this to the traditional cultural factors of *Ahimsa* and bovine reverence; but this would be an over-simplification.   There would, nevertheless, seem to be some support for the notion of cultural continuity expressed through popular cultural forms.

In spite of a general perception of football, and the positive attitude towards it, participation amongst the South Asians at Parkview School was relatively low. The reasons for this are related to the position of football as the single most popular playground activity; and it became a reflection of school life more generally. The way that young South Asians were confronted by racist abuse in football was the same as other aspects of their daily lives.   Football was frequently the means through which young working-class males asserted some form of identity - either through participating in it or as spectators; but it was also a vehicle for the expression of ethnic antagonism. Ramesh (one of the Straights) even speculated about the sort of abuse that might await South Asian professional footballers: "They'd probably throw curry powder at them or something! [laughs] ... Nah, they couldn't do that, maybe they'd just boo 'em. Call 'em "Paki" and that".

The Victims, as the most recent 'immigrants' and a clearly identifiable group, suffered most. Football became a metaphor for ethnic antagonism and hostility. Not only was a certain amount of verbal insult tolerated here in a way that it perhaps would not have been tolerated elsewhere, but also as a physical contact sport, violence was actually legitimised through the game. With a different exposure to football during the early formative years in Bangladesh, their experiences of the game were very different from their British peers. When Rashid spoke of his childhood in rural Bangladesh, and of making a ball out of "feathers and stuff", it is clear that his experience was not the same as that of young children in working class inner-city areas of Britain.

One or two of the young South Asians were reasonably competent in relation to the peers, and the manner in which the former were perceived by the latter was considerably more favourable than it might otherwise have been:

> 9/2/1989 The gym is being used for mocks exams. So half of the first year were in the sports hall. They were given a choice of activities, and not surprisingly many of the lads wanted to play football. Qasim is a Bangladeshi who has just started at the school and he played reasonably well. That in itself was interesting because the difference in his playing ability and that of the rest of the group is not as great as the difference between the second year Bangladeshis and the rest of their year. Additionally though, there were clearly certain forces of expectation at work. The others [i.e., non South Asians] were surprised at Qasim's ability - though he is really no better than slightly below average. They were clearly impressed and commented "Qasim's a good player", as if this was unusual. (Field-notes)

In short, football occupied a central place in the lifestyles of many working-class youngsters at Parkview, and it also provided the means through which ethnic antagonisms were expressed. The participation patterns for young South Asians in football reflected this.

Elsewhere too, in spite of a real commitment to football and interest in it, there is evidence of disproportionate under-representation at more elite levels: there are around 1,900 professional footballers in the Premiership and the Football League, 300 are African-Caribbean (significant over-representation), none are South Asian (G. Hodgson, 1995); and only 27 out of 8,000 youngsters at football centres of excellence are of South Asian origin (BBC TV, 1995).

The overall picture is equivocal and reflects extremes of attitude. Parental involvement is just one good example of the heterogeneity amongst South Asian communities, and of the dangers of 'false universalism'. At the one end of a continuum is the view of Moulana Ashraf Hafesji (father of Mohammed, a South Asian non-league footballer who aspires to the professional ranks): "Kids nowadays are more interested in football and cricket than they are in education. I don't really approve of this, as knowledge is important" (BBC TV, 1995). This indifference was seen as a major handicap to the development of young South Asian footballers (G. Hodgson, 1995). But there is also evidence of almost obsessive commitment amongst some other parents to the nurturing of their sons' footballing potential (BBC TV, 1995).

Explaining participation and non-participation in sport

(i)   'Home-based Sport'?

In her examination of the changing work and leisure patterns of the 1980s, Lloyd (1986) identified differences in the leisure lifestyle of South Asians and non-Asians. One of the trends that emerged from her research was the tendency amongst South Asian shiftworkers to engage in more home-centred leisure than their non-Asian peers (see also Parry, 1988; Gahir, 1984). Indeed for many Hindus in particular, the home also acts as a place of worship (Jackson, 1981).

This pattern of participation in sport was replicated in some measure by the young South Asian males at Parkview School, in that snooker/billiards, table tennis and weight training were all widely and frequently practised in the home. Both table tennis and snooker/billiards conform to the stereotype of the "skilful South Asian blessed with natural hand-to-eye co-ordination". But such a facile explanation does not adequately account for the actual participation in table tennis, and more especially in snooker/billiards which was generally very high amongst all the young males at Parkview School. This popularity reflected, in part, the accessibility of a suitable facility. The Youth Club close to Parkview was visited by large numbers of students from the school during the day as well as after school, and in it, there was a table tennis table and a pool table as well as table-football. Yet the Youth Club was not used by some of the South Asians. The Victims, for instance, did not visit the Youth Club with any great frequency or regularity, for there are certain associations with 'youth clubs' that some cultural groups find unacceptable (Mukherjee, 1988; Parmar, 1988). Parmar (1988) elaborates:

> The term 'Youth Club' occasionally has unacceptable connotations for Asian parents. Clubs are seen as places where there is smoking, drinking, gambling and dancing, and also places girls and boys move freely with each other. (p.202)

For the Victims in particular, it was like some of the other public spaces, something of a 'no-go' area:

> Akbar: "We don't go there, we don't want to".
> SF: 'Why not ?'
> Akbar: "We play on the grass on our own".

Furthermore, the context in which some games were played reflected upon the games themselves. For example, the experiences that most of the Parkview pupils had of table tennis were directly related to their use of the Youth Club. It acted as a social centre for the pupils, and as such reinforced values and standards from the social institution of the school. Here, racism directed against the most disadvantaged group in the school - the Victims - was as prevalent as elsewhere. They did not use the Youth Club, and therefore did not to have access to table tennis in the way that their peers did. More importantly, the Victims associated the venue itself with this sort of behaviour, and table tennis with the venue. Consequently there was a negative perception of the activity on the basis of their experiences - either real or anticipated - in the Youth Club.

(ii)   'Looking after themselves'

Carrington et al. (1987) have observed that in their use of leisure-time, South Asian teenage males participated in the martial arts more frequently than a national sample group of males with an ethnically mixed composition. From the same case-study data Carrington and Williams (1988) also hypothesised a causal link between sporting activities and self-defence. The emphasis was placed on weight training as a means of fulfilling that purpose, though it seems reasonable to suppose that the analysis applies equally to the martial arts. This pattern was replicated amongst the some of the South Asians at Parkview. As Suman - a 13 year-old Boffin - explained his own involvement in self-defence classes at his local sports centre:

> I was getting bored at home. So I decided to go and do something, that's why I started self-defence. There was an advertisement pushed through the door at home, and I saw one here [at school]. I wasn't doing anything else, so I said to my dad "Why don't I do that ?", and he said "OK"... My dad thought it might come in useful, so when I'm older and if I am mugged, I can fight.

(iii)   No time

The absence of available time for South Asians was first identified as a constraining factor on leisure participation by Lloyd (1986), but her study was concerned with adults. Amongst the young South Asians at Parkview, there was general consensus that they believed their participation in sport to be restricted by the time constraints. One of the Victims, 12 year-old Massur, indicated how there were religious and cultural commitments that he had that were not shared by his peers from other ethno-cultural groups:

> I don't have very much time because I am very religious, I pray five times a day. I pray at school as well, every lunchtime. Every Friday I leave school early at lunchtime to go to the Mosque for special prayers. I also learn the Qur'an at the Islam School.

Another Victim, 14 year-old Rashid, also explained how his time was prioritised for certain activities before any leisure pursuit:

> I haven't got time to do athletics. I asked my dad about it, and he said that there's not enough time to pray, do my homework, read the Qur'an, go to the Mosque and do athletics.

There was a clear expectation among all three of the main South Asian religions that daily prayer took place, and for some Muslims the timing of such prayer prevented participation in certain leisure activities. The concept of leisure time being residual was something that many of the young South Asians identified with;

and significantly, many also considered that residual leisure time was defined by religious and cultural commitment, rather than by the activities that were pursued in it. In short, residual leisure time was the time that remained after cultural and religious commitments had been fulfilled. This emphasis on the absence of available time has been used widely in the media to account for the failure of Muslims in particular to become elite level professional sportsmen (c.f., BBC TV, 1991b; 1992; ITV, 1995), and the implications are clear: with prayer, attendance at the Mosque, and supplementary education in Islam, as well as commitment to fasting during *Ramazan*, "it is no easy task fitting playing [and training] commitments around Islam" (BBC TV, 1995).

Other features of South Asian family lifestyle also served to restrict the time that was available for sporting activity. Briefly, in seeking the independence, security, respect and recognition that discrimination in the white-controlled jobs market denies them, many South Asians have turned to self-employment and entrepreneurial experimentation - long and unsociable working hours are not uncommon (Forester, 1978). When working for an employer outside the kinship network South Asian employees are very willing to work overtime, thereby sacrificing leisure time; and are tolerant of shifts at unsociable hours, indicating an acceptance of restricted leisure choices (Kew, 1979; Lloyd, 1986). The exploitation of South Asian women as 'outreach' homeworkers has also been identified as an important factor affecting the overall quality of life (Mitter, 1987). For young South Asians there are serious implications. There is often the expectation that they share the workload in the family business, though the stereotype of the small entrepreneurial South Asian business, was almost non-existent among the South Asian families represented amongst the students at Parkview.

There are, however, other variables to consider. There is evidence to suggest that the leisure activities of the extended family are central to South Asian lifestyle (cited Kew, 1979), and that giving support to family and friends is a valid leisure-time activity (Karmi, 1988). Furthermore the informed guesses of Usha Prashar of the Runnymede Trust (in Kew, 1979) indicate that weddings, birthdays and anniversaries are of major significance to South Asian communities. Indeed, Lloyd suggests that the leisure choices that South Asians do make are often home-based, and her evidence indicates that:

> Asian [men] had less leisure because they devoted more time to personal care - eating and sleeping. According to the evidence, Asian meals were more prolonged, and native-born whites spent less time in bed. (Lloyd, 1986, p.120)

She also found evidence for South Asians spending a lot of their leisure time viewing and listening, visiting friends, and socialising in their homes. Community leader, Mr Mukherjee explains:

> Usually, the whole family goes on family occasions. Most weekends they are busy in this type of occasion - social gathering or religious or seeing friends. So it does hinder their commitments to sports. And in this context, Asian family life is still different to the present system here - the British system of family life.

These are the sorts of factors that influenced the lifestyles of young South Asians as well as the older members of their family. It is not surprising, therefore, that of the reasons given to Carrington et al. (1987) for not participating in sport and physical recreation, 'lack of time' was the most common among young South Asian men. The sorts of reasons outlined above were the same as those reported by the young South Asian males at Parkview. Jitendra elaborated on the way that he uses his 'free time':

> I don't have time to go out to sports clubs and that. In the evenings I do my homework for about an hour, I watch television - I do a lot of that. Sometimes I go upstairs and play on my computer if there's nothing on television; and sometimes I might go round to my cousins' and watch an Indian film. The day my aunt had a baby we had a big party there and everyone came round.

Unlike Suman, a boffin , who enjoyed a range of leisure interests, and either had or made sufficient time for them, much of Jitendra's leisure was restricted to home-based pursuits due - amongst other things - to a lack of available time. The important feature that is common to both though, is that even when time was spent in 'leisurely' activities, there were alternatives to sport that were pursued.

(iv)   Parental disapproval

In comparative studies of South Asian youth, both DES (1983) and Carrington at el. (1987) identified 'parental approbation" as an important constraint on the participation of South Asians in sporting and leisure activities. This also proved to be a central concern among the young South Asian males at Parkview, and seemed to be operating in two ways: actual parental approbation - when parents expressed their disapproval about the nature of the sport and leisure participation habits of their sons; and perceived parental approbation - when the young South Asians thought that their parents disapproved.

In the latter instance - perceived parental disapproval - some of the young South Asian respondents were clear in their own minds that their parents did not like them doing sport, but when the matter was followed up in discussion, they were unable (or unwilling) to explain the reasons for this. For some it was just a general impression:

> Ramesh: "I don't think my mum and dad would want me to play more [sport]".
> SF: Why not ?"
> Ramesh: "Dunno. I suppose it's 'cos they want me to work hard - at school an' that. So I can get a job. Dad thinks it's a waste of time".

Interestingly, though, Ramesh's father actually explained that this was not the case:

> Sport and physical education is good for young people; I'd always encourage Ramesh to get involved, but he doesn't seem to be that interested". (Mr Parmar)

113

Some also believed that their parents thought that sports participation reflected badly on the family. Akram explained this in response to a very vague question that was posed:

> SF: "Is there a problem for you doing sport ?"
> Akram: "Yea, like people saying 'this boy at this age and he is still behaving like a children - going there and doing that'... You see, my parents would like to get respect from other people; for example if my parents send me to play football everyday or whatever I like, the other people will say "his father is very stupid, he lets his son do what he likes - freedom'".

In the face of these sorts of objections to participation in sport, and in the light of the traditional South Asian family loyalty and respect for parents (especially fathers) that was evident, it is perhaps not surprising that this would act as an inhibiting factor in sports participation patterns.

Parental disapproval was not only a perceived phenomenon though, in some instances it was very real. Often the barriers placed in front of young South Asians wishing to pursue an interest in sport are a response to factors other than a mere objection to sport per se. For some parents (especially the recent arrivals from Bangladesh) who were struggling to escape from the poverty trap, the cost of funding a sporting interest was prohibitive. But even some parents in higher socio-economic groups found the cost of funding a leisure interest an inhibiting factor; as Mr Kumar, a credit controller, explained:

> We can not afford to pay these exorbitant fees for our children. Like say for example my son is interested in music lessons, and when I find a teacher and ask her the fees, even the least is fantastic - even more than driving tuition per hour. I mean how can we afford for one hour £15 ? Even £10 per hour, how could we afford that ? And how my lessons will he need ? Ten lessons is £100 straight away. I mean, how can we afford that ? ... My son's interested in and very keen in learning music, or when he wants to learn sports, the fees just put off. The children are getting the problem because they feel the parents are not 'putting' them, but the parents can't afford it. (Mr Kumar)

Clearly, young people, economically and financially dependent on their parents, were at a relative disadvantage in their pursuit of sporting interests. The danger for some, as Mr Kumar remarked, was that the children did not fully comprehend the financial situation, and saw the parents as denying them access to certain sporting activities.

A second very real concern for some South Asian parents and one that has already been discussed in relation to swimming, was the nature of the sporting environment, and the risk to the safety of their children. In a society in which violent crime is on the increase, and racial abuse is commonplace, many South Asian parents feared for the safety of their children. Those venues where young people collect in large numbers - swimming pools, leisure centres, skating rinks - were all places of potential conflict and confrontation. Mr Singh explains: "They

[South Asians] are a bit scared of those sort of environment. There aren't many Indian families coming there. They're just scared". But, as Mr Singh indicated, it is not the venues that South Asians were afraid of; rather it was the people who frequented them, and the fear of racially motivated attacks.

(v)   "It's not safe!"

The findings of the Bradford Youth Research Team (1988, p.57) indicate that: "White racism limits access to material opportunities and resources for black minorities, and importantly access to safe public spaces". In the East End of London, an area of high South Asian population density, the situation is particularly severe. Bangladeshis avoid places of social interaction with other groups for fear of racial hostility (Carey and Shukur, 1985). This pattern of behaviour has been seen elsewhere, and affects some South Asian groups very acutely. There are fears of perceived discrimination (Roberts et al., 1992), and even public transport has become the site of conflict as South Asians are subjected to abuse on buses and trains (Cohen, 1987).

Concerns about safety were shared by the young South Asian males at Parkview, and many of them expressed the view that they didn't feel safe going out to play sport. This fear for personal safety is perhaps the most telling indictment of a hostile and violent society.

> Jayant: "You'd be mad if you were an Indian and you went out to the youth club on your own at night".
> SF: "Why's that ?"
> Jayant: "'Cos you'd get yer 'ead kicked in. I'd only go out with Justin and Sammy, and most of the Indians don't go out at all".

Sport, class and ethnicity at Parkview School

As a general overview, the sporting participation patterns of many of the young South Asian males at Parkview School were not greatly different from those of their peers from other ethno-cultural groups; and this is important for it stands in contradistinction to much of the 'popular wisdom' of the PE profession and sports policy-making bodies. The same sorts of activities did seem to be both favourably perceived and actively pursued. Differences that did exist, were concerned more with those activities perceived unfavourably, and those that were low in participation. The young South Asians at Parkview School were, however, a heterogeneous population. Their participation in sporting and leisure activities reflected this, for different groups demonstrated different attitudes towards, and participation in, various sporting activities. Many, of course, were actually British-born, and shared many of the leisure lifestyle characteristics of other ethno-cultural youth groups in Britain. A brief socio-economic analysis of sports participation in relation to ethnicity helps to further elucidate the situation at Parkview more fully.

The demographic profile of the families of the young people at Parkview School revealed some broad patterns and trends: a quarter of the families were involved in non-manual occupations, over half were in manual occupations, and that nearly a fifth were unemployed. These data have some important implications for patterns of involvement in sport, but it is important to recognise that sports participation amongst a school-based population is, of course, mediated by common experiences of physical education and the extra-curricular sporting opportunities that exist. In this regard the experiences that young people have of sport are not directly representative of an adult population; and predictably, participation patterns were characterised by similarity rather than difference among different socio-economic groups - both in terms of the levels and frequency of participation, and in the activities that were pursued.

This phenomenon requires particular attention, as the large number of young people from families experiencing unemployment might be expected to experience participation in sporting and leisure activities rather differently. As Paul Corrigan explains (1982):

> Firstly, it is only possible to understand any aspect of leisure as a result of the major material themes contained within work, domestic labour or school. Secondly, the major material experiences of unemployment are humiliation, poverty, isolation and uselessness. Thirdly, the leisure activities of unemployed people will be inevitably affected by the above and not by the progressive elements of 'choice'. (p.27)

It is very evident that as a direct consequence of being unemployed (and/or dependent on state benefits) is a shortage of disposable income (BYRT, 1988); and that, in turn, constrains and restricts participation in sporting and leisure activities. Yet poverty, and its implications for leisure, did not seem to have affected the participation in sport of the youngsters of unemployed families at Parkview School. Part of the explanation for this is that the activities in which these young people participated most were all activities that were catered for during the school day, either in the school facilities themselves, or in the nearby youth centre. Thus the impact of poverty, in terms of access to facilities and prohibitive cost of participation was often ameliorated for these young people.

The reality for the students of Parkview School was that sports participation was experienced differently by different groups. But it was not just 'class' that accounted for the differences that existed. As Sadhna Raval (1989) has indicated, in failing to locate specific findings in relation to 'race', class and gender positions, causal links and explanations are over-simplified and potentially even bogus. Raval's argument is that by neglecting class, all differences between South Asian and other groups are attributed to ethnicity; and because class clearly does influence participation in sport, this focus on ethnicity is not necessarily a valid basis on which to proceed. Yet the converse is also true, that by failing to accommodate ethnicity, all differences between socio-economic groups are attributed to class. A solely class-based analysis is therefore also flawed. The example of swimming illustrates the point. Participation amongst young people from unemployed families was disproportionately low, and an analysis based solely on class might lead to the conclusion that social disadvantage prevents participation in swimming as a leisure or sporting activity; and that links might exist between poverty and paying for admission to swimming pools. This may, of course, provide part of the explanation. But a large proportion of the families experiencing unemployment were from the South Asian communities, and many of them were the families of the Victims (i.e., newly arrived from Bangladesh and committed Muslims). The implications of participation in swimming for Muslims have already been considered in previous chapters; and without accommodating both class and ethnicity, causal links run the risk of being over-simplified and/or inaccurate.

The Victims - a socially disadvantaged group

In studies of British children (Wedge and Prosser, 1973; Wedge and Essen, 1982), three factors have been identified as central to an understanding of social disadvantage: family composition, low income, poor housing. The class-ethnicity relation is important with regard to this social disadvantage, for it is clear that,

> Asians locked into working-class structures employed in types of work particularly sensitive to downswings in the economy, and confined in their residence to inner-city areas with decaying infrastructures and serious economic and social problems. (Holmes, 1991, p.4)

The broad concept of social disadvantage, when defined in this way, and in relation to these factors, is experienced acutely by nearly all of the Victims at Parkview School. Many of the families were large and living in poor quality over-crowded housing. With an unemployment rate of nearly four in five amongst the families of the Victims, income was generally low. These social conditions and material deprivation impacted very directly on sports participation.

The sporting participation patterns of the Victims indicate that, as a group, they were among the least involved, particularly in out-of-school teams and clubs; and the frequency of their participation was disproportionately low. In particular, amongst some of the most popular activities (American football, football, table tennis, boxing and basketball), the Victims were clearly under-represented. In explanation of these kinds of patterns of participation, or more precisely non-participation, Wedge and Prosser (1973) observe:

> Socially disadvantaged children were less likely to have access to swimming baths or to indoor play centres, clubs and the like, or to take advantage of them where they were reported to be available. (p.29)

Part of the explanation for this is purely the lack of disposable income, which clearly restricts certain sporting pursuits. This economic explanation, however, does not fully account for the sports participation patterns of the Victims. For if social disadvantage and the class position were the key determinants, then there would be no differences between the Victims and other young people in situations of equal adversity and deprivation. The economic argument in relation to South Asians is developed by Taylor and Hegarty (1985). They assert that:

> Even when earnings are similar to those of white workers, they may have to be spread further. The greater average size of Asian families and number of dependants per working adult, sending remittances to support relatives in the country of origin, and the overwhelming trend for owner-occupied

accommodation, which, though it may be inferior in quality, requires maintenance and repayments of housing finance, are all factors likely to contribute to a greater prevalence of poverty among Asian families. (p.66)

Furthermore, such factors not only create a greater prevalence of poverty, but also mean that the effects of poverty are felt more acutely among socially disadvantaged South Asians.

The sports participation patterns of the Victims are clearly influenced by this economic position; though they are not adequately explained by economic reasons alone. There are other considerations related to ethnicity that cannot be ignored, and the most important of these for the Victims is personal racism. Social interaction in public spaces often results in the Victims being verbally and/or physically abused. When this occurs in conjunction with the simple economics of participation, it is not difficult to see how the Victims' sporting participation would be affected.

Straights, Boffins and Street-kids: just like their white British peers?

The experiences of social disadvantage were felt most acutely by the Victims at Parkview School. In very simple terms, in contrast to an unemployment rate of more than three in four among the families of the Victims, only one in ten of the other young South Asians reported that their families had similar socio-economic status. Moreover, the Straights, Boffins and Street-kids collectively suffered from fewer social disadvantages, and less material deprivation than the Victims.

Socio-economic status amongst the Straights, Boffins and Street-kids did not indicate any trends based on the sub-cultural groups. That is to say, there were no distinctive differences amongst these three groups in terms of class criteria. Broadly speaking, overall participation in sporting activities amongst these young South Asians had characteristics in common both within as well as between broadly defined ethno-cultural groups; and the levels of involvement in extra-curricular teams and out-of-school sports clubs were comparable with - though slightly less than - those of the general population at Parkview School.

The reasons offered for not participating either more frequently, more regularly, or in a wider range of activities concerned a perceived lack of time, and anxieties about personal safety. These are evidence of the centrality of ethnicity and cultural factors in defining the life-styles of young South Asians in Britain. For many young South Asian males, their perception of their situation was that they had little residual leisure time for sporting and leisure. The point is well made by a BBC television documentary about the absence of South Asians in professional football, which in other respects tended to over-simplify some very complex social phenomena:

> Whatever the family business is, the Asian culture can be restrictive. **Young Asian boys have so many commitments, they simply don't have time to perfect the art of kicking a football.** They're expected to study hard for a profession which will help support the family. **Muslim men are also required to pray five times a**

day, and spend two hours in the Mosque every night. (BBC
TV, 1991d, emphasis added)

Social mobility through educational achievement might be an aspiration of
working-class people of all ethnic groups, but daily prayer and attending the Mosque
is a characteristic of particular ethnic groups. It is this type of ethno-culturally
specific activity that creates relatively less residual leisure time for South Asians
than their white British peers. Though not stated explicitly in the remarks from the
documentary, the same principle of relatively less residual leisure time also applies
to Hindus, Sikhs and other South Asian religions as well as the example of
Muslims that is cited.

The issue of personal safety also affects the Straights, Boffins and Street-kids in
relation to their participation in sport and leisure activities in a way that is not the
general experience of their peers from other ethno-cultural groups. Thus, while the
argument might be advanced that young people generally are concerned about their
safety on the streets and in public spaces, young South Asians experience this fear
very acutely. This is a function of their ethnicity, and for many it is a fear of
personal racist abuse. Even the Street-kids, who in many ways seem less adversely
affected by racism in their leisure life-styles, reported this fear for personal safety as
an inhibiting factor in their sports participation.

South Asian male youth and sports participation: more than ethnicity or class

The sports participation patterns of the young South Asians at Parkview School
were clearly affected by both ethnicity and class. Set in a context of wide-ranging
and high-quality sports amenity provision in and around the school, problems of
access that are often encountered by working-class people were not encountered by
Parkview pupils to the same extent. From the socio-economic status of the
Victims, and their experiences of multiple social disadvantage, it could be argued
that their sports participation patterns were a product of their class position. Yet
there were certain features of their sports participation that can not be explained with
recourse to class as a solitary factor. In short, an analysis of sports participation
based on class alone, is not sufficient.

In the wider context of Britain's black population, Roberts (1983, p.148) has
remarked that, "Ethnic minority youth face the disadvantages of being working
class, only more so"; and more recently, with colleagues, that: "it is widely
recognised that Britain's black population faces social class disadvantages in addition
to any specifically racial barriers" (Roberts et al., 1992, p.219). Here, in essence, is
the position of the sports participation patterns of the Victims. For they were
affected by their class position and social disadvantage, but also by ethno-cultural
factors that are specific to first-generation rural Bangladeshi Muslim males, and by
their experiences of racism.

For first-generation South Asians more generally, experiences of sport on the
Indian sub-continent provide the context against which sports participation patterns
of migrants to Britain must be set. On one level, there are parallels between the
two societies: sport in Britain is dominated by young, middle class males (Lamb et
al., 1991), and sport in the sub-continent is characterised by elitism and patriarchal
domination. Yet in comparative terms, access to sporting opportunities is a

119

reflection of the macro-economic position of Britain as a developed nation in relation to the developing, but poverty-stricken and exploited nations of the sub-continent. Quite simply, South Asians in the sub-continent have relatively restricted opportunities, and set their expectations accordingly. It is these expectations, attitudes and perceptions that help to define their participation patterns on settling in Britain.

For British-born South Asians, perceptions of sport are influenced by values from the culture of origin transmitted by first generation family members and significant others. But the processes of socialisation also include some of the influences of the role of sport in British society; and with subsequent generations born in Britain, it seems that the impact of the culture of origin will take on a different (though not necessarily lesser) importance.

Accepting the fundamental premise that the leisure interests of minority ethnic groups reflect a wide range of strategies of conciliation and reaction to the dominant host - white - culture (Rojek, 1995); and the further premise that minority groups do not necessarily aspire to the leisure habits of white middle-class males (Roberts, 1983), there are two important conclusions. First, that South Asians generally do not, in fact, wish to emulate white middle-class sports participation patterns. Ethno-cultural factors give sport a different place in the lifestyle of South Asians; experiences from the culture of origin create different expectations of sport and leisure; and there are often different sets of economic priorities amongst groups for whom social disadvantage shapes daily life.

Second, as Jarvie (1991a, 1991b) points out, that in spite of the claims made by liberal-minded sports enthusiasts, and certain academics and aficionados, that sport provides democratisation and equality, experiences of racism and discrimination on both personal and institutional levels deny real equality of opportunity for South Asians. He concludes:

> We might all be equal on the starting line, but the resources (political, **economic and cultural**) that people have and the hurdles that people have to leap to get there are inherently unequal. Sporting relations themselves are vivid expressions of privilege, oppression, domination and subordination. (p.2, emphasis added)

Jarvie's analysis is a useful starting point, for he locates racism and discrimination centrally, and suggests different barriers for different groups of people. Yet it is not entirely adequate as an explanation of the sports participation patterns of the young South Asian males at Parkview School. It is certainly true to say that access to economic resources affected participation in sport, but for the Straights, Boffins and Street-kids, levels of involvement were broadly comparable with the general population. For the Victims, though, participation in sporting and leisure activities was affected by both cultural and economic resources - their ethnicity and their socially disadvantaged position in society.

The analogy of the track race is not sufficient, however, because there are at least three implicit assumptions that can not be sustained. First, that everyone wants to take part in the race; and there is evidence from the South Asians at Parkview that not everyone is equally interested in sporting activities generally. Second, that everyone who wants to take part actually gets to the starting line; but for the key reasons associated with racism in its various forms, this is not the case. Third, that all of those who reach the starting line are taking part in the same race, and for the same reasons; yet it is clear that sport occupies different roles both between and within different cultural groups.

8 'At the end of the day...': some concluding comments

Sport and South Asian male youth at Parkview School

The South Asian males at Parkview provided rich case-study data for an analysis of the sport-ethnicity dynamic. Collectively, they exhibited heterogeneity in the usual constructs of ethnicity: place of origin, religion, and language; as well as in generation and class. These factors clearly influenced South Asian lifestyles in the school, and they provided a complex web of inter-related variables that no thorough analysis of South Asian participation in sport and leisure activities should ignore. Yet these were not the variables that directly influenced the social differentiation amongst the young South Asian males in the school environment. Rather, there were other aspects of lifestyle that determined the social order of the school, and the part played by the South Asians in it. A typological framework for analysing the South Asians at Parkview School evolved during a period of intensive fieldwork. It was based on the various modes of social interaction that the South Asians adopted, the way that they were perceived by others, and their status amongst peers in the school.

This analytical tool provided an organising structure for understanding South Asians' leisure lifestyles; and an important feature of it was the concept of 'cultural differentness'. There was broad corroboration for the somewhat over-simplified causal link that Holmes (1991) identifies - between the tendency to prefer what is familiar, and the level of antagonism experienced by minority groups. That is to say, when members of a minority group are compared to the desired norms of the dominant culture, the closer they are, the greater the likelihood that the minority group members will be considered 'normal' and non-threatening.

Amongst the South Asians at Parkview, the Victims could hardly have been more different. They were subjected to racist abuse, both verbal and physical; and through their failure to confront the hostility and antagonism that was directed at them, they were considered even further at odds with the working-class culture of youthful masculinity. The other groups - Straights, Boffins and Street-kids - demonstrated greater cultural and behavioural similarity to the dominant culture, and they were more widely accepted. Amongst them, it was the Street-kids that adopted many of the features of working-class male youth sub-cultures; and their day-to-day leisure lifestyle was significantly influenced by an informal multi-ethnic 'gang' of which they were a part.

Participation in sport by the South Asians at Parkview School was considerably influenced by the characteristics of their lifestyles; and central to these were their experiences of racism. Sporting involvement outside their own immediate group of friends was denied to the Victims as they retreated submissively. The Straights avoided conflict situations which inevitably took them away from some public sporting domains. The Boffins, paradoxically, engaged in sport as a direct coping strategy for dealing with racism (but were marginalised because of their intellect by the prevailing anti-school ethos). The Street-kids tackled racism head-on, but their sports participation was restricted by the apparent reluctance of their immediate circle of friends to conform to the structured pattern of competitive formalised sport.

In their attitudes towards sport, and in the sporting participation patterns that were reported, the young South Asian males at Parkview manifested some important trends. Firstly, there was evidence of cultural continuity. Aspects of religious and cultural behaviour significantly influenced the leisure choices made; and interestingly, continuity was evident amongst first, second and third generation South Asians. Inevitably, there was also evidence of cultural discontinuity and change. This was not so much a 'dilution' of cultural values, as a rejection of those that were not seen as important, and an affirmation of those that were.

Secondly, contrary to some of the popular stereotypes, broad patterns of participation in sport amongst all ethno-cultural groups were characterised as much by similarity as by difference. The one group for whom there was very distinctive difference and variance in sports participation was the Victims. Their experiences of sport were a product of their cultural differentness, their rejection and alienation, and their socio-economic position which had trapped them in a state of social adversity and powerlessness.

Thirdly, the heterogeneity apparent in a single case-study school highlighted the very real risks of stereotyping and 'false universalism', which can operate on (at least) three levels: collective treatment of all minority groups as the same; mistaken assumptions about all South Asians; and the failure to acknowledge the full complexity of South Asian cultures lifestyles within as well as between groups (for a fuller discussion, see Fleming 1994).

Fourthly, as a factor of social stratification, social class is central to the understanding of the leisure lifestyles and sports participation of young South Asians; and as such, should not be divorced from ethnicity. It applied most obviously to the Victims, for patterns of participation suggested that neither a class analysis nor a cultural analysis was sufficient. Rather, that sports participation was a product of these two together.

Research and policy

Case-study research is characterised by being particularistic, and when conducted effectively, it produces high-quality and valid data. If such data then help to generate, modify or consolidate some sort of theoretical framework, then the more general application of case-study research is in providing 'projective models' for others to explore their unique situations (Elliott, 1990). Parkview School

123

represents a single case-study, but the analytical construct generated has wider applications. The importance of this kind of research is not restricted to one school, it "extends to general problems in sociology and education" (Lacey, 1970, p.xi). Hence, an understanding derived from a single case-study situation increases the understanding of other such situations, and can be used to inform more general debates. Indeed if there was no wider application for this kind of work, then, as Cashmore (1982c) discovered, the whole enterprise might be seen as rather indulgent:

> "What will you do next?" a black youth recently asked me. "I suppose you'll finish this project and then look around and think, 'Oh yes, there's the Asians, they've got a few problems. I think I'll go and study them'". His remark was intended to undermine, even devastate, my whole commitment to the area of race relations, a term I find increasingly restrictive. He was indicating - not unreasonably - that my work was futile. (p.14)

The seemingly obvious response to this kind of criticism is that the usefulness of such research is in helping to inform professionally relevant discourse, and in guiding policy-making decisions. Moreover, in view of the observation by the Sports Council (1991) that communication between researchers and policy-makers had hitherto been absent, this was always an explicit aim of the work. It is therefore to some of the key issues in sporting and educational policy and provision that the discussion now turns.

Sports policy and provision

The rhetoric of sports provision places sport as a central - and even crucial - aspect of an individual's quality of life: "It is widely recognised that sport and recreation have an important role to play improving the quality of life for people living in inner city areas" - Colin Moynihan, Minister for Sport (DoE, 1989, p.iii). Sport and recreation have a uniquely important role in society today as no other fundamentally voluntary activity comes close to matching their impact on the economy, the media, the health and well-being of communities, and even the mood of the nation. The importance of sport and recreation as an integral part of society is now widely recognised and accepted.

It is assumed by sports providers therefore that under-represented groups must be encouraged - and even coerced - into improving their quality of life by engaging in some form of sport. Relatively recent policy documents concerned with the provision of sport and active recreation have given some indication of the state of current thinking (Pote-Hunt, 1987; DoE, 1989; LCSR, 1989); and the research conducted at Manchester University provides a particular focus on minority ethnic groups (Verma et al., 1991). Each of these documents contains extensive recommendations for a broad spectrum of agencies on a wide range of issues. Naturally enough, there are some eminently sensible suggestions dealing with good practice in "equal opportunities" (Pote-Hunt, 1987, pp.32-33, Verma et al., 1991, pp.340-341); and there is some sound advice to various key institutions and partners

(Pote-Hunt, 1987, pp.33-37; LCSR, 1989, pp.35-37, DoE, 1989, pp.55-59; Verma et al., 1991, pp.341-346). But all are based on certain assumptions; and with reference specifically to South Asians, the evidence from the young males at Parkview School, indicates that these assumptions may be flawed in at least three different ways.

First, it is assumed that South Asians generally (and women in particular) are under-represented in sports participation. The difficulty here is in the definition of terms, for the conceptualisation of sport as generally "structured, goal-oriented, competitive, contest-based and ludic" (McPherson et al., 1989, pp.15-17), is too narrow for the young South Asian males at Parkview School. A number of them engaged in informal, though physically active, recreation. When, for example the Street-kids took part in an informal kick-about (as they often did), the participation would not have been acknowledged in the 'official' participation statistics.

With the exception of the Victims, the young South Asian males at Parkview had roughly similar participation patterns as their peers from other ethno-cultural groups. That might, of course, indicate that all ethnic groups are not taking part in sufficient sport and physical recreation in the interests of their own health; but that is an entirely different issue from having South Asians identified as a special 'target group'. Sports participation takes many forms, and people attach different meanings to them. Just because sports participation is not being monitored by official statisticians, docs not mean that it is non-existent or irrelevant. Neither does it mean that it should be marginalised or ignored.

Second, it is assumed that given freedom to choose, South Asians would select sport as an activity for leisure time. But sport does not occupy the same central role in the lives of all South Asians that it does for some other ethnic groups. Cashmore (1982a) comments that sport is a "central life interest" for many African-Caribbean youngsters, but for many South Asians it is no more than a very peripheral interest. The implication here is that in attributing values associated with a typically white British middle-class perspective on sport to other groups, there is a clearly Eurocentric perspective of sport presented to South Asian groups. The attitudes of providers are often paternalistic, and attempts to promote sport amongst misunderstood ethnic groups betray an assumed cultural superiority.

Third, it is assumed that South Asians would experience a 'healthy and productive life' if they could be encouraged to engage in some form of sport or active recreation (Malik, 1988; Verma et al., 1991). Yet for socially disadvantaged groups, like the Victims, there are economic realities that have to be faced, and the priorities for money and time might, quite understandably, lie elsewhere.

The wider picture of South Asians' involvement in sport indicates that if levels of participation in formal organised sporting activity are to be increased, then attention to the real detail of provision is essential. Dixey (1982) reported a pioneering scheme in which South Asian women were catered for, in the sporting sense, by addressing some of the important religious and cultural concerns that some South Asian community groups had. The procedure has been replicated elsewhere (David, 1991; Sports Council, 1994), and is a clear articulation of the spirit of "unequal effort for equal opportunity". It is important to note too, as Carrington and Williams (1988) indicate, that when such attention to detail lapses, disengagement is likely.

It has been suggested that South Asians will, in time, emulate the patterns of participation and success of African-Caribbeans in Britain (BBC TV, 1991d). This, however, seems an unlikely prognosis, and the reasons for its improbability are explained by a central theme of much of Cashmore's analysis of African-Caribbean sportsmen:

Social deprivation breeds sporting prowess. That if you live in .the ghetto and you've got blocked opportunities, and you don't see that you've a chance in any other area of society. Yet sport surfaces as the one area in which you just might make it, and there's a glimmer of hope there, then you take it, you go for that goal. And I think a lot of blacks do exactly that. They think they haven't got much chance in the rest of society, but sport is the one area that they can make it, and so they go for it with everything. (BBC TV, 1990b, emphasis added)

The important point is that the experiences of blocked opportunities from which some African-Caribbeans suffer, are not experienced by South Asians in the same way - and perhaps, in many instances, not to the same extent. Hence social adversity, disadvantage and deprivation have failed to foster the development of sporting South Asians in the way that African-Caribbean sports-stars have been mass-produced.

A final comment about the specific role that sport plays in South Asian lifestyles is set in the context of a macro-view of sport. Carrington (1986) and Jarvie (1991a, 1991b) have both noted the propensity for functionalist sociologists and liberal-minded sports enthusiasts to argue that sport is a 'great equaliser', that it is free from racism, that it is essentially 'fair for all', and that it has acted as a means of enhancing inter-ethnic harmony. The reality is that it has often failed to deliver any of these.

To emphasise the point, Cashmore reinforces one of his main arguments about African-Caribbeans by asserting that:

I think sport is very much a litmus test, in the sense that if we see a lot of blacks succeeding in numbers in sport, it's usually a fairly reliable indicator that race relations are not going to well. (BBC TV, 1990b)

It is a theme to which he has repeatedly returned (Cashmore 1982a, 1983, 1990a, 1990c); but his analysis is not completely adequate as it fails to fully accommodate the position of South Asians. To pursue the analogy from chemistry, sporting success is not a 'universal indicator' because the same would not necessarily be true of South Asians. Moreover, sporting success is not a 'reversible indicator' either, for the absence of South Asian sports-stars does not imply that 'race relations' with South Asians are in a well-adjusted state, nor does it indicate that they are less affected by personal and institutional racism. On the contrary, the evidence from Parkview School and elsewhere (BYRT, 1989; LSCR., 1989; Lashley, 1991; Lovell, 1991; Verma et al., 1991) indicates that sport is afflicted by racism as much as any other aspect of society; and that fear of racial discrimination and harassment is a fundamental block to participation in sport and recreational leisure.

In order to dismantle the barriers to participation, Lashley (1991) advances the ideology of anti-racism. In so doing, racism is located as a problem for white people that is experienced by black people. It is a principle that applies equally to education, schooling and PE

South Asian male youth, schooling and sport

PE in a culturally pluralist society: from monoculturalism to multiculturalism

For some considerable time the approach of the PE profession to educating young people of minority groups was firmly fixed in the ideology of assimilation and the practices of monoculturalism. This has inevitably meant a 'colour-blind' approach to PE curricula and pedagogy, which has been justified by the articulation of the view that: "Children 'want to be treated the same, not differently'" (cited in Bayliss, 1989, p.19). As Troyna and Carrington (1990, p.2) indicate, the message that was conveyed to minority groups was abundantly clear: "Forget the culture of your parents, discard any affiliation to your ethnic background and blend in".
Of greater concern, as Anne Williams (1989, p.163) confirms:

> Treating all the children the same means treating them all like white children and probably like white middle class children. This will inevitably mean that all children's needs are not being equally met.

Yet in spite of this, the ethos of monoculturalism became embedded in PE, and the inherent conservatism of PE and sport in Britain meant that PE was somewhat resistant to change, and slow to react to wider ideological influences and political pressures (John Hargreaves, 1982; Leaman and Carrington, 1985)
Since then, however, the National Curriculum Council (1990, p.3) has commented that:

> Introducing multi-cultural perspectives into the curriculum is a way of enriching the education of all our pupils. It gives pupils the opportunity to view the world from different standpoints, helping them to question prejudice and develop open-mindedness.

This is a view that now seems to have found favour with physical educators, who have often adopted a multi-cultural approach to PE rather unquestioningly. The evidence from Parkview School suggests that minority groups are not well served by this approach.

Multicultural PE: A Critique

The philosophical basis of multicultural education assumes assimilation (Cole, 1986a; Donald and Rattansi, 1992). Mullard (1985) has argued that within the ideology of assimilation, there is an implicit notion of the cultural - and even 'racial' - superiority of the 'host' society. It implies both a politically and culturally indivisible unitary nation, and a universally shared set of values to which all should assimilate; and also acts as a means of coercion and control. More specifically:

> Traditionally multicultural education has been seen (overwhelmingly) as 'teaching' children about other cultures, thereby instilling respect for such cultures by white indigenous children and improving the self-image of non-white immigrant and indigenous children, partly as a result of the positive images thus engendered. It was also expected to have had the spin-off of generating tolerance and understanding between minority groups. (Cole, 1986a, p.124)

As a critic of multicultural education, Cole's description might be an over-simplification, but in it, he does identify some of the basic elements of its rationale. These have implications for PE

First, the 'teaching about other cultures' is, as Cole (1986a) suggests, a gargantuan task. Dance, for example, is one aspect of the PE curriculum which is often touted as a vehicle through which awareness and tolerance of minority groups might be increased (Kansara, 1984; Todryk, 1988; Gajadhar, 1990). There are also claims that it develops a greater level of understanding of the cultures and lifestyles of the Indian sub-continent (Leaman, 1984; BAALPE, 1990). Yet without the necessary depths of cultural insight into the subject matter being taught, material is often delivered based on "meaningless platitudes or racist stereotypes" (Cole, 1986a, p.124). Furthermore, the prevalent stereotypes about South Asians are often couched negatively in terms of lack of ability. This being the case, the argument that multicultural PE develops greater understanding and respect for minority groups is fundamentally flawed.

The process of stereotyping has further importance because of the way that racist ascription can occur based on bogus logic - what Troyna and Carrington (1990) refer to as 'false syllogisms'. For example, starting from the evidence of sporting success, the process might be as follows:

> (The Pakistanis are the world cricket champions);
> Pakistanis are good at cricket;
> Iqbal is a Pakistani;
> *ergo*, Iqbal is good at cricket.

A very significant danger is that this kind of flawed reasoning becomes the basis for damaging physiological and/or psychological prejudices. For example:

> The Pakistanis are good at cricket;
> Pakistanis have 'natural ability' at cricket;
> *ergo*, Pakistanis are physiologically and psychologically well equipped for cricket.

The further implication of an 'argument by example' to illustrate natural ability ('they do because they can'), is the argument by example to illustrate natural inability ('they don't because they can't'). In this way 'benign stereotypes' can be very damaging too (Klein, 1993).

Second, multicultural education focuses on what Cole (1986a, p.124) calls "safe cultural sites". Again dance is an example from PE. The failure to place dance in its full cultural context is clearly tokenistic and exoticising, and is an example of practice that has been described as the "Three S's Syndrome: saris, samosas and steel bands" (Carrington and Troyna, 1990, Donald and Rattansi, 1992).

Third, the contention that multicultural education will enhance the self image of the members of minority groups is another illustration of the pathological 'black youth in crisis'. It is assumed that enhancement of self image is both possible and required, which, in itself is debatable. But there are also real concerns about the relevance of the curriculum for meeting that end. For if the curricula are not relevant, and have no meaning for the respective minority groups, then it is hard to imagine how enhancement of self image might occur.

The final point about multicultural PE is made by Anne Williams (1989, p.161). She suggests that: "teaching children about cultural differences for example, may reinforce not reduce their sense of distinctiveness". That may not necessarily be undesirable; but by reinforcing cultural distinctiveness, there is a danger of consolidating racist stereotypes, and of exacerbating ethnic antagonism.

The most telling indictment of multicultural PE comes from Leaman (1984) who observes that in spite of attempts to implement a multicultural PE curriculum, the attempts have often been unsuccessful. He explains:

> Physical activities which tend to be offered in British schools have a well-defined position in the majority culture which give those activities their social meaning, and the implantation of different activities from other cultures may fail to get a grip. (p.216)

The way forward: an anti-racist approach to PE

Multicultural education does not adequately acknowledge the central issue of racism, and instead focuses on the issues of culture. But Brandt (1986) warns against the perils of concentrating on culture in the hope that racism will go away. An anti-racist approach to PE would not only confront the kind of incidents of overt racism that the Victims in particular were subjected to, but would also place the issue of racism at the heart of practice and pedagogy.

The curriculum In order to challenge some of the damaging stereotypes that exist about minority groups (and South Asians in particular), a reappraisal of the PE curriculum is necessary. As Brandt (1986) explains, such a reappraisal should be an attempt to eradicate ethnocentrism. It is time for the PE profession to rid itself of its preoccupation with the 'problems' approach to minority groups, and replace it with a commitment to an understanding of each pupil as an individual. That is, teachers should be sensitive (and sensitised) to individual needs, and be disabused of the prevalent and enduring stereotypic notions attached to different cultural groups.

The specific detail of the curriculum therefore needs to be re-examined, for it is in the different elements of the PE curriculum that the stereotypes about cultural groups are often reinforced and perpetuated. Grinter (1990b, 217) expands on this proposition:

Competitive team games as group activities often reflect the divisive effects of these stereotypes. The power of these stereotypes where they have not been questioned demands a quite fundamental reassessment, and a restructuring of PE and sport onto a more individualistic basis from which to explore the reality of differences and skills behind the stereotypes.

The same principle is true of other prevalent stereotypes associating different cultural groups with other aspects of the PE curriculum. Some of the stereotypes about the sporting abilities of particular groups are positive, but because of the flawed logic of ascription to stereotypes, these must also be confronted and challenged,

Curriculum material If reappraisal of the curriculum is undertaken, the material of the curriculum must be subjected to close scrutiny and inspection. Brandt (1986, p.131) suggests that:

It seems clear that materials used ... must reflect our diverse society and in a positive light. They must relate to the experience of the pupils while aiding the transition or extrapolation to a global perspective. They must also be the basis for challenging the stratification and inequitable distribution of society's resources. Therefore, there is a clear shift away from the fallacious notion of 'neutral' to the notion of material which can be useful in challenging inequality, injustice and in challenging racism.

The concept of curricular relevance is one that forms part of the critique of multicultural education, but Brandt touches the same concept in his proposals for curriculum material. The point is illustrated by Williams (1989, p.163):

In the context of physical education, a narrowly focused games curriculum may reflect on white middle class culture in contrast to a curriculum which introduces children to a variety of game forms and in so doing offers something with which children from many different cultures can identify.

Yet PE is perhaps the one aspect of the entire curriculum in which, with sensitive and imaginative curriculum planning, culturally neutral material could be presented as part of a culturally balanced programme without loss of identity.

The 'hidden curriculum' Many of the institutional procedures of the organisation and administration of PE are potentially racist (Rattansi, 1992). For an indication of the widespread nature of this subtle and unintentional discrimination, recourse to Bayliss' (1983, 1989) exposition of the 'problems' approach indicates just how widespread the 'problems' encountered by cultural minority groups actually are. For many of the 'problems' there is an explanation grounded in the racism of the hidden PE curriculum.

To illustrate the point, there is "indirect discrimination", in the compulsory nature of PE kits (Rattansi, 1992, p.23), and also in the "procedures and expectations" of the physical educator (Williams, 1989, p.169). These too are matters for re-examination and re-evaluation. In order to combat this type of inherent discrimination, the hidden curriculum must be made blatant (Brandt, 1986), so that racist practices can be identified and deconstructed.

A final thought

It is clear that many of the experiences that different groups of young South Asians have of sport in the widest sense are often characterised by intolerance and a lack of real understanding. Sports providers and policy-makers have at last recognised the 'gaps in their knowledge' and some attempts have been made to plug them. There has been a temptation, however, to adopt white, middle-class and male values in the understanding of sport, and apply typically Eurocentric models to the full range of culturally diverse groups in Britain. It is critically important to recognise that equality of opportunity does not necessarily require equal participation. Neither does it necessarily mean participation at the same time, in the same place, and in the same way. The key principle is that sports participants should be granted real dignity in a climate of mutual and general respect. At the risk of over-simplifying the situation, it is vitally important that particular individuals and groups are not oppressed because of their cultural values, ethnicity and physical appearance. An explicitly anti-racist approach to PE, if implemented with tact and sensitivity, would significantly alter for the better the experiences of many otherwise oppressed individuals from all sections of Britain's minority populations.

Bibliography

Abercrombie, N., Hill, S. and Turner, B.S. (1984), *The Penguin dictionary of sociology*, Penguin, Harmondsworth, Middlesex

Acland, T. and Siriwardena, S. (1989), 'Integration and segregation in an Asian community'. *New Community* 15 (4), 565-576.

Ahsan, H. (1989), 'Pakistan's toughest tour', *Cricket Life International* December, p.11.

Alexander, P. (1987), *Racism, resistance and revolution*, Bookmarks, London.

Allen, S. (1979), 'Pre-school children: ethnic minorities in England', *New Community* 7 (2), 135-142.

Amritraj, V. and Evans, R. (1990), *Vijay!*, Libri Mundi, London.

Asian Times (1988), 'Asian family terrorised', 18th November, p.2.

Asian Times (1990), 'Hindu half marathon attracts over 2,000', 25th September, p.36.

Asian Times (1991), 'Bhangra can help prevent heart attacks', 2nd April, p.3.

Bagley, C. (1976), 'Behavioural deviance in ethnic minority children. A review of published studies', *New Community* 5 (3), 230-238.

Bains, H.S. (1988), 'Southall youth: an old-fashioned story', in Cohen, P. and Bains, H.S. (eds.), *Multi-racist Britain*, Macmillan Education, London, pp.226-243.

Bale, J.R. (1983), 'Geography, sport and geographical education', in Widmeyer, W.N. (ed.), *Physical activity and the social sciences*, Mouvement Publications, Ithaca, pp.114-129.

Ball, S.J. (1981), *Beachside Comprehensive*, Cambridge University Press, Cambridge.

Ball, S.J. (1990), 'Self-doubt and soft data: social and technical trajectories in ethnographic fieldwork', *International Journal of Qualitative Studies in Education* 3 (2), 157-171.

Ballard, R. (1973), 'Family organisation among Sikhs in Britain', *New Community* 2 (1), 12-24.

Ballard, R. (1976), 'Ethnicity: theory and experience', *New Community* 2 (1), 196-202.

Ballard, R. (1990), 'Migration and kinship: the differential effect of marriage rules on the processes of Punjabi migration to Britain', in Clarke, C., Peach, C. and

Vertovec, S. (eds.), *South Asians overseas*, Cambridge University Press, Cambridge, pp.219-250.

Bayliss, T. (1983), 'Physical education in a multiethnic society', *Physical Education*, I.L.E.A., London.

Bayliss, T. (1989), 'PE and racism: making changes', *Multicultural Teaching* 7 (5), 18-22.

BBC Television (1977), *Five views of multi-racial Britain*, BBC2.

BBC Television (1990a), *The Lane - Bangla town*, BBC1.

BBC Television (1990b), *Inside story - the race game*, BBC1.

BBC Television (1991a), *Black Britain*, BBC1.

BBC Television (1991b), *Lowdown - Yorkies*, BBC1.

BBC Television (1991c), *Birthrights - who's batting for Britain?*, BBC2.

BBC Television (1991d), *On the line*, BBC2.

BBC Television (1992), *Standing room only*, BBC2.

BBC television (1995), *East - out of the game*, BBC 2

Beckerlegge, G. (1991), '"Strong culture" and distinctive religions: the influence of imperialism upon British communities of South Asian origin', *New Community* 17 (2), 201-210.

Beetham, D. (1968), *Immigrant school leavers and the youth employment service in Birmingham*, Institute of Race Relations, London.

Benn, M. (1991), 'Ancient roots of a turbulent state', *Education Guardian* 11th June, p.2.

Berry, S. (1987), 'Qadir: my art is not for sale', *The Observer* 6th December, p.16.

Berry, S. (1992), 'Mushtaq spins mystical webb', *The Independent on Sunday* 3rd May, p.26.

Bhaura, K. (1989), *Towards greater participation in sport amongst black and ethnic minorities*, speech at launch of London Council report 'black and ethnic minority participation', Westminster Central Hall, 10th May.

Bhandari, R. (1991), 'Asian action', *Sport and Recreation* 32 (5), 24-25.

Blease, D. and Bryman, A. (1986), 'Research in schools and the case for methodological integration', *Quality and Quantity* 20, 157-168.

Boneham, M.A. (1989), 'Ageing and ethnicity in Britain: the case of elderly Sikh women in a Midlands town', *New Community* 15 (3), 447-459.

Bose, M. (1970), *Classical Indian dancing: a glossary*, General Printers and Publishers, Calcutta.

Bose, M. (1990), *A history of Indian cricket*, Andre Deutsch, London.

Boseley, S. (1990), 'Action urged to move Asians from ghettos', *The Guardian* 10th September, p.3.

Botholo, G., Lewis, J., Milten, J. and Shaw, P. (1986), *A sporting chance, GLC sports sub-committee 1983-85 and review of Brixton Recreation Centre*, Greater London Council, London.

Bourke, J. (1994), *Working-class culture in Britain 1890-1960*, Routledge, London.

Bowen, D.G. (1981), 'The Hindu community', in Bowen, D.G. (ed.), *Hinduism in England*, Bradford College, Bradford, pp.33-60.

Bradford Youth Research Team, (1988),*Young people in Bradford - survey 1987*, Bradford and Ilkley Community College, Ilkley.

Brah, A. (1978), 'South Asian teenagers in Southall: their perceptions of marriage, family and ethnic identity', *New Community* 6 (3), 197-206.

Brah, A. and Minhas, R. (1985), 'Structural racism or cultural difference: schooling for Asian girls', in Weiner, G. (ed.),*Just a bunch of girls*, Open University Press, Milton Keynes, pp.14-25.

Brandt, G.L. (1986), *The realization of anti-racist teaching*, Falmer Press, Lewes, East Sussex.

British Association Advisers and Lecturers in Physical Education (1990), *Perceptions of physical education*, BAALPE, Dudley.

Brown, J.M. (1985), *Modern India - the origins of an Asian democracy*, Oxford University Press, Oxford.

Bryman, A. (1988), *Quantity and quality in social research*, Unwin Hyman, London.

Burley, M. (1994), *Welsh, gifted and black: a socio-cultural study of racism and sport in Cardiff*, unpublished MA dissertation, Cardiff Institute of Higher Education.

Caldwell, G. (1982), 'The role of sport in the development of national identity', in Howell, M.L. and Mckay, J. (eds.), *Proceedings of the VII Commonwealth and international conference on sport, physical education, recreation and dance, Vol. 9 - socio-historical perspectives*, University of Queensland, Queensland, pp.113-118.

Callaghan, J. (1991), *The control and development of sport in the sub-continent - the challenge for India*, a paper presented at the ICHPER 34th World Congress, Limerick, Ireland.

Camerapix (1989), *Spectrum guide to Pakistan*, Camerapix, Nairobi, Kenya.

Carey, S. and Shukur, S. (1985), 'A profile of the Bangladeshi community in East London', *New Community* 12 (3), 405-417.

Carrington, B. (1983), 'Sport as a sidetrack. An analysis of West Indian involvement in extra-curricular sport', in Barton, L. and Walker, S. (eds.), *Race, class and education*, Croom Helm, London, pp.40-65.

Carrington, B. (1986), 'Social mobility, ethnicity and sport', *British Journal of Sociology of Education* 7, 3-18.

Carrington, B., Chivers, T. and Williams, T. (1987), 'Gender, leisure and sport: a case-study of young people of South Asian descent', *Leisure Studies* 6, 265-279.

Carrington, B. and Williams, T. (1988), 'Patriarchy and ethnicity: the link between school physical education and community leisure activities', in Evans, J. (ed.), *Teachers, teaching and control in physical education*, Falmer Press, Lewes, East Sussex, pp.83-96.

Carrington, B. and Wood, E. (1983), 'Body talk: images of sport in a multi-racial school', *Multi-Racial Education* 11 (2), 29-38.

Carroll, R. (1993), 'Physical Education: challenges and responses to cultural diversity', in Pumfrey, P.D. and Verma, G.K. (eds.), *The foundation subjects and religious education in secondary schools*, Falmer Press, London, pp.176-187.

Carroll, R. and Hollinshead, G. (1993), 'Ethnicity and conflict in physical education', *British Educational Research Journal* 19 (1), 59-76.

Cashman, R. (1979), 'The phenomenon of Indian cricket', in Cashman, R. and McKernan, M. (eds.), *Sport in history*, University of Queensland Press, Queensland, pp.180-204.

Cashmore, E. (1981), 'The black British sporting life', *New Society* 6th August, 215-217.

Cashmore, E. (1982a), *Black sportsmen*, Routledge & Kegan Paul, London.

Cashmore, E. (1982b), 'Black youth, sport and education', *New Community* 10 (2), 213-221.

Cashmore, E. (1982c), 'Black youth for whites', in Cashmore, E. and Troyna, B. (eds.), *Black youth in crisis*, George Allen & Unwin, London, pp.10-14.

Cashmore, E. (1983), 'The champions of failure: black sportsmen', *Ethnic and Racial Studies* 6 (1), 90-102.

Cashmore, E. (1984), *Dictionary of race and ethnic relations*, 2nd edition, Routledge, London.

Cashmore, E. (1986), 'Glove puppets', *New Socialist* 40, 24-25.

Cashmore, E. (1987), *The logic of racism*, Allen & Unwin, London.

Cashmore, E. (1988), *Dictionary of race and ethnic relations*, 2nd edition, Routledge, London.

Cashmore, E. (1990a), 'The race season', *New Statesman and Society* 1st June, 10-11.

Cashmore, E. (1990b), *Making sense of sport*, Routledge, London.

Cashmore, E. (1990c), 'No more room at the top', *New Statesman and Society* 3 (114), 17th August, pp.10-11.

Cashmore, E. (1991), 'Bowled over', *New Statesman and Society* 3 (135), 25th January, pp.30-32.

Cashmore, E. and Troyna, B. (1981), 'Just for white boys? Elitism, racism and research', *Multiracial Education* 10 (1), 43-48.

Castles, S., Booth, H. & Wallace, T. (1987), *Here for good - Western Europe's new ethnic minorities*, 2nd edition, Pluto, London.

Channel 4 TV (1986), *The Khans of Pakistan - a squash dynasty*, C4.

Channel 4 Television (1991a), *Kabaddi*, Endboard production.

Channel 4 Television (1991b), *Critical eye - Great Britain united*, C4.

Cherrington, D. (1975), 'Physical education and the immigrant child', in Glaister, I.K. (ed.), *Physical education - an integrating force?*, NATFHE, London, pp.33-45.

Child, E. (1983), 'Play and culture: a study of English and Asian children', *Leisure Studies* 2, 169-186.

Chisti, M. (1991), 'Birmingham Pakistan sports forum', *Sport and Recreation* 32 (5), 28.

Chivers, T.S. (1990), *Can we study racism in an anti-racist way?*, a paper presented at the British Sociological Association Annual Conference, University of Surrey.

Clarke, C., Peach, C. and Vertovec, S. (1990), eds., *South Asians overseas*, Cambridge University Press, Cambridge.

Coalter, F., Dowers, S. and Baxter, M. (1995), 'The impact of social class and education on sports participation: some evidence from the General Household Survey', in Roberts, K. (ed.), *Leisure and social stratification*, Leisure Studies Association, Eastbourne, pp.59-73.

Cole, M. (1986a), 'Teaching and learning about racism: a critique of multicultural education in Britain', in Modgil, S., Verma, G.K., Mallick, K. and Modgil, C.

(eds.),*Multicultural education - the interminable debate*, Falmer Press, London, pp.123-148.

Cole, M. (1986b), 'Multicultural education and the politics of racism in Britain', *Multicultural Teaching* 5 (1), 20-24

Cole, M. (1987), *Racism and the political and ideological origins of the welfare state*, unpublished paper, Brighton Polytechnic.

Cole, M. (1989), ed., *Education for equality*, Routledge, London.

Cole, M. (1993), "Black and ethnic minority' or 'Asian, black and other minority ethnic': a further note on nomenclature', *Sociology* 27 (4), 671-673.

Cole, W.O. (1985), 'Sikhism', in Hinnells, J.R. (ed.), *A handbook of living religions*, Ward Lock Educational, London, pp.237-255.

Cole, W.O. (1991), 'Common threads in the matter of faith', *Education Guardian* 30th April, pp.6-7.

Collins, D. (1988), 'Dear diary, today we were firebombed', *The Guardian* 13th September, p.16.

Colson, M-L. (1991), 'Le dib, dib, dib, dob, dob, dob', *The Guardian* 6th September, p.24.

Colwill, B. (1995), 'Contributors to clubs but not country', *The Independent* 10th February, p.38.

Community Relations Commission (1976), *Between two cultures: a study of relationships between generations in the Asian community in Britain*, C.R.C., London.

Community Relations Commission (1977), *The education of ethnic minority children*, C.R.C., London.

Cook, S. (1991), 'Race attacks put Asian families under seige', *The Guardian* 12th September, p.3.

Corrigan, P. (1979), *Schooling the Smash Street kids*, Macmillan Education, London.

Corrigan, P. (1982), 'The trouble with being unemployed is that you never get a day off', in Glaister, I.K. (ed.),*Physical education, sport and leisure: sociological perspectives*, NATFHE, London, pp.27-32.

Coventry Local Education Authority (1980), *Physical education in a multi-cultural society*, Elm Bank Teachers' Centre, Coventry.

Crace, J. (1992), *Wasim and Waqar - Imran's inheritors*, Boxtree, London.

Craft, A. and Klein, G. (1986), *Agenda for multi-cultural teaching*, School Curriculum Development Committee Publications, Longman, York.

Craft, M. (1989), 'Teacher education in a multicultural society', in Verma, G.K. (ed.), *Education for all*, Falmer Press, Lewes, East Sussex, pp.132-150.

Critcher, C. (1986), 'Radical theories of sport: the Sstate of play', in Tomlinson, A. (ed.), *Leisure and social relations*, Leisure Studies Association, Eastbourne, pp.95-106.

Crooks, G. (1991), 'Route to rout racism', *The Independent* 10th September, p.30.

Dahya, B. (1973), 'Pakistanis in England', *New Community* 2 (1), 25-33.

Daley, D. (1988), 'GCSE PE and the bilingual child', *British Journal of Physical Education* 19 (6), 222-223.

Daley, D. (1991), 'Multicultural issues in physical education', *British Journal of Physical Education* 22 (1), 31-32.

Datar, R. (1989), 'An elusive goal for theEast End Pele', *The Guardian* 28th June, p.20.

David, C. (1991), 'Success in the long term', *Sport and Recreation* 32 (5), 18.

Department of Education and Science (1983), *Young people in the 80s. A survey*, HMSO, London.

Department of Education and Science (1985), *Education for all* (The Swann Report), Command 9453, HMSO, London.

Department of Education and Science and the Welsh Office (1991), *Physical education for ages 5 to 16*, O/N 15695, HMSO, London.

Department of the Environment (1977), *Recreation and deprivation in inner urban areas*, HMSO, London.

Department of the Environment (1989), *Sport and active recreation provision in the inner cities*, Crown, London.

Deshpande, S.H. (1970), 'Exercise therapy in ancient India', *Asian Journal* 2 (2), 20-24.

Dev, K. (1987), *Kapil: the autobiography of Kapil Dev*, Sidgwick & Jackson, London.

Dixey, R. (1982), 'Asian women and sport, the Bradford experience', *British Journal of Physical Education* 13, 108 & 114.

Donald, J. and Rattansi, A. (1992), eds., *'Race', culture and difference*, Sage, London.

Dosanjh, P.S. (1969), *Punjabi immigrant children - their social and educational problems in adjustment*, Educational Paper no. 10, University of Nottingham.

Dove, L. (1975), The hopes of immigrant children, *New Society* 10th April, 63-65.

Drew, D. and Gray, J. (1990), 'The fifth-year examination achievements of black young people in England and Wales', *Educational Research* 32 (2), 107-117.

Drew, D. and Gray, J. (1991), 'The black-white gap in examination results: a statistical critique of a decade's research', *New Community* 17 (2), 159-172.

Driver, G. (1980), 'How West Indians do better at school (especially the girls)', *New Society* 17th January, 111-114.

Duncan, C. (1985), 'One school's response to the needs of Muslim children', *Multi-Cultural Teaching* 3, 20-23.

Dunnett, R. (1991), 'Open access', *Sport and Recreation* 32 (5), 23-24.

Edgell, S. (1993), *Class*, London, Routledge.

Eitzen, D.S. and Sage, G.H. (1983), 'Sport and religion', in Widmeyer, W.N. (ed.),*Physical activity and the social sciences*, Mouvement Publications, Ithaca, pp.268-299.

Elliott, J. (1990), 'Validating case studies', *Westminster Studies in Education* 13, 47-60.

Eriksen, T.H. (1993), *Ethnicity and nationalism - anthropological perspectives*, Pluto Press, London.

Fairall, B. (1995), 'A matter of time, perseverence and the melting pot', *The Independent* 10th February, p.38.

Fetterman, D.M. (1989), *Ethnography step by step*, Sage, London.

Field, F. and Haikin, P. (1971), *Black Britons*, Oxford University Press, Oxford.

Figueroa, P. (1993), 'Equality, multiculturalism, antiracism and physical education in the National Curriculum', in Evans, J. (ed.), *Equality, education and physical education*, Falmer Press, London, pp.90-102.

Fine, G.A. and Sandstrom, K.L. (1988), *Knowing children*, Sage, London.

Fleming, S. (1987), *The practical considerations of a large Muslim population within a secondary school, with reference to the curricular implications for physical education*, Unpublished paper, Loughborough University.

Fleming, S. (1993), 'Ethnicity and the physical education curriculum: towards an anti-racist approach', in McFee, G. and Tomlinson, A. (eds.), *Education, sport and leisure - cultural and curricular aspects: connections and controversies*, Chelsea School Research Centre, Eastbourne, pp.109-123.

Fleming, S. (1994), 'Sport and South Asian youth: the perils of 'false universalism' and stereotyping', *Leisure Studies* 13, 159-177.

Fleming, S, (1995 - in press), in Tomlinson, A. and Fleming, S. (eds.), Ethics in sport, Chelsea School Research Centre,

Folkert, K.W. (1985), 'Jainism', in Hinnells, J.R. (ed.), *A handbook of living religions*, Pelican, Harmondsworth, Middlesex, pp.256-277.

Ford, J. (1977), *This sporting land*, New English Library, London.

Forester, T. (1978), 'Asians in business', *New Society* 23rd February, 420-423.

Freeman, S. (1986), 'How sport helps blacks clear the high hurdles', *The Sunday Times*, 14th September, pp.28-29.

Frith, S. (1984), *The sociology of youth*, Causeway, Ormskirk, Lancs.

Gahir, N. (1984), 'Gone West', *Sport and Leisure*, January, 46-47.

Gajadhar, J. (1990), 'Dance brings down barriers', *New Zealand Journal of Health, Physical Education and Recreation* 23 (4), 16.

Gati, F.A. (1988), 'Miandad - the master batsman', *Asian Times* 9th December, p.40.

Ghuman, P.A.S. (1991a), 'Best or worst of two worlds? A study of Asian adolescents', *Educational Research* 33 (2), 121-133.

Ghuman, P.A.S. (1991b), 'Have they passed the cricket test? A 'qualitative' study of Asian adolescents', *Journal of Multilingual and Multicultural Development* 12 (5), 327-346.

Giddens, A. (1989), *Sociology*, Polity Press, Cambridge.

Gidoomal, R. and Fearon, M. (1993), *Sari 'n' chips*, MARC, Sutton, Surrey.

Gillborn, D. (1990), *'Race', ethnicity and education*, Unwin Hyman, London.

Gilroy, P. (1990), 'The end of anti-racism', *New Community* 17 (1), 71-83.

Gilroy, P. (1992), 'The end of antiracism', in Donald, J. and Rattansi, A. (eds.), *'Race', culture and difference*, Sage, London, pp.49-61.

Gilroy, P. and Lawrence, E. (1988), 'Two-tone Britain: white and black youth and the politics of anti-racism', in Cohen, P. & Bains, H.S. (eds.), *Multi-racist Britain*, Macmillan Education, London, pp.121-155.

Glaister, I.K. (1975), ed., *Physical education - an integrating force?*, London, ATCDE.

Glaister, I.K. (1982), ed., *Physical education, sport and leisure: sociological perspectives*, NATFHE, London.

Glanville, B. (1990), 'Black players still uffer the taunts of morons', *The Sunday Times* 7th October, p.2.3.

Glyptis, S. (1985), 'Women as a target group: the views of the staff of Action Sport - West Midlands', *Leisure Studies* 4, 347-362.

Gordon, P. (1989), 'Just another Asian murder', *The Guardian* 20th July, p.23.

Greenidge, G. and Symes, P. (1980), *Gordon Greenidge - the man in the middle*, David & Charles, Vermont.

Griffiths, J. (1982), ed., *Asian links*, Commission for Racial Equality, London.

Grinter, R. (1990a), 'Developing an antiracist National Curriculum: constraints and new directions', in Pumfrey, P.D. and Verma, G.K. (eds.), *Race relations and urban education*, Falmer Press, London, pp.199-213.

Grinter, R. (1990b), 'Developing an antiracist National Curriculum: implementing antiracist strategies', in Pumfrey, P.D. and Verma, G.K. (eds.), *Race relations and urban education*, Falmer Press, London, pp.217-230.

Hadfield, D. (1995), 'Butt breaks new ground with an air of distinction', *The Independent* 10th February, p.38.

Hall, S. (1986), Popular culture and the state, in Bennett, T., Mercer, C. and Wollacott, J. (eds.), *Popular culture and social relations*, Open University Press, Milton Keynes, pp.22-49.

Hamilton, A. (1982), *Black pearls of soccer*, Harap, London.

Hammersley, M. and Atkinson, P. (1983), *Ethnography - principles in practice*, Tavistock Publications, London.

Hardman, K. and Khan, N.M. (1989), 'The structure and organization of interschool sport in England and Pakistan', in Fu, F.H., Ng, M.L. and Speak, M. (eds.), *Comparative physical education and sport*, The Chinese University of Hong Kong, pp.93-100.

Hargreaves, Jennifer (1994), *Sporting females - critical issues in the history and sociology of women's sports*, Routledge, London.

Hargreaves, John (1982), 'Sport, culture and ideology', in Hargreaves, Jennifer (ed.), *Sport, culture and ideology*, Routledge & Kegan Paul, London, pp.30-61.

Hargreaves, John (1986), *Sport, power and culture*, Polity Press, London.

Harrison, T. (1991), *Kriss Akabusi on track*, Lion Publishing, Oxford.

Huynes, J.B. (1985), *The reawakening of sport and physical education in India: some interesting perspectives*, The 28th ICHPER World Congress Proceedings, West London Institute of Higher Education, London.

Hedayatullah, M. (1977), 'Muslim migrants and Islam', *New Community* 5 (4), 392-396.

Henderson, M. (1992), 'Tendulkar to break mould', *The Guardian* 28th March, p.21.

Hill, D. (1976), *Teaching in multiracial schools*, Methuen, London.

Hill, Dave (1987), 'Black on red', *New Society* 11th December, pp.19-21.

Hill, Dave (1989), *"Out of his skin": the John Barnes phenomenon*, Faber & Faber, London.

Hill, Dave (1991), 'The race game', *The Guardian Guide* 31st August, pp. viii-ix.

Hill, Dave (1995), 'Unlevel fields', *Guardian 2* 21st March, p.2.

Hiro, D. (1969), 'Asians in school - a survey', *The Slough Observer*, 11th July.

Hiro, D. (1973), *Black British, white British*, revised edition, Monthly Review Press, London.

Hodgson, D. (1995), 'No home heroes for young hopefuls', *The Independent* 10th February, p.38.

Hodgson, G. (1995), 'More than just faces in the crowd', *The Independent* 10th February, p.38.

Hoggett, P. and Bishop, J. (1984), 'A voluntary sector in leisure', in Tomlinson, A. (ed.),*Leisure: politics, planning and people*, Leisure Studies Association, Eastbourne.

Hoggett, P. and Bishop, J. (1985), 'Leisure beyond the individual consumer', *Leisure Studies* 4 (1), 21-38.

Holmes, B. (1990), 'Building bridges', *Cricket Life International* January, 20-22.

Holmes, C. (1991), *A tolerant country?*, Faber & Faber, London.

Holt, R. (1989), *Sport and the British*, Oxford University Press, Oxford.

Homan, R. (1991), *The ethics of social research*, Longman, London.

Hopps, D. (1989), 'Black Yorkshiremen crossing the boundary', *The Guardian* 13th October, p.21.

Hopps, D. (1992), 'Javed the brave, maker of runs more than friends', *The Guardian*, 21st February, p.19.

Hughes, R. (1989), 'Blacks race to catch up', *The Sunday Times* 1st October, pp. F6-F7.

Hurst, P. (1985), 'Critical education and Islamic culture', in Brock, C., Tulasiewicz, W. (eds.), *Cultural identity and educational policy*, Croom Helm, Surry Hills, pp. 189-198.

Husband, C. (1987), ed., *'Race' in Britain continuity and change*, 2nd edition, Hutchinson Education, London.

Ibrahim, H. (1982), Leisure and Islam, *Leisure Studies* 1 (2), 197-210.

Ibrahim, H. (1991), *Leisure and society: a comparative approach*, Wm. C. Brown, Dubuque, Iowa.

Iganski, P. (1990), *Challenging racism: the role of the white researcher*, a paper presented at the British Sociological Association Annual Conference, University of Surrey.

Independent Television (1995), *Sunday Live*, HTV Wales.

Inner London Education Authority (1989), *Ethnic monitoring in Further and Higher education*, ILEA, London.

Iqbal, M. (1981), Drawing on Islam for the school curriculum', in Lynch, J. (ed.), *Teaching in the multi-cultural school*, Ward Lock, London, pp.202-215.

Jackson, R. (1981), 'The Shree Krishna Temple and the Gujarat Hindu community in Coventry', in Bowen, D.G. (ed.), *Hinduism in England*, Bradford College, Bradford, pp.61-85.

Jackson, R. and Nesbitt, E. (1991), 'The Hindu experience in Britain', *Education Guardian* 6th July, pp.6-7.

Jackson, R. and Nesbitt, E. (1993), *Hindu Children in Britain*, Trentham Books, Stoke-on-Trent.

Jarvie, G. (1990), 'The sociological imagination', in Kew, F. (ed.), *Social scientific perspectives on sport*, BASS monograph no.2, Sports Science Education Programme, Leeds, pp.8-12.

Jarvie, G. (1991a), 'Introduction: sport, racism and ethnicity', in Jarvie, G. (ed.), *Sport, racism and ethnicity*, Falmer Press, London, pp.1-6.

Jarvie, G. (1991b), 'Ain't no problem here', *Sport and Recreation* 32 (5), 20- 21.

Jeffrey, P. (1972), 'Pakistani families in Bristol', *New Community* 1 (5), 364-369.

Kanitkar, H. (1981), 'Caste in contemporary Hindu society', in Bowen, D.G. (ed.), *Hinduism in England*, Bradford College, Bradford, pp.86-97.

Kanitkar, H. and Jackson, R. (1982), *Hindus in Britain*, Occasional Papers VI, Extramural Division, School of Oriental and African Studies, University of London.

Kansara, B. (1984), 'Indian dance in London schools', *Impulse* Summer, 22-24.

Karmi, G. (1988), 'Stress', *Heart-health and Asians in Britain*, Health Education Authority & Coronary Prevention Group, London, p.8.

Kelly, E. (1988), 'Pupils, racial groups and behaviour in schools', in Kelly, E. and Cohn, T. *Racism in schools - new research evidence*, Trentham Books, Stoke-on-Trent, pp.5-28.

Kelly, E. (1990), 'Transcontinental families - Gujarat and Lancashire: a comparative study', in Clarke, C., Peach, C and Vertovec, S. (eds.), *South Asians overseas*, Cambridge University Press, Cambridge, pp.251-268.

Kelly, E. and Cohn, T. (1988), *Racism in schools - new research evidence*, Trentham Books, Stoke-on-Trent.

Kelsey, T. (1992), 'New rivalries divide the East End', *The Independent* 20th April, p.4.

Kemp, J.H. and Ellen, R.F. (1984), 'Informal interviewing', in Ellen, R.F. (ed.), *Ethnographic research*, Academic Press, London, pp.229-236.

Kerawalla, G.J. (1980), 'Socio-economic differences and educational opportunities - the Indian experience', *Proceedings of the IVth world congress of the world council of comparative education studies*, Korean Comparative Education Society, Seoul, Korea, pp.216-220.

Kerridge, R. (1989), 'Oy! for England...', *Midweek* 5th January, pp.10-13.

Kew, S. (1979), *Ethnic groups and leisure*, Sports Council and Social Science Research Council, London, London.

Keysel, F. (1988), 'Ethnic background and examination results', *Educational Research* 30 (2), 83-89.

Khan, H. and Randall, R.E. (1982), *Squash racquets The Khan game*, British Edition, Souvenir Press Ltd., London.

Khan, I. (1988), *All round view*, Chatto & Windus, London.

Khan, I. (1990), *Indus journey*, Chatto & Windus, London.

Khan, I. and Murphy, P. (1983), *Imran*, Pelham Books, London.

Khan, S. (1985), 'The education of Muslim Girls', *Multi-Cultural Teaching* 2, 30-33.

Khan, V.S. (1976), 'Pakistanis in Britain: perceptions of a population', *New Community* 5 (3), 222-229.

Khanum, S. (1991), 'Naked ambition', *New Statesman and Society* 4 (174), 12-14.

Klein, G. (1993), *Education towards race education*, Cassell, London.

Kureishi, O. (1989a), 'The patriot game', *Cricket Life International* August, 27-28.

Kureishi, O. (1989b), 'Indo-Pakistan cricket: more than a game', *Cricket Life International* December, 14.

Lacey, C. (1970), *Hightown Grammar*, Manchester University Press, Manchester.

Lamb, K.P., Asturias, L.P., Roberts, K. and Brodie, D.A. (1991), 'Sports participation - how much does it cost?', *Leisure Studies* 11 (1), 19-30.

Lashley, H. (1980a), 'The new black magic', *British Journal of Physical Education* 11, 5-6.

Lashley, H. (1980b), 'Rhythms of life', *British Journal of Physical Education* 11, 71-72.

Lashley, H. (1990), 'Black participation in British sport: opportunity or control', in Kew, F. (ed.), *Social scientific perspectives on sport*, BASS monograph no.2, Sports Science Education Programme, Leeds, pp.36-41.

Lashley, H. (1991), 'Promoting anti-racist policy and practice', *Sport and Recreation* 32 (5), 16-17.

Lawrence, E. (1981), 'White sociology, black struggle', *Multiracial Education* 10 (1), 3-17.

Leaman, O. (1984), 'Physical education, dance and outdoor pursuits', in Craft, A. and Bardell, G. (eds.), *Curriculum opportunities in a multicultural society*, Harper & Row, London, pp.210-222.

Leicestershire Education Authority Working Party on Multi-Cultural Education (1983), *Report and findings*, Leicestershire Education Authority, Leicester.

Levine, N. and Nayar, T. (1975), 'Modes of adaption by Asian immigrants in Slough', *New Community* 4 (3), 356-365.

Lewis, T. (1979), 'Ethnic influences on girls' PE', *British Journal of Physical Education* 10, 132.

Liston, R. (1993), 'Can blacks win the power race?', *The Observer*, 6th June, p.41.

Livingstone, P. (1978), *The leisure needs of Asian boys aged 8-14 in Slough, Berkshire*, The Scout Association, London.

Lloyd, N. (1986), ed., *Work and leisure in the 1980's. The significance of changing patterns*, Sports Council & Economic and Social Research Council, London.

London Council for Sport and Recreation (1989), *Black and ethnic minority participation*, A report from the London Regional Council for sport and recreation, London.

Longmore, A. (1988), *Viv Anderson*, Heinemann Kingswood, London.

Lovell, T. (1991), 'Sport, racism and young women', in Jarvie, G. (ed.), *Sport, racism and ethnicity*, Falmer Press, London, pp.58-73.

Lyon, M.H. (1973), 'Ethnicity in Britain: the Gujarati tradition', *New Community* 2 (1), 1-11.

Lyons, A. (1989), *Asian women and sport*, West Midlands Regional Sports Council, Birmingham.

Lyons, A. (1991), 'Inside Pakistan', *Sport and Leisure* 32 (2), 33.

Mac an Ghaill, M. (1988), *Young, gifted and black*, Open University Press, Milton Keynes.

Mac an Ghaill, M. (1991), 'Young, gifted and black: methodological reflections of a teacher/researcher', in Walford, G. (Ed.), *Doing educational research*, Routledge, London, pp.101-120.

MacDonald, I., Bhavnani, R., Khan, L. and John, G. (1989), *Murder in the playground - the Burnage report*, London, Longsight Press.

Maguire, J.A. (1991), 'Sport, racism and British society: a sociological study of England's elite male Afro/Caribbean soccer and rugby union players', in Jarvie, G. (ed.), *Sport, racism and ethnicity*, Falmer Press, London, pp.94-123.

Malik, K. (1989), 'The 'sleeping demons' awake', *Living Marxism* 7, 24-25.

Malik, R. (1988), 'Exercise', in *Heart-health and Asians in Britain*, Health Education Authority & Coronary Prevention Group, London, pp. 4-5.

Mandell, N. (1991), 'The least-adult role in studying children', in Waksler, F.C. (Ed.), *Studying the social worlds of children*, Falmer Press, London, pp.38-59.

Mangan, J. A. (1985), *The games ethic and imperialism*, Viking, Harmondsworth.

Marshall, M. (1987), *Marshall arts*, Queen Anne Press, London.

Mason, T. (1988), *Sport in Britain*, Faber & Faber, London.

Mason, T. (1989a), 'Introduction', in Mason, T. (ed.), *Sport in Britain - a social history*, Cambridge University Press, Cambridge, pp.1-11.

Mason, T. (1989b), 'Football', in Mason, T. (Ed.), *Sport in Britain - a social history*, Cambridge University Press, Cambridge, pp.146-186.

Mason, T. (1990), 'Football on the Maidan: cultural imperialism in Calcutta', *International Journal of the History of Sport* 7 (1), 85-96.

Matheson, J. (1991), *Participation in sport - GHS 1987*, Series GHS. no.17 Supplement B, HMSO, London.

Matthews, J. (1992), '"It's alright Miss, init?" Racial abuse in secondary schools', *Multicultural Teaching* 10 (2), 28-29 & 35.

McCrystal, G. (1989), 'Is Rushdie just the beginning?', *Sunday Times Magazine*, 25th May, p.27.

McDermott, M.Y. and Ahsan, M.M. (1980), *The Muslim guide*, The Islamic Foundation, Leicester.

McDonald, T. (1984), *Viv Richards - the authorised biography*, Sphere Books, London.

McDonald, T. (1986), *Clive Lloyd - the authorised biography*, Grafton, London.

McFee, G. (1994), *The concept of dance education*, Routledge, London.

McNab, T. (1990), 'The race debate', *Athletics Weekly* 23rd May, p.12.

McNeill, P. (1985), *Research methods*, Tavistock Publications, London.

McPherson, B.D., Curtis, J.E. and Loy, J.W. (1989), *The social significance of sport*, Human Kinetics Publishers, Champaign, Illinois.

Michaelson, M. (1979a), 'The moral dimensions of leisure: attitudes of Indian immigrants to leisure', in Strelitz, Z. (ed.), *Leisure and family diversity*, Leisure Studies Association, Eastbourne, pp.66-69.

Michaelson, M. (1979b), 'The relevance of caste among East African Gujaratis in Britain', *New Community* 7 (3), 350-360.

Miles, K. and Khan, R. (1988), *Jahangir and the Khan dynasty*, Pelham Books, London.

Miles, R. (1982), *Racism and migrant labour*, Routledge & Kegan Paul, London.

Miles, R. (1989), *Racism*, Routledge, London.

Mills, C.W. (1959), *The sociological imagination*, Pelican, Harmondsworth, Middlesex.

Mitchell, K. (1991), 'Passing the cricket test', *The Guardian* 19th April, p.38.

Mitchell, K. (1991), 'Mean streets feel the pace of change', *The Observer*, 21st May, pp.18-19.

Mitter, S. (1987), *Black women and unemployment*, a paper presented to The Centre for Multicultural Studies, Brighton Polytechnic, Brighton, 5th November.

Modood, T. (1988), "'Black', racial equality and Asian identity', *New Community* 14 (3), 397-404.

Moore, R. (1977), 'Becoming a sociologist in Sparkbrook', in Bell, C. and Newby, H. (eds.), *Doing sociological research*, Allen & Unwin, London, pp.87-107.

Morison, M. (1986), *Methods in sociology*, Longman, London.

Morrison, C. (1976), *As they see it*, Community Relations Council, London.

Mott, S. (1992), 'Mean streak forged in the mean streets', *Sunday Times* 12th April, p.2.12.

Muir, K. (1989), 'No reprieve for the prisoners of racial hatred', *The Sunday Correspondent* 1st October, p.8.

Mukherjee, S. (1988), *Playing for India*, 2nd edition, Sangam Books, London.

Mukherjee, T. (1988), 'The journey back', in Cohen, P. and Bains, H.S. (eds.), *Multi-racist Britain*, Macmillan Educational, London, pp.211-225.

Mullard, C. (1985), 'Multiracial education in Britain: from assimilation to cultural pluralism', in Arnot, M. (ed.), *Race and gender - equal opportunities policies in education*, Pergamon Press, London, pp.39-52.

Murphy, J. (1989), 'Race, education and intellectual prejudice', in Macleod, F. (ed.), *Parents and schools: the contemporary challenge*, Falmer Press, Lewes, East Sussex, pp.31-44.

Murshid, T.M. (1990), 'Needs, perceptions and provisions: the problem of achievement among Bengali (Sylhetti), pupils', *Multicultural Teaching* 8 (3), 12-15.

National Curiculum Council (1990), *The whole curriculum*, National Curriculum Council, London.

Nazar, M. (1989), 'The way I see it', *Cricket Life International* October, pp.22-23.

Nesbitt, E. (1991), 'The Sikh experience in Britain', *Education Guardian* 26th November, pp.6-7.

Newby, H. (1977), 'In the field: reflections on the study of Suffolk farm workers', in Bell, C. and Newby, H. (eds.), *Doing sociological research*, Allen & Unwin, London, pp.108-129.

Nielsen, J. (1987), 'Muslims in Britain: searching for an identity', *New Community* 13 (3), 384-394.

Nixon, H.L. (1986), 'Social order in a leisure setting: the case of recreational swimmers in a pool', *Sociology of Sport Journal* 3, 320-332.

Nugent, N. and King, R. (1979), 'Ethnic minorities, scapegoating and the extreme right', in Miles, R. and Phizacklea, A. (eds.), *Racism and political action in Britain*, Routledge & Kegan Paul, London, pp.28-49.

Oakley, R. and Carey, S. (1986), 'Street life, youth and ethnicity in inner city areas', *New Community* 13 (2), 214-223.

Oldfield, G. (1991), 'Outdoor action', *Sport and Recreation* 32 (5), 22.

Parekh, B. (1978), *Asians in Britain - problem or opportunity in multi-cultural Britain*, Commission for Racial Equality, London.

Parker-Jenkins, M. (1991), 'Muslim matters: the educational needs of the Muslim child', *New Community* 17 (4), 569-582.

Parmar, P. (1981), 'Young Asian women', *Multi-Racial Education* 9, 3.

Parmar, P. (1988), Gender, race and power: the challenge to youth work practice, in Cohen, P. and Bains, H.S. (eds.), *Multi-racist education*, Macmillan Educational, London, pp.197-210.

Parry, J. (1988), *Participation by black and ethnic minorities in sport and recreation - a review of literature*, Social and Community Services Group, London Research Centre.

Peeke, G. (1984), 'Teacher as researcher', *Educational Research* 26 (1), 24-26.

Phillips,E.M. and Pugh, D.S. (1987), *How to get a Ph.D.*, Open University Press, Milton Keynes.

Pilkington, A. (1986), 'Responses - the state, the mass media and racial minorities', in Cohen, L. and Cohen, A. (eds.), *Multicultural education*, Harper & Row, London, pp.130-158.

Pirani, M. (1974), 'Aspirations and expectations of English and immigrant youth', *New Community* 3 (1-2), 73-78.

Pollard, A. (1985), 'Opportunities and difficulties of a teacher-ethnographer: a personal account', in R.G. Burgess (ed.), *Field methods in the study of education*, Falmer Press, Lewes, East Sussex, pp.217-233.

Pote-Hunt, B. (1987), *Black and other ethnic minority sports policy issues*, London Strategic Policy Unit Recreation and Arts Group, London.

Pringle, D. (1991a), 'The 'Banyani brothers'', *The Cricketer International* 72 (6), 34-36.

Pringle, D. (1991b), 'The dangers of duality', *The Cricketer International* 72 (6), 29.

Pryce, K. (1986), *Endless pressure*, 2nd edition, Bristol Classical Press, Bristol.

Pumfrey, P.D. and Verma, G.K. (1990), eds., *Race relations and urban education*, Falmer Press, London.

Pumfrey, P.D. (1993), 'The whole, basic, and National Curriculum in secondary schools: contexts, challeges and responses', in Pumfrey, P.D. and Verma, G.K. (eds.), *The foundation subjects and religious education in secondary schools*, Falmer Press, London, pp.28-53.

Rakhit, K. (1989), 'Fighting fear with fun', *The Guardian* 25th July, p.23.

Ramdin, R. (1987), *The making of the black working class in Britain*, Wildwood House, Aldershot, Hants.

Rattansi, A. (1992), 'Changing the subject? Racism, culture and education', in Donald, J. and Rattansi, A. (eds.), *'Race', culture and difference*, Sage, London, pp.11-48.

Raval, S. (1989), 'Gender, leisure and sport: a case study of young people of South Asian descent - a response', *Leisure Studies* 8, 237-240.

Ray, A. (1987), *Great moments of Indian cricket from 1932-1986*, Virgin Vision.

Reason, M, and Bath, R. (1993), 'Blackballed', *Rugby News* October, pp.12-14.

Regis, J. (1990), 'The race debate', *Athletics Weekly* 23rd May, pp.12-13.

Reid, I. (1989), *Social class differences in Britain*, 3rd edition, Fontana Press, London.

Rex, J. (1981), 'Errol Lawrence and the sociology of race relations: an open letter', *Multiracial Education* 10 (1), 49-51.

Rex, J. (1982), 'West Indian and Asian youth', in Cashmore, E. and Troyna, B. (eds.), *Black youth in crisis*, George Allen & Unwin, London, pp. 53-71.

Reynolds, J. (1990), *Occupation groupings: a job dictionary*, The Market Research Society, London.

Rhodes, P.J. (1994), 'Race of interviewer effects in qualitative research: a brief comment', *Sociology* 28 (2), 547-558.

Richards, V. and Foot, D. (1982), *Viv Richards*, W.H. Allen, London.

Riley, K. (1985), 'Black girls speak for themselves', in Weiner, G. (ed.), *Just a bunch of girls*, Open University Press, Milton Keynes, pp.63-76.

Roberts, K. (1981), *Leisure*, 2nd edition, Longman, Harlow, Essex.

Roberts, K. (1983), *Youth and leisure*, George Allen & Unwin, London.

Roberts, K., Connolly, M. and Parsell, G. (1992), 'Black youth in the Liverpool labour market', *New Community* 18 (2), 209-228.

Robins, D. (1984), *We hate humans*, Penguin, Harmondsworth, Middlesex.

Robinson, M. (1989), 'The junior years', in Cole, M. (ed.), *Education for equality*, Routledge, London, pp.122-138.

Robinson, V. (1990), 'Boom and gloom: the success and failure of South Asians in Britain', in Clarke, C., Peach, C. and Vertovec, S. (eds.), *South Asians overseas*, Cambridge University Press, Cambridge, pp.269-296.

Rojek, C. (1989), ed., *Leisure for leisure*, Macmillan, London.

Rojek, C. (1995), *Decentring Leisure*, Sage, London.

Rose, D. (1989), 'Bitter questions of racial violence', *The Guardian* 13th December, p.25.

Ross, A. (1983), *Ranji - prince of cricketers*, Collins, London.

Rotherham Metropolitan Borough Council (1988), *Physical education in a multi-cultural and multi-religious society*, 2nd edition, Rotherham MBC, Rotherham.

Rowbottom, M. (1995), 'Unravelling Britain's Asian mystery', *The Independent* 10th February, p.38.

Ruddock, J. (1993), *Racial attacks - time to act*, Labour Party, London.

Runnymede Trust and Radical Statistics Race Group (1980), *Britain's black population*, Heinemann Educational, London.

Ruthven, M. (1991), *A satanic affair: Salman Rushdie and the wrath of Islam*, Hogarth Press, London.

Sanderson, T. and Hickman, L. (1986), *My life in athletics*, Willow Books, London.

Sargant, A.J. (1972), 'Participation of West Indian boys in English schools' sports teams', *Educational Research* 14 (3), 225-230.

Sarwar, G. (1983), *Muslims and education in the U.K.*, The Muslim Educational Trust, London.

Scraton, S. (1987), '"Boys muscle in where angels fear to tread" - girls' sub-cultures and physical activities', in Horne, J., Jary, D. and Tomlinson, A. (eds.), *Sport, leisure and social relations*, Routledge & Kegan Paul, London, pp.160-186.

Semple, M. (1992), 'Cultural diversity, physical education and dance', *British Journal of Physical Education* 23 (2), 36-38.

Semple, M. (1993), 'Physical education and dance',*The multicultural dimension on the National Curriculum*, Falmer Press, London, pp.162-172.

Sharma (1983), 'Mohinder and Mudassar - the amazing parallels', *The Cricketer* July, 30.

Siraj-Blatchford, I. (1993), 'Ethnicity and conflict in physical education: a critique of Carroll and Holinshead's case study', *British Educational Research Journal* 19 (1), 77-82.

Sivanandan, A. (1976), *Race, class and the state*, Institute of Race Relations, London.

Sivanandan, A. (1982), *A different hunger*, Pluto Press, London.

Skillen, A. (1993), 'Racism: Flew's three concepts of racism', *International Journal of Applied Philosophy* 10 (1), 73-89.

Small, S. (1994), *Racialised barriers - the black experience in the United States and England in the 1980s*, Routledge, London.

Socialist Party (1988), *Racism*, Socialist Party, London.

Solomos, J. (1988), *Black youth, racism and the state*, Cambridge University Press, Cambridge.

Sports Council (1979), *People in sport*, The Sports Council, London.

Sports Council (1982), *Sport in the community... The next ten years*, The Sports Council, London.

Sports Council (1988), *Into the 90s*, The Sports Council, London.

Sports Council (1991), *Sports equity - ethnic minorities and sport policy statement*, The Sports Council, London.

Sports Council (1994), *Black and ethnic minorities in sport: policy and objectives*, Sports Council, London.

Standeven, J. (1991), 'International perspectives on leisure bathing as an interpretation of sport for all', in Standeven, J., Hardman, K. and Fisher, D. (eds.), *Sport for all - into the 90's*, Meyer and Meyer Verlag, Aachen, pp.304-309.

Stanley, L. and Wise, S. (1983), *Breaking out. Feminist consciousness and feminist research*, Routledge and Kegan Paul, London.

St John-Brooks, C. and Greenwood, L. (1988), 'A new generation of Asians widens the learning gap', *The Sunday Times* 16th October, p.H1.

Stoddart, B. (1982), 'Sport and cultural imperialism: some exploratory thoughts', in Howell, M.L. and Mckay, J. (eds.), *Proceedings of the VII Commonwealth and international conference on sport, physical education, recreation and dance*, University of Queensland, Queensland, pp.79-85.

Sugden, J. (1987), 'The exploitation of disadvantage: the occupational sub-culture of the boxer', in Horne, J., Jary, D. and Tomlinson, A. (eds.), *Sport, leisure and social relations*, Routlege & Kegan Paul, London, pp.187-209.

Syal, R. and Gilligan, A. (1995), 'Asian stars ignored by 'racist' football clubs', *The Sunday Times*, 8th January, p.2.20.

Tambs-Lyche, H. (1975), 'A comparison of Gujarati communities in London and the Midlands', *New Community* 4 (3), 349-355.

Tanna, K. (1990), 'Excellence, equality and educational reform: the myth of South Asian achievement levels', *New Community* 16 (3), 349-368.

Taylor, D. (1994), 'Walking away from football', *Sports Magazine*, March, 36-38.

Taylor, J.H. (1976), *The half-way generation*, NFER Publishing, Windsor.

Taylor, M.J. and Hegarty, S. (1985), *The best of both worlds...?*, NFER-Nelson, Windsor.

Tennant, I. (1994), *Imran Khan*, Witherby, London.

Terrill, C. (1990), 'Unsporting chance', *The Listener* 25th March, pp.14-15.

Thanki, M. (1989), *Towards greater participation in sport amongst black and ethnic minorities*, speech at launch of London Council report Black and Ethnic Minority Participation, Westminster Central Hall, 10th May.

Thomas, S. (1990), 'Through whose eyes', *The struggle is my life - multi-cultural issues in education perspectives* 42, School of Education, University of Exeter, pp.41-43.

Thompson, M. (1974), 'The second generation - Punjabi or English', *New Community* 3 (3), 242-248.

Thornley, E.P. and Siann, G. (1991), 'The career aspirations of South Asian girls in Glasgow', *Gender and Education* 3 (3), 237-248.

147

Todd, R. (1991), *Education in a multicultural society*, Cassell Educational, London.

Todryk, D. (1988), 'Multiculturalism and dance', *Impulse* Summer, 20-21.

Tomlinson, A. (1982), 'Physical education, sport and sociology: the current state and the way forward', in Glaister, I.K. (ed.), *Physical education, sport and leisure: sociological perspectives*, NATFHE, London, pp.44-53.

Tomlinson, A. (1984), 'The sociological imagination, the new journalism and sport', in Theberge, N. and Donnelly, P. (eds.), *Sport and the sociological imagination*, Christian University Press, Fort Worth, Texas, pp.21-39.

Tomlinson, A. (1986), 'Playing away from home: leisure, disadvantage and issues of income and access', in Golding, P. (ed.), *Excluding the poor*, Child Poverty Action Group, London, pp.43-54.

Tomlinson, A. (1988), 'Good times, bad times and the politics of leisure', in Cantelon, H., Hollands, R., Metcalfe, A. and Tomlinson, A. *Leisure, sport and working class cultures*, Garamond press, Toronto, pp.41-64.

Tomlinson, S. (1983), 'The educational performance of children of Asian origin', *New Community* 10 (3), 381-391.

Tomlinson, S. (1986a), *Ethnic minority achievement and equality of opportunity*, University of Nottingham School of Education, Nottingham.

Tomlinson, S. (1986b), 'Ethnicity and educational achievement', in Modgil, S., Verma, G.K., Mallick, K. and Modgil, C. (eds.), *Multicultural education - the interminable debate*, Falmer Press, London, pp.181-193.

Townsend H.E.R. and Brittan, E.M. (1973), *Multi-racial education: need and innovation*, Evans/Methuen Educational, London.

Troyna, B. (1991), 'Children, 'race' and racism: the limitations of research and policy', *British Journal of Education Studies* 39 (4), 425-436.

Troyna, B. and Carrington, B. (1990), *Education, racism and reform*, Routledge, London.

Vadgama, K. (1984), *India in Britain*, Robert Royce Ltd., London.

Van Dalen, D.B. and Bennett, B.L. (1971), *A world history of physical education*, 2nd edition, Prentice Hall, Englewood Cliffs, New Jersey.

van den Berghe, L. (1988), 'Caste', in Cashmore, E. *Dictionary of race and ethnic relations*, 2nd edition, Routledge, London, pp.44-46.

Vatsyayan, K. (1976), *Traditions of Indian folk dance*, Indian Book Company, New Delhi.

Verma, G.K. (1983), 'Consciousness, disadvantage and opportunity: the struggle for South Asian youth in British society', in Bagley, C. and Verma, G.K. (eds.), *Multicultural childhood*, Gower, Aldershot, Hants., pp.110-123.

Verma, G.K. and Mallick, K. (1981), Hinduism and multi-cultural education, in Lynch, J. (ed.), *Teaching in the multi-cultural school*, Ward Lock, London, pp.184-201.

Verma, G.K., MacDonald, A., Darby, D. and Carroll, R. (1991), *Sport and recreation with special reference to ethnic minorities*, University of Manchester, Manchester.

Vitale, R. (1990), 'I'm frightened - tormented soccer star victimised', *Caribbean Times* 13th February, p.40.

Wade, B. and Souter, P. (1992*), Continuing to think - the British Asian girl*, Multilingual Matters, Clevedon, Avon.

Walia, Y (1991), *Kabaddi*, Channel 4 Television, London.

Walsh, M. (1991), 'Coming through the hard way', *Sport and Recreation* 32 (5), 26-27.

Wedge, P. and Essen, J. (1982), *Children in adversity*, Pan Books, London.

Wedge, P. and Prosser, H. (1973), *Born to fail?*, Arrow Books Ltd., London.

Weightman, S. (1985), 'Hinduism', in Hinnells, J.R. (ed.), *A handbook of living religions*, Pelican, Harmondsworth, Middlesex, pp.191-236.

Weinreich, P. (1979), 'Ethnicity and adolescent indentity conflicts: a comparative study', in Khan, V.S., *Migration and social stress: Mirpuris in Bradford*, Bradford College, Bradford, pp.86-92.

Welch, A,T. (1985), 'Islam', in J.R. Hinnells (ed.), *A handbook of living religions*, Pelican, Harmondsworth, Middlesex, pp.123-170.

Werbner, P. (1990), 'Manchester Pakistanis: division and unity', in Clarke, C., Peach, C. and Vertovec, S. (eds.), *South Asians overseas*, Cambridge University Press, Cambridge, pp.331-348.

Werbner, P. (1992), *Fun spaces: on identity and social empowerment among British Muslims*. Paper presented at Institute of Social and Cultural Anthropology, Oxford University.

Whannel, G. (1983), *Blowing the whistle*, Pluto, London.

White, J. (1990), 'Yorkshire's biggest test', *The Independent* 26th May, p.29.

Williams, A. (1989), 'Physical education in a multicultural context', in Williams, A. (ed.), *Issues in physical education for the primary years*, Falmer Press, Lewes, East Sussex, pp.160-172.

Williams, J. (1989), 'Cricket', in T. Mason (ed.), *Sport in Britain - a social history*, Cambridge University Press, Cambridge, pp.116-130.

Williams, J. (1994), 'South Asians and cricket in Bolton', *Sports Historian* 14, 56-65.

Williams, J.A. (1962), Ed., *Islam*, George Braziller,New York .

Williams, J., Dunning, E. and Murphy, P. (1984), *Hooligans abroad*, Routledge & Kegan Paul, London.

Willis, P. (1977), *Learning to labour*, Gower, Aldershot, Hampshire.

Willis, P. (1978), *Profane culture*, Routledge & Kegan Paul, London.

Willis, P. and Team (1990), *Moving culture: an enquiry into the cultural activities of young people*, Calouste Gulbenkian Foundation, London.

Wilson, A. (1983), 'Blame the victim', *New Internationalist* 128, 14-15.

Wilson, N. (1990), 'Blacks 'playing racists' game', *The Independent* 2nd May, p.30.

Wilson, P. (1991), 'The black man's burden', *The Observer* 22nd September, p.41.

Wissmann, H. (1972), 'Sport and non-Christian religions', in Gruppe, O., Kurz, D. and Teipel, J.M. (eds.), *The scientific view of sport*, Springer-Verlag, Berlin, pp.99-103.

Wolverhampton Borough Council (1985), *The social condition of young people in Wolverhampton in 1984*, Wolverhampton BC, Wolverhampton.

Wood, E.R. and Carrington, L.B. (1982), 'School, sport and the black athlete', *Physical Education Review* 5 (2), 131-137.

Woolnough, B. (1983), *Black magic - England's black footballers*, Pelham Books, London.

Wrench, J. (1989), *Gatekeepers in the urban labour market*, a paper presented at the British Sociological Association annual conference, Plymouth Polytechnic.

Wright, C. (1992), 'Early education: multiracial primary school classrooms', in Gill, D., Mayor, B. and Blair, M. (eds.), *Racism and education*, Sage, London, pp.5-41.

Yates, P.D. (1986), 'Figure and section: ethnography and education in the multicultural state', in Modgil, S., Verma, G.K., Mallick, K. and Modgil, C. (eds.), *Multicultural education - the interminable debate*, Falmer Press, London, pp.61-76.

Yusuf Ali, A. (1946), *The Holy Qur'an. Translation and commentary*, Islamic Propagation Centre International, Birmingham.

Author index

Abercrombie, N. 41
Ahsan, M.M. 12, 26
Amritraj, V. 37, 38
Atkinson, P. 51, 58
Ballard, C. 30
Ballard, R. 32
Bayliss, T. 2, 26, 27
Bishop, J. 50
Bradford Youth Research Team 33, 118
Brandt, G. 130
Brown, J.M. 15
Carrington, B. 49, 97, 129
Cashman, R. 11, 17
Cashmore, E. 43, 65-67, 72, 99, 124
Cherrington, D. 22, 27
Chivers, T. 49
Cole, M. 128, 129
Cole, W.O. 13
Connolly, M. 119
Corrigan, P. 52, 116
Coventry Local Education Authority 25
Craft, M. 31, 36, 141
Curtis, J.E. 125
Daley, D. 102
Darby, D. 21-22, 31, 124
Department of the Environment 124
Dixey, R. 25-26, 98, 125
Eitzen, D.S. 10
Ellen, R.F. 54
Evans, R. 37, 38

Fetterman, D.M. 58, 59
Field, F. 3
Folkert, K.W. 11
Frith, S. 30
Giddens, A. 5, 32
Gillborn, D. 60
Grinter, R. 129
Haikin, P. 3
Hall, S. 3
Hammersley, M. 51, 58
Hargreaves, John 32
Hedayatullah, M. 13
Hegarty, S. 32, 118
Hill, S. 41
Hiro, D. 36-37
Hoggett, P. 50
Holt, R. 7, 8
Holmes, C. 117, 122
Homan, R. 63-64
Ibrahim, H. 11, 12
Inner London Education Authority 93
Jarvie, G. 4, 41, 42, 120
Kemp, J.H. 54
Kerawalla, G.J. 15
Khan, H. 10, 15
Khan, I. 10, 16, 37
Khan, S. 23
Khan, V.S. 5
Klein, G. 36, 41
Lashley, H. 22, 41
Lawrence, E. 72
Leaman, O. 129

Livingstone, P. 22
Lloyd, N. 112
Lovell, T. 20
Lyon, M.H. 5
Mangan, J.A. 7
McDermott, M.Y. 12, 26
McNab, T. 43
McPherson, B.D. 125
Mills, C.W. 3
Modood, T. 5
Murshid, T.M. 31
National Curriculum Council 127
Newby, H. 61
Parmar, P. 110
Parsell, G. 119
Pilkington, A. 32
Pryce, K. 62
Ramdin, R. 89
Rex, J. 96
Roberts, K. 1, 30, 89, 119
Robinson, M. 2-3, 26
Ross, A. 7, 9
Sage, G.H. 10

Schatzman, L. 61
Solomos, J. 52, 80
Sports Council 2, 50
Standeven, J. 105-106
Stanley, L. 4
Stoddart, B. 9, 11
Strauss, A.L. 61
Taylor, M.J. 118
Tomlinson, A. 3, 4, 34
Tomlinson, S. 21, 86
Troyna, B. 67, 129
Turner, B.S. 41
van den Berghe, L. 15
Verma, G.K. 21-22, 31, 124
Weightman, S. 16-18
Williams, A. 24, 25, 27, 39, 40,
    127, 129, 130
Williams, T. 49
Willis, P. 60
Wise, S. 4
Wissmann, H. 10, 11
Wright, C. 69
Yates, P.D. 26

Subject index

adaption 73, 80
aerobics 50, 102, 104
African-Caribbeans 2, 42-43, 99
Akabusi, Kriss 44
Anglicisation 7
anti-racism 53
assimilation 79, 86
athleticism, cult of 7
athletics 43-44
Bannerjee, Suvra 18
Bassett, Dave 40
'between two cultures' 29-32, 80-81
bhangra 27, 102
'Boffins' 85-88, 94, 111
boxing 101
Butt, Ikram 12, 44
caste 15-16
class 32-34, 71, 114, 115-121
Close, Brian 46
clothing (and identity) 58, 72, 76, 89
cricket 46-48, 100-101
dance 12-13, 27, 78, 102-104
data collection 60-63
education 36, 95, 96-97
    achievement 74, 81, 86, 90, 118
    single-sex 24
Elm Park Swimming Club 55-56
England v India (Oval, 1971) 9
ethics 63-65
ethnic identity 1, 6, 10
ethnicity 5
ethnography 52-65

Eurocentrism 23, 101, 105-106
Fairfax Scheme 25, 98
Fleming, Scott 52-53
football 45, 75, 76, 83, 84, 85, 87, 91, 108-109
gate-keeper 53-54
Gavaskar, Sunil 14
gender-roles 22, 35-36, 102-104
health related exercise 104
Hinduism and Hindus 11-12, 27-28, 79-80, 119
Ahimsa 11-12, 28, 105, 108
hockey 50, 102
immigration 34-35
Indian civilisation 6
interviewing 61-62
Islam and Muslims 12-13, 23-27, 70, 80-81, 106, 107
    Hadith 12
    modesty 23-25, 105-107
        see also 'dance'
    Mosque 70, 79, 112-113, 119
    prayer 70, 112, 113, 119
    Qur'an 13, 70, 74, 112, 113, 119
    Ramazan 26
    Shari'a 13
izzat 24
Jainism 11, 28, 105
kabaddi 11, 18, 85, 105
Khan, Hashim 9-10, 15
Khan, Imran 14
leisure 12, 34-37, 48-50, 82-83, 86-87, 110, 114

153

see also 'work and employment'
masculinity 4
multi-culturalism 103
  tokenism 103-4
Muslims
  see 'Islam'
National Curriculum 36
national identity 8-10
  see also 'ethnic identity'
Northbridge Amateur Boxing Club
55
Parkview School 69-95
Parkview Sports Centre 98
Parkview Youth Club 68
physical education 115
  curriculum 97, 102, 107
  extra-curricular activities 97
  kit 24, 77, 83, 90-91, 107
  lessons 62, 77-78, 97
  'Problems approach' 2, 23-24, 26, 78, 103
  showering 78, 107
    see also 'dance', 'modesty'
play 35, 74-75, 97
professionalism of teacher 58-59
questionnaire 62-63
'race' and natural ability 37-38, 104
racism
  definition 41
  in sport 41-48
  institutional 46-67
  personal 44-46, 72, 75, 82, 84, 86, 90, 92-95, 108, 110, 115, 118
  spectator 45-46, 108
Ranjitsinhji 9
religion 10-14, 28, 79, 107
researcher
  acceptance 53-60
  blunders 54
  least-authoritative role 58
  roles 53, 56-59
  white 65-57
role models 40-41, 88, 91, 100
rugby 102
Sikhism and Sikhs 13-14, 27, 84, 85, 99, 107, 118
  temple 84, 98
  turban 99, 107

socialisation 100, 119
social mobility 36-37
'sociological imagination' 3-4
South Asian
  definition 5
  stereotypes 89-90, 97
South Asians and sport in Britain
  home-based 49, 83, 110-112
  parental disapproval 113-114
  personal safety 82, 106, 115, 117
  self-defence 88, 110
  stereotypes 38-40, 48, 49, 98-99, 101-102
  time constraints 79, 111-112, 113, 118-119
  women 22, 24, 49, 50, 97, 98
    see also 'dance', 'modesty'
South Asian youth
  attacks on 71
  family origin 21-13, 71
  generation 29-32, 80, 103 119
    see also 'between two cultures', 'caste'
  heterogeneity 20-21, 41-42, 68, 96
'Sport for All' 2, 50
sports clubs and teams 97, 118
sport in the Indian sub-continent
  badminton 97
  cricket 7, 9, 14, 16-17
  elitism 14-15
  football 19, 11, 109
  gender 17-19
  Hindu-Muslim relations 10
  hockey 7-8, 9, 14
  hunting 12
  Indo-Pakistan 10
  military 7
  nationalism 9, 10
  nepotism 16-17
  physical education 22
  polo cult 8
  the Raj 6-8
  regionalism 17
  squash 10
  urbanism 17
'Straights' 79-85, 92, 118-119
'Street-kids' 88-92, 118-119

swimming 25, 50, 55-56
Sylhettis 30-32
tennis 100
terminology 4
typology 69
uniformed organisations 36-37, 49
'Victims' 70-79, 94, 102, 108, 109, 110, 117-118
violence 104-5
  see also *Ahimsa*

work and employment 34-36, 81-82, 91-92, 112
Yorkshire County Cricket Club 46-47
youth Club 110
  see also 'Parkview Youth Club'
Zoroastrians 87